African American Almanac:
Day-by-Day Black History

African American Almanac

Day-by-Day Black History

Leon T. Ross *and*
Kenneth A. Mimms

McFarland & Company, Inc., Publishers
Jefferson, North Carolina, and London

This work is dedicated to the hundreds of people
from Cooperstown, New York, to San Diego, California,
who helped us in our research, but especially
to our wives and families
who endured the long process with us.

LIBRARY OF CONGRESS CATALOGUING-IN-PUBLICATION DATA

Ross, Leon T., 1931–
     African American almanac : day-by-day black history / Leon
T. Ross and Kenneth A. Mimms.
          p.   cm.
     Includes bibliographical references and index.

     ISBN 0-7864-2629-2 (softcover : 50# alkaline paper) ∞

     1. Afro-Americans—History—Chronology.   I. Mimms,
Kenneth A., 1935–   .   II. Title.
E185.R815   2006
973'.0496073'00202—dc20   96-44832

British Library cataloguing data are available

Cover photograph: Sojourner Truth, 1864 *(Library of Congress)*

Manufactured in the United States of America

McFarland & Company, Inc., Publishers
  Box 611, Jefferson, North Carolina 28640
  www.mcfarlandpub.com

Table of Contents

Preface

The task of compiling this book presented several complex problems. Primary among these were the matters of definition, limitation and identification, each of which needed a logical and consistent approach developed before we could consider taking pen in hand and writing about African American history. While it is true that these problems exist in any field, they are compounded when inquiring into the history of African Americans. Because of the social position that Americans and many Europeans assign to people of African descent, they are often ignored or overlooked when history is written.

The first problem we considered was that of definition, which involved several subordinate issues. First was to determine what term to use. In America persons of African origin have been politely referred to as negro, Negro, colored, black, Black, Afro-American and African American (with and without a hyphen). Since African Americans are defined as Americans who are descended from the Black people of Africa, our first task became that of attempting to define the word "Black." As an adjective, Black has been defined as "of or relating to a group or race characterized by dark pigmentation as the Negro race or the Afro-American people." However, for the purposes of this work, we considered the word "Black" to be a noun, a proper noun, the name of a people, Black people. On this point we took our cue from Amiri Baraka (formerly Leroi Jones) who said "In America, Black is a country."

The noun form of the word "Black" has been defined as "a person belonging to a dark skinned race or one stemming in part from such a race, a Negro or Afro-American."

This definition itself raises further questions of what exactly is meant by "one stemming in part from such a race." The answer is simultaneously simple and complex. One who is part Black is Black. Popular American usage has made the term "part Black" an oxymoron.

To verify this convoluted logic that says that part Black is all Black, one has merely to look at the people who are designated as Black Americans. Their skin colors range from a dark ebony to a pale beige. This enormous range of hues led one member of the British royalty to exclaim, "I am fascinated by your American Negroes. They are like roses in a garden, no two of them are the same color."

1

It is true that Black Americans come in many colors, hues and tones, but they are all labeled with the same general term: "Black."

The term "black" fits into the American culture as the symbolic contrast to the term "white." White carries the connotations of pure, good, holy, and desirable. Black, the opposite, is used to indicate something that is dirty, bad, evil or undesirable. Muhammad Ali, the boxer, once pointed out that "Angel food cake is white, but devil's food cake is chocolate."

For centuries it was understood that White people had souls, but Black people did not. This was an item fit for high school debates in the 1930s: "Do Colored people have souls?" Black people were generally considered less than human. Sexual intercourse between Whites and Blacks was a crime and labeled miscegenation. It was considered only slightly less perverse than bestiality, though no evidence is needed to know that such unions did take place. In fact an entire lexicon of terms arose to identify the children of these unions. There were mulattoes who were half Black, quadroons who were one-fourth Black and octoroons who were one-eighth Black. Any American who is one-eighth Black was, and is, legally Black.

The American federal government has done little to simplify the definition of Black people. In the 1960s the United States Bureau of the Census listed as Black all persons living in a household the head of which was identified as Black. By contrast, in the 1970s the United States Department of State shocked a White woman from Louisiana by issuing her a passport declaring her as Black. It seems government records showed she was three-sixteenths Black and was therefore Black, according to the State Department, whether she liked it or not. In the 1980s a political candidate in California claimed to be Black even though both the Black opposition candidate and his own mother claimed he was White. In this same decade the United States Equal Employment Opportunity Commission defined a Black person as anyone having origins among the people of Africa. Yet if one is to believe the findings of the British anthropologist Louis S.B. Leaky, all of humanity originated in Africa. In other words, all people belong to a dark skinned race or stem in part from such a race.

For the purposes of this book, African American people have been defined as United States residents descended entirely or in at least one-eighth part from the Black people of Africa. No one certain term has been favored in this book as the only and correct terminology for the U.S. descendants of the Black people of Africa. The capitalized "Black" is, however, the term of preference (and thus the term "White" is also used).

The definition of the word "history" offered yet another challenge. History can be defined as a chronological record of significant events. It can be studied by reviewing the conflicts of the past and the solutions that people have applied to these conflicts. By further considering the effectiveness of the solutions to attain the desired results, it is then possible to apply these solutions to similar and current conflicts.

A second way to look at history is to review the lives of those men and women who made significant contributions to the advancement of society. This may be done through biographical sketches and reports about the lives of noteworthy individuals.

The third approach to history, the one taken by textbooks, is to review a chronicle of events presented in sequential order. From this account one can draw conclusions as to cause, motivation, reaction and results. Facts are presented in order of their occurrence with opinions and analysis being limited by the fairness and objectivity of the writer. A lack of these two qualities can alter both the character and accuracy of the reporting of fact, and indeed much historical literature is so damaged. The insidious injection of bias and prejudice into chronicles and news accounts in historical documents leaves the reader with the impression that throughout recorded history, Blacks have contributed nothing of good to humanity.

This book presents history in a somewhat unconventional manner: It is arranged by day of the year, with events arranged chronologically under each day, rather than in a standard chronological format. To discover what significant events in African American history occurred on March 28, for example, one would simply turn to the entry for that day. Most entries include several events, so the March 28 listing might include occurrences from March 28 of many different years. (All dates are based on the Gregorian calendar.) Since this is not the order of real time, and since history does not follow this sequence, the events of one day on the almanac are not usually related to those of the next.

When compared to the problem of definition, the problem of limitation was perhaps the easiest to resolve. The guiding principle was that this almanac should record events initiated by or associated with African American persons that have had a significant impact on other African Americans. It is obvious, however, that a number of events which have importantly affected African Americans have been initiated by persons of other races, so this book does include events associated with such significant persons as John Brown, Abraham Lincoln, Harriet Beecher Stowe and John F. Kennedy.

The third and final hurdle to overcome was the twofold problem of identification. The first part of this problem was in identifying African Americans. Again this problem existed because most historical writing has lacked fairness and objectivity. When recording positive accomplishments by Black persons, many of the writers did not think it was significant to say that the person who accomplished the act was Black. As a result, many Black persons who have made a favorable impact on the development of American society have not been identified by their African lineage. This effect is seen in the reporting of history outside the United States as well. Aesop, for example, is most often described as a Greek slave from Thrace; few sources indicate that he was a Black person originally from northeast Africa. Few American histories mention that Pedro Alonso Niño, the navigator on Columbus's ship the *Nina*, was a Black person. The story of the adventures of Estevan the Black has been preserved principally by the

Indians of the Southwest. African Americans who distinguished themselves in the Revolutionary War, such as Crispus Attucks, the first to die in the Boston Massacre, and Peter Salem, the hero of the Battle of Bunker Hill, are seldom mentioned. Explorers such as York, who traveled with the Lewis and Clark expedition, and Matt Henson, who was the first in Admiral Perry's party to reach the North Pole, are generally unknown. These are a few examples of the magnitude of the problem of identification.

The second part of the identification problem was centered on the scarcity of detailed chronological records of African Americans. Many Blacks did not have their births recorded. There was no recognized need to record the births of slaves. Because of this, many Black historical figures had only the date of their deaths recorded. And this was done only because they had reached a significant level of prominence in the eyes of the American majority race.

In the years since the emancipation of the slaves, many African Americans began to live in isolated rural areas or impoverished urban ghettos where the importance of registering home births was not considered a priority. Many other African American births went unregistered until years later when a certificate was required for some government purpose. By that time the exact dates were often only vaguely remembered or invented to meet the needs of the person filing for the certificate.

The almanac that has resulted from our attempts to resolve the problems of definition, limitation and identification may be used either as a standard reference book or as a calendar. Used either way, it may serve as a reminder that the heritage of African Americans is continuous. It goes forward day by day, year after year, and it goes back many centuries. Probably no book can encompass its fullness, but it is the authors' hope that the present work will serve as a good start.

Significant Events Not Associated with a Single Day, By Year

I have a dream that one day this nation will rise up and live out the true meaning of its creed: "We hold these truths to be self-evident: That all men are created equal."—Martin Luther King, Jr.

1401–1800

1492—PEDRO ALONSO NIÑO, a navigator and member of Columbus' crew when America was discovered, was one of many Africans who labored as an explorer, servant, or slave in the "New World" with Spanish and French Expeditions.

1500—Believed to be year of birth, in Azamore, Morocco, of ESTEVANICO, a Spanish-African companion of the Spanish explorer Dorantes. Estevanico discovered Arizona and New Mexico while looking for the legendary Cities of Gold.

1513—African sailors were with Balboa during his journey across what is now the United States to the Pacific Ocean. They contributed significantly to the expedition which took Balboa from the Atlantic Ocean to the Pacific Ocean.

1539—African crew members were with the Spanish explorer Desoto during his trip to the Mississippi River.

1540—Alabama's second settler was an African American who entered the territory with Hernando De Soto. He remained in the "New World" and settled among Native Americans.

1565—African sailors were with the explorer Mendez when he founded St. Augustine, Florida.

1620—The first public school for African Americans and Native Americans opened in Virginia.

1624—The birth of WILLIAM TUCKER, the first African American child born and baptized in Jamestown, Virginia. Tucker reportedly lived to be 108 years of age.

1628—The first African indentured servant was sold to a Canadian settler in Quebec Province.

1638—The Northeastern territories of New England received their first African slaves.

1704—The first New York City school for African Americans was opened by French immigrant Elias Nau.

1753— SCIPIO MOOREHEAD, the earliest known African American artist, was born in this year.

1762— JAMES DERHAM — Derham is generally recognized as the first African American physician in the United States. He was born a slave outside Philadelphia.

1773— Slaves living in Massachusetts petitioned the State Legislature for freedom. Eight petitions were offered during the Revolutionary War. No grants of freedom resulted from the petitions.

1774— Benjamin Franklin became president of the first anti-slavery organization formed in Philadelphia.

1776— Gen. George Washington invited poet PHILLIS WHEATLEY to visit his Cambridge, Massachusetts, headquarters. Washington personally expressed his appreciation for poems Wheatley had written in his honor.

1777— Vermont became the first state to abolish slavery.

1778— In Virginia, 30,000 slaves escaped from the state, according to Thomas Jefferson.

1780— A law for the "gradual" abolishment of slavery was passed by the Pennsylvania Legislature.

1781— Slave QUORK WALKER won freedom by quoting a passage from the Constitution of the State of Massachusetts, asserting: "the Massachusetts State Constitution says, 'All men are born free and equal.'"

1792— The first African American Catholic Sisterhood was established in the United States by ANTOINE BLANC.

1793— The importation of slaves to Canada was banned in 1793 by a law enacted by the Upper Canadian Parliament. The same law ordered children of slave mothers freed at age 25.

1797— In England a law was repealed that had permitted the sale of African Americans with other property to satisfy bankruptcy. Canadian lawmakers interpreted this to mean the revocation of all slavery laws and by 1800 slavery was near history in Canada.

1801–1850

1808— Slavery was prohibited in the United States by a law that took effect this year.

1809— The third census put the national population at 7,239,881 million and included 1.2 million slaves and 186,746 free African Americans.

The first African Methodist Episcopal (AME) Church for African Americans was established in Philadelphia.

In Philadelphia, the African Baptist Church was formed by African Americans.

The birth year, in New York City, of journalist PHILIP ALEXANDER BELL, who was active in the Colored Movement. A friend of Frederick Douglass, Bell moved to San Francisco in 1862 and founded *The Pacific Appeal*, a weekly newspaper published until 1864. *The Appeal* and *The Elevator* were merged after Bell's death in 1869.

1814— Two African American (military) Regiments were authorized by the New York State Legislature.

1816— BARNEY FLETCHER was born a Maryland slave in this year and later was lured to California by the Gold Rush of 1849. Fletcher settled in Sacramento where, in 1850, he founded the first African Methodist Episcopal Church on the Pacific Coast. He was a minister and a civil rights leader.

Former slave RICHARD ALLEN became Bishop of the AME Church.

An African American seaman, known only as BOB, and his European shipmate, one Thomas Doak of Boston, both believed to have been born in this year, deserted the ship Albatross at Monterey, California. Bob was baptized JUAN CRISTOBAL and remained in the city along with Doak who was baptized as Felipe Santiago. Bob and Doak were the first U.S. citizens to settle in California, which was then a Spanish possession.

1820— A free African American, DAVID WALKER, angered southern Whites by writing "12 armed African American men could best 50 whites."

1821— WILLIAM STILL was born on a New Jersey farm. He was the son of a free father and a mother who was a runaway slave from Maryland. Characterized as one of the "foremost leaders" of the Underground Railroad, Still also helped organize the first YMCA for African Americans. Still moved to Philadelphia in 1844 and was hired by the Anti-Slavery Society as a clerk/janitor. In 1872, Still published the first edition of his book *The Underground Railroad*, which sold out immediately. Still died in 1895.

JEREMIAH BURKE SANDERSON, African Methodist Episcopal Church minister and educator, was born in this year. A native of Massachusetts, Sanderson migrated to California in 1854. He worked eight years as principal of a San Francisco school for African American children before moving, in 1868, to a similar job in Stockton, California. Sanderson was ordained an Elder in the Stockton AME Church in 1872, but later left the Central Valley city to lead an Oakland Church. He died in 1875.

THOMAS L. JENNINGS became the first African American to patent an invention, a dry-cleaning process.

1822— WILLIAM ROBISON was born in Virginia during this year. Robison migrated to California in 1847 and became an activist for civil rights in Stockton. He worked as a Pony Express rider between Stockton and the gold mines in the foothills of the Sierra Nevada Mountains. Robison died in 1902.

1825— FRANCES ELLEN WATKINS HARPER — Poet, anti-slavery lecturer, and first African American woman to have a full-length novel published. Harper was born free, in 1825, in Baltimore, Maryland. She was orphaned early and brought up by an aunt. As a teenager, Harper began writing poetry, some of which was published in the local newspaper. Harper moved to Ohio in 1850, after opting to live in a free state. While there she taught domestic science for an African American Seminary in Columbus. Harper later moved to Little York, Pennsylvania, where, after becoming acquainted with the Underground Railroad, she began crusading against slavery. In 1853, Maryland legislators approved a law banning free northern people of color from entering the state, a move which prevented Harper from returning there. Instead she became a lecturer for the Anti-Slavery Movement of Maine. In 1856, Harper wrote *Bury Me in a Free Land*. Four years later she married Fenton Hughes and was widowed in 1864. Her novel, *Lola Leroy — The Shadows Uplifted*, was published in 1860.

Birth year of RICHARD H. CAIN, congressman, minister and educator. Cain was born free, in Greenbrier County, Virginia. He was licensed to preach in 1844 and ordained a deacon 15 years later. In 1865, Cain was sent to South Carolina to work for freed slaves. Along with Robert B. Elliott, Cain was elected to the House of Representatives after four years as a South Carolina state senator during the Continental Congress of 1868. Cain served two terms, 1873–75 and 1877–79. He died in 1887.

1826— JAMES MADISON BELL, a native of Ohio, was born this year. Bell was a civil rights advocate and a friend and aide to abolitionist John Brown. Bell migrated to San Francisco in 1860. He wrote the poem *The Progress of Liberty* in celebration of the Emancipation Proclamation.

1827— *Freedom's Journal*, the first African American newspaper published in the United States, was first distributed in this year. The printers and journalists were SAMUEL CORNISH and JOHN RUSSWURM.

1830— Birth year of JAMES A. HEALY, the son of an Irish planter who settled in Georgia and a slave. Healy and his brothers attended Quaker schools in New York and New Jersey. Healy was the first African American ordained a priest in the Roman Catholic Church.

1831 — WILLIAM LLOYD GARRISON published the first issue of *The Liberator,* an abolitionist newspaper.

1834 — HENRY BLAIR invented the corn husker and became one of the first African Americans to receive a patent.

1836 — THEODORE R. WRIGHT received the first U.S. theological degree awarded to an African American minister. Wright earned the doctorate degree from Gammon Theological Seminary in 1928.

1837 — Year of birth, in Mississippi, for ARCHY LEE, a slave brought to Sacramento, California, in 1857 by his "owner" Charles Stovall. Lee later became the principal subject in the last and most celebrated fugitive slave trial held in California. Under state law, it was illegal to own slaves if the owner moved to California with intent to remain. The legal battle was joined when Stovall tried to send Lee back to Mississippi. In order to avoid returning to Mississippi, Lee took refuge in Hackett House, an African American owned hotel. It wasn't long before Lee was found and hauled into Judge Robert Robinson's courtroom. The initial hearing was held Jan. 7, 1858; others were scheduled for Jan. 23 and Jan. 26, after which Robinson ordered Lee freed.

But Lee's tenure as a free man lasted only seconds. Stovall's appeal to Robinson's ruling resulted in Lee's re-arrest and the case sent to the state Supreme Court. The high court ruled in Stovall's favor and he made plans to send Lee to Mississippi via ship.

On March 5, 1858, Lee was to be put aboard the *Orizaba,* which was en route to Panama. According to the plan, Lee was to be transferred to the *Orizaba* from a second ship positioned near Angel Island in San Francisco Bay. The minute Lee and his captors boarded the *Orizaba,* he was arrested a third time and Stovall was charged with illegally holding a slave.

California was then home to about 4,000 African Americans who paid Lee's legal expenses. The matter remained in the courts for five weeks. Lee was freed April 14 by U.S. Commissioner William Penn Johnston. Several weeks later, Lee teamed up with a group of African Americans and left California for British Columbia. He died in 1873.

1838 — The Underground Railroad became fully operational.

The first issue of the *Mirror of Freedom,* the first African American periodical, was published in New York City.

1839 — OCTAVIUS VALENTINE CATTO was born in Charleston, South Carolina. An educator and political leader, Catto was assassinated in 1871.

1840 — Birth year of MICHAEL HEALY, brother of priests Patrick and James Healy, and Captain of the U.S. Revenue Cutter Service ship *Bear, Rush and Corwin,* which patrolled Alaskan waters from 1884 to about 1899. Early in 1884, the *New York Daily Sun* described Healy: "Captain Mike Healy is a good deal more distinguished person in the waters of the far Northwest than any President of the United States or any potentate of Europe has yet become." In addition to being a sea captain, Healy also was a Deputy U.S. Marshal, and the only law enforcement officer in Alaska. The number of reindeer grew to an estimated half million by 1940. Healy, at age 64, was the third ranking officer in the Cutter Service at the time of his mandatory retirement where he was cashiered for drunkenness and impossible behavior. He was restored as a captain in 1898. Healy, died August 31, 1904, a year after retiring. (See also 6/2; 7/31).

1841 — Artist GRAFTON TYLER BROWN was born in Harrisburg, Pennsylvania. Brown moved to San Francisco in 1855 and became a student of Charles C. Kuchel. He later worked for Kuchel as a lithographer. Brown opened his own lithograph shop in San Francisco about 1867, but closed it some five years later. He then left San Francisco to travel as an artist throughout the west, settling finally in Wyoming. Brown died in 1918.

1842— Pony Express rider GEORGE MONROE was born in Georgia. Monroe, who was brought to California as a child, rode a regular route between Merced and Mariposa. He later became the driver of a Yosemite Valley stage coach. Monroe Meadows, part of the valley, was named for him.

1845— MACON B. ALLEN became the first African American admitted to the bar in Worcester, Massachusetts.

Baptists split over the question of slavery. Anti-slavery baptists did not permit slaveholders to become missionaries, an act that created the Southern Baptist Convention.

1847— The population of San Francisco was estimated at 459 and included nine African American males and one female.

FREDERICK DOUGLASS, a fugitive slave, published the first issues of the *North Star*, an abolitionist newspaper.

1848— The Free Soil Party, organized in this year, called for the prohibition of slavery in new U.S. territories.

In Massachusetts, blacksmith LEWIS TEMPLE invented a harpoon with a movable head that prevented harpooned whales from slipping free. Temple failed to patent the new harpoon and died penniless.

Gold Rush Camps Settled by African Americans, 1849–1850

California historian Erwin G. Gudde, in *California Gold Camps* defines Negro as: (a) term frequently used in geographical names since the presence of one blackamoor was often sufficient to call the place for him. The nickname "nigger" was still more often used, even in modern nomenclature. See Nigger.

In alphabetical sequence it defines "nigger" as "The nickname for negro, was frequently used in mining days. The same (settlements known as Nigger this or that) were often also called Negro." The antiquated term "Negro" will be used herein to identify 20 settlements Gudde found that

were established by African American miners. Some of the men became wealthy after working claims in the Sierra Nevada Mountains of Eastern California.

NEGRO BAR, Nevada County, California

NEGRO BAR, Placer County, California, north fork of American River

NEGRO BAR, Placer County, on Bear River

NEGRO BAR, Plumas County, California

NEGRO BAR — A Gold Rush era African American settlement also known as NIGGER BAR, was founded in 1849, in Sacramento County, California. Although destroyed, in 1850, by the Virginia Mining Company, the site is known now as the City of Folsom, and is the home of one of California's toughest prisons which bears the same name.

NEGRO BAR, Sierra County, California

NEGRO BAR, Yuba County, California

NEGRO BLUFF, El Dorado County, California

NEGRO CAMP, Nevada County, California

NEGRO CREEK, Siskiyou County, California

NEGRO DIGGINS, Sacramento County, California

NEGRO FLAT, Siskiyou County, California

NEGRO FLAT, El Dorado County, California

NEGRO FLAT, Nevada County, California

NEGRO GULCH, Calaveras County, California

NEGRO GULCH, Tuolumne County, California, near Columbia

NEGROHEAD BAR, Placer County, California, north fork of the American River

NEGRO HILL, Calaveras County, California

NEGRO HILL, El Dorado County, California, now covered by Folsom Lake

NEGRO HILL, El Dorado County, California, three miles east of Placerville

NEGRO HILL, Placer County, covered now by Folsom Lake

NEGRO HILL, Shasta County, California

NEGRO HILL, Siskiyou County, California, on Salmon River

NEGRO JACKS POINTS, Tuolumne County, California

NEGRO RAVINE, Nevada County, California

NEGRO SLIDE, Sierra County, California, north of Camptonville

NEGRO SLIDE, Yuba County, California

NEGRO TENT, Sierra County, California

NEGRO's BLUFF, Placer County, California

NEGROVILLE CREEK, GULCH, Siskiyou County, California

1850— African American Californians established churches in Sacramento.

It was reported that by the end of this year some 20,000 African Americans escaped slavery and the south on the Underground Railroad.

1851–1900

1852— Mormon migration from Utah to the San Bernardino area of Southern California, set the stage for the most significant slavery issue heard in the state courts.

African American Californians established churches in San Francisco.

1853— African American Californians established churches in the California foothill communities of Grass Valley and Marysville.

In California, African American Californians held the first state Convention of Colored Citizens, at Sacramento.

In Georgia, freed slaves reportedly owned more than 350,000 acres; equal to 546.9 square miles.

DARIUS STOKES was born in Baltimore, Maryland. An AME minister, Stokes pastored churches in the California cities of Sacramento, San Francisco, and Marysville, where Stokes was a leading citizen.

1854— JOHN JACKSON, best known as John W. "Bud" Fowler, was the first African American to play professional baseball with white teammates. The child of free field hands, Jackson was born at Cooperstown, New York. His baseball debut came in the spring of 1872 when he joined a white team in New Castle, Pennsylvania, and established himself as the first paid African American baseball player. From *Sporting Life* magazine, May 14, 1884: "The Stillwater Club has a colored player named Fowler who pitches, catches and plays left field in good shape." Fowler pitched the Stillwater Minnesota team to its first victory in the Northwestern League. Fowler earned a new suit and a $10 bonus for that game … enough to make Fowler a paid professional baseball player.

James A. Healy was ordained a priest in the Roman Catholic Church in this year. The ordination was held in Paris' Notre Dame Cathedral.

1855— The matter for judicial resolution was the status of slaves HANNAH (X) and BIDDY (X), who later took MASON as her surname. Hannah and Biddy, and their 12 children and grandchildren, were owned by a Mississippi Mormon named Robert Smith.

Smith's problems began when he decided to move to Texas after living in San Bernardino for three years. En route to Texas, Smith and his party stopped to rest outside Los Angeles, near what is now Santa Monica. It was during this rest stop, with help from a San Bernardino resident— a Mrs. Rowen—that Hannah and Biddy filed a petition for their freedom in the Los Angeles Courts. Mrs. Rowen also told authorities that "African Americans were being held as slaves" in the Los Angeles area. Slavery was outlawed in California by legislative action in 1852. Nonetheless, the law was not rigidly enforced and African Americans in some areas of the state were retained in slave status.

Acting on Mrs. Rowen's report, the Los Angeles County Sheriff took Hannah, Biddy, their children and grandchildren into custody pending a hearing on a freedom petition. During the hearing, according to court records, Hannah and Biddy had different opinions about slavery and going to Texas with Smith. Despite this, the trial judge freed all the slaves.

In his written decision, Judge Hayes criticized Smith, telling his slaves that "in Texas, of all places, they could expect an unbinding relationship." The judge further took issue with Smith in the case of four children who had been born free in California.

San Francisco attorney and author ROBERT CHARLES O'HARA BENJAMIN, was born in the British West Indies. Benjamin practiced law in Los Angeles where he also edited a newspaper.

1856—*Mirror of the Times*, a weekly newspaper, and the Athenaeum, a library, were established by African Americans living in San Francisco.

1857—A slave blacksmith/mechanic in Pike County, Mississippi, known only as NED, invented a cotton scraper.

Slave mechanic BENJAMIN MONTGOMERY designed a propeller for steamboats operating in shallow water.

1858—African American Californians established churches in Oakland.

1859—EDWARD PARKER DUPLEX was the first elected African American municipal official and later elected mayor of a California city, Wheatland, in Yuba County. He was born in Connecticut in 1888 and migrated to California in 1859.

1860—Census records show there were 4.44 million African Americans in the United States. However, 89 percent of them, 3.95 million, were slaves.

Military records of 1860 indicate there were 178,975 African American soldiers in the Union Army. Of this number, 16 were awarded the Congressional Medal of Honor for bravery in action during the Civil War.

One of every four Union sailors was an African American.

1862—Slavery was abolished in the District of Columbia with the passage of appropriate legislation by the U.S. Senate.

1864—ANTHONY OVERTON was born in this year. Overton was a jurist, newspaper publisher and banker. He manufactured Overton Hygienic products, baking powder, flavor extracts and toiletries. He received the Harmon Award in 1927 and the Spingarn Medal two years later. Overton, who died in 1946, also started Victory Mutual Life Insurance Co., which still exists.

1865—The 13TH AMENDMENT, which abolished slavery, became part of the U.S. Constitution.

Rev. ADAM CLAYTON POWELL, SR., was born in Franklin County, Virginia. He died in 1953. An author and clergyman, Powell was educated at Virginia Union College and Yale School of Divinity.

After the Civil War, but prior to Reconstruction, the Freedman's Bureau assumed responsibility for former slaves from various departments of "Negro affairs," created by President Lincoln. The federal law establishing the bureau gave it the power to give one mule and 40 acres of confiscated southern land to former slaves by January of 1866. The land and the animals were never distributed in Georgia, but from this plan came the phrase: "I'm still waiting for my 40 acres and mule," often said in jest among contemporary African Americans. Much of the land that could have been given to former slaves was in Georgia. Thus, to avoid shunting African Americans into one state, federal authorities offered tracts (in 80 acre parcels) to African Americans in Alabama, Arkansas, Florida, Louisiana and Mississippi.

The potato chip was accidentally discovered by an unknown African American chef when a wafer thin slice of the pome de terre fell into a vat of boiling oil. The location, somewhere in the United States. The chip proved to be a successful business venture.

1866—Freed African Americans owned and occupied 160,960 acres, or 251.5 square miles of the state of Florida.

Fr. JAMES A. HEALY was named pastor of Boston's St. James Catholic Church during the year.

Congress passed the first Civil Rights Act.

African American historian and journalist DELILAH LEONTIUM BEASLEY was born this year in Ohio. Beasley became a leader in the movement for women's rights after her 1909 arrival in Oakland. Beasley authored *The Negro Trailblazers of California*, a history of California African Americans, which was written in 1919.

Lyricist and signer HARRY THACKER BURLEIGH was born in Erie, Pennsylvania, this year. One of this best known songs is the spiritual *Nobody Knows the Trouble I've Seen*.

1867— The Pennsylvania State Legislature approved a law that allowed African American passengers on Philadelphia street cars (public transportation).

MAGGIE LENA WALKER, founder and president of St. Luke Penny Savings Bank, Richmond, Virginia, was born in Richmond. St. Luke's bank is the oldest African American-owned and African American-managed bank in the nation. Walker joined the Independent Order of St. Luke at age 14 and, eight years later became Grand Secretary-Treasurer. In 1903 Walker oversaw the construction of the St. Luke Building and was made president of the fledgling bank, which had nearly one-half million dollars in assets when the 1929 Depression struck. The following year, Walker was instrumental in negotiating mergers with other African American-owned Richmond banks. She later became chairman of the board of Consolidated Bank and Trust Company, a position Walker held until she died late in 1934.

SARA BREEDLOVE WALKER, believed to be the first female millionaire in the United States, was born in Louisiana. Married at 14 to C. J. Walker, "Madam C. J. Walker," as she became known, was widowed six years later. The widow Walker moved to St. Louis in 1887 and worked as a wash woman to support herself and her daughter. In 1905, Madam Walker began selling cosmetics and hair straightener to African Americans.

What began as a door-to-door business in Denver boomed. A mail order service was added just before 1913 when the business was incorporated, and franchises were sold across the United States and four foreign countries. Madam Walker built a home in New York where her daughter A'Lelia became the first African American debutante in Harlem. Madam Walker died in 1919.

1868— Classes began at Hampton Institute with MARY S. PEAKE as the first African American teacher. The institute is now known as Hampton University.

1870— JAMES WEBSTER SMITH of South Carolina became the first African American appointed to West Point. In June, 1874, after enduring four years of discrimination, social ostracism and racism, Smith was found "deficient in natural and experimental philosophy" and dismissed from the academy. He returned to South Carolina, became a mathematics instructor and commandant of cadets at South Carolina Agricultural and Mechanics Institute. Smith died of tuberculosis two years later.

HIRAM R. REVELS succeeded Jefferson Davis as the U.S. Senator from Mississippi.

1872— JOHN H. CONYERS was the first African American appointed to the U.S. Naval Academy.

1873— JOHN HENRY, the legendary African American railroad worker died in 1873 while at work on the Big Bend Tunnel in West Virginia.

1874— Vaudeville comedian EGBERT AUSTIN WILLIAMS was born on the Island of Antigua in the British West Indies and raised in Riverside, California. It is believed that Williams began performing in San Francisco around 1895. References to Williams in books about African Americans indicate he lived in San Francisco for "a time" before moving to New York where he was successful. Williams died in 1922.

1875— BLANCHE K. BRUCE was elected the U.S. Senator from Mississippi.

Fr. JAMES A. HEALY was named Bishop of the Catholic Diocese of Portland, Maine.

1878— LUTHER ROBINSON, later known as tap dancer Bill "Bojangles" Robinson, was born in Richmond, Virginia, during this year. Robinson's original goal was to become a jockey. So, in 1886 he quit school and travelled to the District of Columbia where he took a job in a stable. The veteran stable boys taught Robinson the Buck and Wind and several more dance steps. Working as a team, the boys sometimes performed on the streets for money. Robinson's professional dancing career began with minstrel Eddie Leonard. However, it was 1928 before Robinson was noticed by critics as he performed *Blackbirds of 1928*. He began appearing in movies two years later and after nine years had dazzled movie goers with his fancy footwork in 14 films.

1880— Birth year of former Assemblyman FREDERICK MADISON ROBERTS, the first African American elected to the California Legislature. Roberts was born in Ohio. A Republican, Roberts was elected to the State Assembly in 1918 from a Los Angeles district. He served eight two-year terms beginning in 1919. A teacher with journalism experience, Roberts edited and published the newspaper *New Age*, in the Los Angeles area.

1881— The first Jim Crow law enacted in Tennessee took effect in this year. It required African Americans to travel in segregated railroad coaches.

1883— ERNEST EVERETT JUST, a zoologist, was born in South Carolina. He left home for New Hampshire's Kimball Academy and Dartmouth College from which he graduated magna cum laude in 1907. Just taught at Howard University and spent summers doing research at Woods Hole, Massachusetts, while doing doctoral work at the University of Chicago. He received his doctorate in 1916. Racism forced Just to leave the United States for Europe,

where he received research fellowships and grants. He worked at the Kaiser Wilhelm Institute for Biology and the Naples Zoological Station. Just died in October 1941.

ARTHUR MITCHELL, former office boy for Booker T. Washington, was born in Chambers County, Alabama. Mitchell was the second African American seated in the House of Representatives. He founded and later was president of the Armstrong Agricultural School in Butler, Alabama.

Mitchell was admitted to the District of Columbia Bar in 1927. After a brief law practice, Mitchell moved to Chicago where he became involved in politics and later was elected to the House. Mitchell was the only African American in the House between 1935 and 1943. He retired to a Virginia farm at the expiration of his third term and died in 1968.

1884— JOHN PARKER received patents for the screw used in tobacco presses.

CHARLOTTE HAWKINS BROWN was born in Henderson, North Carolina. Brown founded Palmer Memorial Institute in North Carolina in 1902. She attended Howard University and Simms College.

An Alabama law made it unlawful for African American and Caucasian convicts to be housed in the same cell or to be chained together.

1885— ELIJAH McCOY invented the first automatic lubricating system.

1886— ALAIN LOCKE, an educator, philosopher and newspaper editor was born in 1886, location unknown. In 1907, he became the nation's first African American Rhodes Scholar.

L. CLARK BROOKS operated the first electric trolley on the North American continent.

Birth year of WILLIAM L. DAWSON, R-Illinois, who served 14 consecutive terms in the House of Representatives, beginning in 1943. Dawson, a lawyer who passed the bar in 1920 was a graduate of Kent College and Northwestern University.

1890— Census data indicate 57% of African Americans were employed in agriculture, hunting and fishing; 31% domestic, personal service; 6% manufacturing; 5% trade and transportation and 1% were professionals.

MORDECAI WYATT JOHNSON was born in Paris, Tennessee. An orator, educator and minister, Johnson was once president of Howard University, and responsible for the rise from humble beginnings in an abandoned tavern and dance hall to a campus valued at $34 million by 1956 — 30 years after he became president. Johnson was a Morehouse College graduate; he earned a master's degree in theology from Harvard Divinity School and his doctorate from Gammon Theological Seminary in 1928.

1891 — Georgia became the first state to invoke segregation on public transportation.

Census data indicates 1.3 million African Americans were members of the National Colored Farmer's Alliance.

1892 — WALTER FRANCIS WHITE was born in Atlanta, Georgia. He was Assistant Secretary to the NAACP, from 1918 to 1931, and Executive Secretary 1931 to 1955, the year of his death. White defied logic and racist Whites by traveling to various southern cities to investigate, firsthand, the lynching of African Americans.

Architect PAUL REVERE WILLIAMS was born in Los Angeles. Williams designed and built pubic and commercial buildings for business and government and homes for movie stars. His designs were noted for their unique Williams style.

GEORGE DIXON, then World Bantamweight boxing champion, defended his title only after refusing to fight at the New Orleans Olympic Club unless 700 seats were set aside for African American fans.

WALTER ARTHUR GORDON — A jurist, Gordon was born in Georgia in 1892. He graduated from the University of California in 1918 and completed law school four years later. He served as governor of the Virgin Islands 1955–58, the first African American in that job, and as the islands' federal district court judge, 1958–76.

CHARLES SPURGEON JOHNSON — A social scientist born in 1892, Johnson was the first African American president of Fisk University. He was appointed in 1946. Johnson was a native of Bristol, Virginia, and was educated at Virginia Union University and University of Chicago. He earned a doctorate from the latter in 1928. Johnson also served as executive director of Chicago's Human Relations Commission in the period of 1923–29. He published several books based on his research projects regarding African Americans and African American issues. Among them were *The Negro in Chicago*, *The Negro in American Civilization*, *Economic Status of the Negro* and *Collapse of Cotton Tenancy*. Johnson died in 1956.

1894 — Congress repealed the 1866 Civil Rights Act.

1896 — Ragtime, a blend of West African and European music made its debut in the Midwestern United States.

1898 — A composer and arranger of music, WILLIAM LEVI DAWSON was born in Anniston, Alabama, during this year. A 1921 graduate of Tuskegee Institute, Dawson also attended Washburn College, the Kansas City, Missouri, Institute of Fine Arts and the Chicago Musical College. Among his songs are: "I Couldn't Hear Nobody Pray," "Talk About a Child That Do Love Jesus" and "My Lord What a Morning."

1901–1950

1900 — Sculptor AUGUSTA SAVAGE was born at Green Cove Springs, Florida. Savage died in 1962.

1902 — The birth year of writer WILHELMINA MARGUERITA CROSSON, in Rutherford, New Jersey. The author of numerous articles on education, Crosson was an assistant to Charlotte Hawkins Brown at the Palmer Memorial Institute, Sedalia, North Carolina.

CHARLIE GRANT masqueraded as a Native American named "CHIEF TOKAHOMA" and played professional baseball with the Baltimore Orioles. Grant was not detected until the team played an exhibition game against the White Sox in Chicago where virtually every African American attended the game to see Tokahoma. The party was over when White Sox manager Charlie Comisky complained about "our boy Charlie Grant." Grant was fired from the Orioles and returned to baseball in the then Negro League.

1903— Poet COUNTEE CULLEN was born this year in New York City. An acclaimed poet at age 21, after *Color*, his first book of poetry, Cullen was brought up by a Methodist minister. He was a Phi Beta Kappa graduate of New York University and also earned a graduate degree from Harvard.

1905— BOB MARSHALL, an athlete with the University of Minnesota varsity football team. He was selected for the 1905 All-American (Collegiate) Football Team.

1909— The National Association of Colored Graduate Nurses was founded in this year. The U.S. Army did not contact the Association for service in World War I until September 1918, two months before the Armistice was signed, despite the use of African Americans in combat divisions.

Slavery formally was abolished by the New York State Legislature.

1910— SHELBY DAVIDSON, inventor of rewind devices for tabulating and adding machines, received a patent in this year.

1912— W. C. HANDY, a composer, published "Memphis Blues" in 1912. It was the first blues composition.

1915— Conductor DEAN DIXON was born in Harlem. Fluent in Swedish, French and German, Dixon became one of Europe's best known conductors after leaving the United States in 1949. He conducted the Goteborg (Sweden) symphony for 10 years before being named conductor for the Hessian Radio Symphony of Frankfurt, Germany. So great was Dixon's ability, he led the New York Chamber Orchestra at age 25 and while still a student at New York's Juilliard School of Music. Dixon died in 1976.

1918— Birth year of child psychologist MAMIE PHIPPS CLARK at Hot Springs, Arkansas. Phipps was a graduate of Howard University and earned a post graduate degree, one of the first African American women to do so, from Columbia University. In 1946, now married, the new Dr. Clark and her husband moved to New York where she opened the Northside Child Development Center in the basement of her Harlem apartment building. She quickly learned that her white counterparts were deliberately classifying many African American children as retarded. Just as quickly, Dr. Clark discovered these determinations were false. Dr. Clark's research of this practice was her contribution to the legal brief which lead to the 1954 U.S. Supreme Court's landmark decision in *Brown vs. Board of Education of Topeka*. She died in 1983.

1919— In California, FREDERICK MADISON ROBERTS, the state's first African American legislator, took his seat in the California Assembly.

1921— The birth year of WHITNEY M. YOUNG, JR. A major civil rights leader and National Urban League executive director, YOUNG was born in Lincoln Ridge, Kentucky. Young died in 1971.

MARCUS GARVEY, a Black Separatist, Garvey announced his organization, the Empire of Africa, of which he was Provisional President. Garvey said it was "futile" for African Americans to expect justice and that they should leave the U.S. and organize a nation of their own.

1923— The first Catholic seminary for African American priests was dedicated at Bay St. Louis, Mississippi.

1924— JOEL E. SPINGARN began the Spingarn Medal awards to recognize the achievements of African Americans. Spingarn was then chairman of the NAACP Board of Directors.

1925— Former Colorado Lt. Gov. GEORGE BROWN was born this year in Lawrence, Kansas.

ADELBERT H. ROBERT became the first African American elected to the Illinois State Legislature since Reconstruction.

1926— Black History Week was introduced to the United States by CARTER G. WOODSON and the Association for the Study of Black Life and History.

1928— OSCAR DE PRIEST became the first African American elected to Congress from a non-southern state.

1929— The Brotherhood of Sleeping Car Porters, a union, was chartered by the American Federation of Labor.

1930— RICHARD B. HARRISON — An actor, Harrison starred as "De Lawd" in 1930 in the Broadway production of *Green Pastures.*

1933— Basketball star MAURICE "MO" STOKES of the Rochester Royals was born in Pittsburgh, Pennsylvania. The NBA Rookie of the Year in 1956, Stokes died in 1970.

The National Association for the Advancement of Colored People launched the first assault on educational discrimination in the United States by bringing a lawsuit against the University of North Carolina.

Actor and comedian GEOFFREY CAMBRIDGE, star of the movie *Watermelon Man* was born in New York City during this year.

1934— AUGUSTUS F. HAWKINS defeated Frederick M. Roberts, California's first African American legislator, in this year's campaign for the state Assembly seat Roberts had held 16 years.

1936— ELEANOR HOLMES NORTON was born in Washington, D.C. A former chairman of the U.S. Equal Employment Opportunity Commission, Norton is a lawyer and earned her juris doctorate from Yale University.

1937— WILLIAM H. HASTIE — Confirmed as a Judge of the Federal District Court, in the Virgin Islands. Hastie thus became the first African American federal judge.

1942— The Congress of Racial Equality (C.O.R.E.) was formed at Chicago, Illinois.

Of the hundreds of so-called Liberty Ships built early in World War II, 18 were named for prominent African Americans. Those so honored included Robert S. Abbott, Robert J. Banks, George Washington Carver, William Cox, Frederick Douglass, Paul Lawrence Dunbar, John Hope, James Weldon Johnson, George A. Lawson, John Merrick, John H. Murphy, Edward A. Savoy, Toussaint L'Ouverture, Harriett Tubman, Robert L. Vann, James K. Walker, Booker T. Washington, Bert Williams. The *Frederick Douglass* was torpedoed in 1943, the *Robert L. Vann* sunk in 1945 after hitting a mine in the Atlantic ocean, the *George Washington Carver* became the U. S. Army Hospital Ship *Dogwood*, and the stern of the *Bert Williams* and the bow of the *Nathaniel Bacon*, also a Liberty Ship, were joined to create the *Bocadasse*, an Italian registry vessel.

Franklin Delano Roosevelt, as president in 1942 signed and issued Executive Order 8802, which ended employment discrimination when work involved government and/or defense contracts and defense training. Roosevelt signed the order after A. Philip Randolph, president of the Brotherhood of Sleeping Car Porters, a union, threatened a massive protest march on Washington, D.C.

1943— The BOOKER T. WASHINGTON, a U.S. merchant ship, was launched this year with Captain Malzoc, an African American, at the helm.

1944— The Rev. ADAM CLAYTON POWELL, JR. became the first African American elected to Congress from the east.

1945— Unlike Liberty Ships, most Victory Ships were built late in World War II and launched in June of this year. Four Victory Ships were named for the African American universities: Fisk and Howard universities, Lane College and Tuskegee Institute. *Fisk Victory* was scrapped in Kaohshung Harbor, on the island of Taiwan; *Howard Victory* was scrapped in Campana, Argentina; *Tuskegee Victory* was taken over by the U.S. Navy in 1957, renamed *Reverend Dutton* and outfitted as a geological survey vessel and is believed to be still in service; and *Lane Victory*, which never saw service during the war, was towed to the Fleet Reserve anchorage in Suisun Bay, CA.

1947— In this year JACKIE ROBIN-SON joined the Brooklyn Dodgers professional baseball team and became the fifth African American to play major league baseball. (See Bud Fowler, Welday Walker, Moses Fleetwood Walker and the Argyle Hotel Waiters)

1948— WILLIAM BYRON RUMFORD was the second African American elected to the State Assembly by California voters. A Democrat, Rumford represented a Berkeley district.

The United Nations Security Council sent envoy RALPHE BUNCHE to mediate a dispute between Israel and its Arab neighbors.

1949— WILLIAM L. DAWSON became chairman of House Expenditures Committee, the first African American to chair a standing Congressional committee. Dawson died in 1970 at Albany, Georgia.

1950— The African American population of California was 462,172; up from 124,306 ten years earlier.

Chicago school teacher and poet GWENDOLYN BROOKS became the first African American to win a Pulitzer Prize. Brooks' *Annie Allen*, a volume of poetry, won her the honor.

1951–present

1951— Army PFC WILLIAM THOMPSON, a native of Brooklyn, New York, was posthumously awarded the Congressional Medal of Honor for heroism in Korea. Thompson was the first African American so honored since the Spanish-American War.

1952— Physician LOUIS TOMKINS WRIGHT died during this year. He was born in La Grange, Georgia. Wright served as a lieutenant in the Army Medical Corps during World War I. He later became a

cancer researcher and founded the Harlem Hospital Cancer Research Foundation.

A report issued by Tuskegee Institute showed 1952 was the first year since 1881 in which no lynching of African American men occurred.

1954— The United States Supreme Court held that racial discrimination in public schools is unconstitutional.

1956— The United States Supreme Court banned segregation in public parks, playgrounds, beaches and golf courses, rejecting the previously accepted "separate but equal" doctrine.

1961— ROBERT C. WEAVER was sworn in as administrator of the Federal Housing and Home Finance Agency. His position, at the time, was the highest federal government appointment ever held by an African American.

1962— Racial and religious discrimination were banned by an Executive Order signed by President John F. Kennedy.

Rep. MERVYN DYMALLY was first elected to a California Assembly seat from the Los Angeles area. Dymally was elected Lt. Governor of California in November 1972, and to the House of Representatives in 1980.

F. DOUGLASS TERRELL was elected to the California Assembly during this election year.

Infielder JACKIE ROBINSON was inducted into baseball's Hall of Fame in this year.

1963— The Rumford Fair Housing Act, known as Proposition 14, became law in California. Written by then Assemblyman BYRON RUMFORD, the Act allowed complaints regarding housing to go directly to the state Fair Housing and Employment Practices Commission for resolution. This provision opened an avenue for housing discrimination grievances and enabled those who could not afford legal counsel to challenge discriminating landlords, real estate agents or property owners.

Employing the initiative process, the

association of California Realtors launched Proposition 14, designed to void the Rumford Fair Housing Act. The electorate embraced Prop. 14 and it passed by a wide margin. However, its mission, to invalidate the Rumford Act, was thwarted. The measure was unable to withstand a court challenge and was thrown out by the State Supreme Court after a hearing. The court action made it possible to reinstate the Rumford Act.

President Kennedy urged the end of segregation with a declaration affirming the practice to be a moral issue.

1964 — California Assembly Speaker WILLIE L. BROWN was first elected to the California Assembly. He emerged as Assembly Speaker in 1980, after a major squabble between two other Democrats seeking the top Assembly job. Brown was Speaker longer than any prior California legislator.

MARTIN LUTHER KING, JR. was awarded the Nobel Peace Prize.

1965 — The Voting Rights Act became law in the United States.

1966 — Massachusetts'   EDWARD BROOKE became the first African American popularly elected to the U.S. Senate since Reconstruction and the third in the history of the nation.

California voters elected YVONNE BRAITHWAITE BURKE, BILL GREEN and LEON RALPH, all of Los Angeles, and JOHN MILLER, of Berkeley, to the California State Assembly.

Economist ANDREW BRIMMER was appointed to the U.S. Federal Reserve Board of Governors.

1967 — MAYME CLAYTON, a former librarian for the University of Southern California and University of California, Los Angeles, began collecting materials for what she now calls the WESTERN STATES BLACK RESEARCH CENTER. The center owns a unique collection of books, film, pamphlets, posters, photographs, phonograph records, video tapes and magazines, all relating to the African American experience. The Center is open to researchers by appointment only.

1969 — The newly elected 91st Congress included ten African American Representatives, among them SHIRLEY CHISHOLM and ADAM CLAYTON POWELL, JR., who was denied his seat in 1967.

CHARLES EVERS was elected mayor of Jackson, Mississippi, his hometown. Evers is the brother of assassinated civil rights leader Medgar Evers.

1970 — California's African American population was estimated at 1.4 million; up from 900,000 a decade earlier.

KENNETH GIBSON was elected mayor of Newark, New Jersey.

1972 — YVONNE   BRAITHWAITE BURKE — In the general election, Burke successfully campaigned for a seat in the U.S. House of Representatives.

JULIAN DIXON was elected to the seat in the California House of Representatives once held by Yvonne Braithwaite Burke.

FRANK HOLOMAN was elected to represent a Los Angeles District in the California Assembly in this year.

1974 — GEORGE L. BROWN was elected Lt. Governor of Colorado. Brown was born in Lawrence, Kansas. He was educated at the universities of Kansas and Colorado.

1988 — LEE ROY YOUNG, a 41-year-old veteran Texas law enforcement officer, received his badge and commission as the first African American Texas Ranger. Texas Rangers are charged only to "protect life and property, by enforcing the Texas Penal Code; put down riots and insurrections; apprehend fugitives, and to investigate major crimes."

In November of this year, efforts were made to upgrade decorations earned in World War I by African American soldiers HENRY JOHNSON and NEEDHAM ROBERTS, the first U.S. soldiers decorated for bravery in France. This plan was to upgrade Johnson's decoration to the Congressional Medal of Honor. The process was stalled in House committees.

WILLIAM B. PURVIS — In Philadelphia, invented the machine used to make paper bags.

THE ALMANAC

January

One's work may be finished someday, but one's education never.—Alexandre Dumas, père

This month:

1920—An all–African American basketball team, now known internationally as the HARLEM GLOBETROTTERS, began nomadic tours of the United States (and later the world as its name implies) under team manager-promoter *Abe Saperstein*. The team earned the nickname the "Clown Princes of Basketball" because of zany on-court antics.

1 January

1808—Congress prohibited slave trading. The illicit trade continued until the Civil War began and, over the next five decades, an estimated 250,000 more Africans were brought to the colonies that became the United States.

1854—Originally chartered as ASHUM INSTITUTE, in Chester, Pennsylvania, LINCOLN UNIVERSITY was the first African American college in the United States. The school is now in Lincoln University, Pennsylvania.

1863—President Abraham Lincoln issued the *Emancipation Proclamation*, which symbolically freed all slaves in the Confederate States. Africans were brought to the colonies in chains and forced into slavery in most states at one time or another until the issue of slavery was resolved, but not finally, by the Civil War.

1916—The first issue of CARTER G. WOODSON's *Journal of Negro History*, a quarterly publication of the Association for the Study of Negro Life and History, was circulated January 1, 1916. (See also 12/19)

2 January

1800—In Philadelphia, free African Americans petitioned Congress, then housed in that city, to abolish slavery. The defeat of the petition focused on the efforts of South Carolinian John Rutledge, Jr. Rutledge said the request was one result of "this new fangled French philosophy of liberty and equality." The petition died in a committee to which it was referred for study.

1954—Kosciusko, Mississippi, was the birthplace of OPRAH WINFREY, television movie producer, actress and talk show hostess. Winfrey's earnings from Harpo, her film production company, and other ventures made her the highest paid person in the American entertainment industry in 1996.

1991—SHARON PRATT DIXON was sworn in as mayor of the District of Columbia. Dixon succeeded Marion Barry who was convicted of cocaine possession during the summer of 1990.

1991—A decision by U.S. District Judge D. Lowell Jensen, prosecutor for the Port Chicago Ammunition Station courts-martial, successfully blocked a proposed federal policy that would have required entrance examinations and established an admissions policy for all potential college students. California community colleges, all 106, traditionally have accepted students without a check of high school academic records or an admissions test.

3 January

1966— SAMMY YOUNGE, JR., 21, was killed in Tuskegee, Alabama. Younge, a Tuskegee Institute student and civil rights activist, was shot to death by Marvin Segrest, a 67-year-old White service station attendant. There are two theories about the shooting:

The men had a long running argument and bickered a great deal but no one seemed to know why, according to the accounts of the shooting in the *Montgomery Advertiser*. However, the shooting was "for no apparent reason," the paper reported. Younge was shot about 11 P.M. The shooting was witnessed by a Greyhound bus driver who reported it to the sheriff. It was later reported that Younge was found with a golf club in his hand. There were no official reports of the bus driver having seen Younge with the club or any other weapon.

A friend of Segrest's reported the incident to the sheriff about an hour after Younge was killed. But then-Sheriff Harvey Sadler said the shooting "is definitely not a civil rights shooting. The boy apparently kept agitating the old man until this happened."

Younge was shot after using the "Whites only" restroom at the service station where Segrest was an attendant, according to the *Tuskegee News*, an African American weekly published in Tuskegee, 40 miles east of Montgomery. (See also 12/9)

4 January

1935— Former world heavyweight boxing champion FLOYD PATTERSON was born in Waco, North Carolina. A 1952 Olympic gold medalist, Patterson fought 64 times and won 40 bouts by knockout. He defeated veteran boxer Archie Moore in 1956 for the then-vacant World Heavyweight Title. After four successful defenses, Patterson lost to Ingemar Johanson in the summer of 1959. He regained the title in a rematch but lost it to Sonny Liston two years later.

1990— Two months shy of the 25th anniversary of the civil rights march on Selma, Alabama, 1,500— 25 percent — of Selma's 6,000 African American students boycott classes to express their concern about the summary dismissal of NORWARD ROUSSELL, the city's first African American superintendent. Roussell was fired by six Whites, who were then the majority on the Selma Board of Education. African American youngsters make up 70 percent of the student population, while their adult counterparts hold only five seats on the school bard. The boycott of classes began when the White majority, appointed by the Selma City Council, refused to renew Roussell's three year contract. The pact expired June 30. The dispute is evidence that little has changed in provincial Selma.

1990— Fashion designer PATRICK KELLY, a 35-year-old native of Vicksburg, Mississippi, died in Paris. The clothing Kelly designed was worn by the Princess of Wales, Jane Seymour, the late Bette Davis, Grace Jones and Madonna.

5 January

1911— At Indiana University, Kappa Alpha Psi fraternity was founded by ELDER W. DIGGS, BRYAN K. ARMSTRONG, JOHN M. LEE, HARVEY T. ASHER, MARCUS P. BLAKEMORE, GUY L. GRANT, PAUL CAINE, GEORGE EDMONDS, EZERA D. ALEXANDER and EDWARD G. IRVIN.

1943— Agricultural scientist GEORGE WASHINGTON CARVER, who discovered hundreds of products within the peanut, died at Tuskegee, Alabama. Carver was born in Diamond Grove, Missouri, but his exact birth date is unknown; however, he was educated at Simpson College in Indianola, Iowa, and later became a professor at Tuskegee Institute. During his lifetime, Carver discovered more than 300 products that could be made from peanuts. He was an early advocate of crop rotation.

1991—In Fresno, California, a U.S. District Court Judge sentenced Thomas D. McCracken, 20, to 21 months in federal prison for helping two juveniles place, ignite and burn a gasoline-soaked, four-foot-tall wooden cross on the front lawn of the Modesto, California, home of an African American mother and her two children.

6 January

1811—The birth date of Charles Sumner, a liberal U.S. senator and abolitionist from Massachusetts. Sumner served one term, 1871–74.

7 January

1901—Writer ZORA NEALE HURSTON, who also was a cultural anthropologist, was born in Eatonville, an all African American incorporated community in Florida. Among Hurston's books were *Mules and Men* and *Tell My Horse*, both of which addressed folk tales and superstitious beliefs among African Americans in the south. Other works by Hurston include *Jonah's Gourd Wine, Their Eyes Are Watching God, Moses, Man of the Mountain*, and her autobiography, *Dust Tracks on a Road*, which was published in 1942. (See also 8/18)

1941—Birthday, in Washington, D.C., of Air Force Col. FREDERICK D. GREGORY, an astronaut assigned to the National Aeronautics and Space Administration. A graduate of the Air Force Academy at Colorado Springs, Colorado, Gregory earned a master's degree in information systems from George Washington University. Gregory, a test pilot, was posted to NASA's Langley Research Center in the summer of 1974. He was selected for the

Astronaut Program in January 1978 and commanded a November 1989 mission of the shuttle *Discovery*.

1955—MARIAN ANDERSON, a mezzo-soprano, sang Ulrica in Verdi's *Masked Ball*. Anderson was the first African American to become a permanent member of the Metropolitan Opera Company of New York. (See also 2/17; 4/9)

1987—New York City police reported significant increases in racial incidents in the 17-day period that began Dec. 20, 1986, when White teens chased MICHAEL GRIFFITH, an African American, onto a freeway. Griffith was hit by a speeding car and later died from his injuries. The incident occurred in Howard Beach, a community in the Borough of Queens, where Griffith and two male companions went into a pizza parlor to telephone for help after their car broke down in the mostly White community. The trio was attacked after leaving the restaurant. (See also 1/23; 12/20; 12/21)

8 January

1815—The Battle of New Orleans, the last of the War of 1812, was fought. African American troops, the Battalion of Free Men of Color and a Battalion from Santo Domingo on the island of Dominica, supporting Gen. Andrew Jackson on the Chalmette Plains, held fast before an enemy attack on their positions. The troop counterattacked and allowed Jackson to successfully defend the city. The role played by African American troops was overlooked since African American veterans were banned from taking part in the annual parades held to celebrate Jackson's victory. Officially, the war ended one week before the battle. The clash took place because neither side knew about the truce.

1875—Virginian GEORGE WASHINGTON, possibly the A. P. Gianini of the Pacific Northwest, having traveled cross country in the company of foster parents and settled in Washington Territory a quarter of a century earlier, founded the city of Centerville. An older settlement, also named Centerville existed in southeastern Washington so, in 1885, Washington's Centerville was renamed "Centralia," as it is presently known. Washington, a successful businessman, was revered because of his willingness to help his neighbors. Regardless of the need — cash, help with crops, or seed money for farmers and fledgling entrepreneurs — Washington never refused a request. He also donated some of his real estate holdings for schools and churches.

1989 — African American and European American White students attended school together for the first time. Integration of St. Helena Parish schools was achieved when Greensburg, Louisiana, school officials settled a 36-year-old lawsuit. Believed to be the nation's oldest integration suit, the complaint was brought in 1952 by JOHN HALL and the National Association for the Advancement of Colored People. Hall complained that his 14 children were required to attend all African American schools.

9 January

1914 — Phi Beta Sigma fraternity was founded at Howard University. Among the founders were LANGSTON TAYLOR, LEONARD F. MORSE and C. I. BROWN. Special charter members included WILLIAM F. VINCENT, I. C. SCRUGGS and WALTER F. TEBLES.

1918 — The last fight between an American Indian tribe and the 4th U.S. Army began on this date when a war party of Yaqui Indians, estimated at slightly more than two dozen braves, opened fire on Troop E of 10th Cavalry Regiment. The Yaqui attack began as the troopers rode through Atasco Canyon west of Nogales, Arizona. According to military historians, the skirmish was overshadowed by World War I and, therefore, attracted little public attention.

10 January

1915 — Classical conductor DEAN DIXON was born in 1915, in Harlem, New York City. Fluent in Swedish, French and German, Dixon became one of Europe's best known conductors after leaving the U.S. in 1949. He conducted the Goteborg (Sweden) Symphony for 10 years before being named conductor for the Hessian Radio Symphony in Frankfurt, Germany. So great was Dixon's ability, he led the New York Chamber Orchestra at age 25 while still a student at Juilliard School of Music in New York. Dixon died in 1976.

1934 — Birthday of FRANK HOLOMAN, who was elected to the California Assembly from the Los Angeles area in 1972.

1938 — Birth date of baseball great WILLIE LEE McCOVEY, in Mobile, Alabama. McCovey joined the San Francisco Giants in 1953 and played with the team for 14 years before moving to the San Diego Padres in 1974. He was Rookie of the Year in 1959 and led the National League in home runs in 1963, 1968 and 1969. McCovey was selected the National League's Most Valuable Player for 1969.

1957 — The Southern Christian Leadership Conference was founded in New Orleans, Louisiana, by five ministers, including MARTIN LUTHER KING, JR., RALPH ABERNATHY, JOSEPH LOWERY, FRED SHUTTLESWORTH and C. K. STEELE. King was founding president, Abernathy president emeritus and Rep. WALTER FAUNTROY, D–District of Columbia, was chairman of the board of directors.

1966 — Because of his opposition to the Vietnam War, the Georgia Legislature refused to seat JULIAN BOND. Bond was re-elected but the Legislature refused to seat him a second time. The issue was resolved by the U.S. Supreme Court, which ruled Bond was entitled to the seat because the act of voicing his political opinion was a right protected by the U.S. Constitution.

1967 — Members of the House of Representatives accused Rep. ADAM CLAYTON POWELL, Jr., D–New York, of misusing public funds (designated for Congressional travel). Powell, author of the first law authorizing educational grants and loans for students, was prevented from taking his seat. He also lost the chairmanship of the House Education and Labor Committee. (See also 3/1; 4/4; 11/25)

11 January

1988— Scientists announced that a woman they call "Eve" was the mother of contemporary society. The "mitochondrial mother" was probably African, the scientists said. Africa is the only area to provide evidence of human life more than one million years ago.

12 January

1944— Former heavyweight boxing champion JOSEPH "Smoking Joe" FRAZIER was born in Beaufort, South Carolina. Frazier was a 1964 Olympic gold medalist who won the vacant New York heavyweight championship from Manuel Ramos in 1968. He lost the title to George Foreman in 1973. Frazier's career included 37 bouts in which 27 opponents were defeated by knock-outs. Frazier was elected to the Boxing Hall of Fame in 1980.

13 January

1966— ROBERT C. WEAVER was appointed Secretary of the Department of Housing and Urban Development and became the first African American member of a presidential cabinet. He was nominated by then President Lyndon B. Johnson.

1987— A federal judge ruled that African American residents of Springfield, Illinois, "have been denied voting rights and suffer the effects" of 70 years of segregation.

1987— Evan Mecham, then governor of Arizona, rescinded the gubernatorial decree by former Gov. Bruce Babbit that established the birthday of the Rev. MARTIN LUTHER KING, JR., as a state holiday. On election day, 1990, the Arizona electorate rejected a ballot measure that would have established King's birthday as a state holiday. Meanwhile, the Arizona Legislature continues to duck the issue. (See also 1/14; 1/15; 1/19; 3/11; 4/4; 4/27; 8/28; 8/29; 10/8; 10/14; 11/6; 11/22; 12/1)

14 January

1940— Former Georgia state senator and civil rights activist JULIAN BOND was born in Nashville, Tennessee.

1943— In Charleston, South Carolina, the birthday of HARVEY B. GANTT, the first African American student enrolled at Clemson University. Gantt is a graduate of Iowa State and Clemson universities and the Massachusetts Institute of Technology. A former lecturer at the University of North Carolina, Gantt became mayor pro tem of Charleston, in 1983 and later served as mayor of Charlotte from 1983 to 1987. (See also 10/5)

1989— In Huntington Beach, California, police officer DONALD JACKSON, having made earlier arrangements with an NBC television news crew, was videotaped during his arrest for no apparent reason by a Long Beach, California, police officer. The arresting officer is suspected of pushing Jackson's head into a plate glass window while going through Jackson's pockets. In interviews following the incident, Jackson, then on leave from the Huntington Beach Police Department, said the so-called sting was set up to prove that White officers harass African Americans, often without probable cause. In November 1989, Jackson filed a $15 million lawsuit naming the arresting officer and his partner and the city of Long Beach as defendants. (See also 11/17)

1990— In Richmond, Virginia, upon completion of inaugural ceremonies, former Lt. Gov. LAWRENCE DOUGLAS WILDER became the first popularly elected African American governor of an American state. A crowd estimated at 30,000 by Virginia state police was on hand when Wilder was sworn in by retired U.S. Supreme Court Justice Lewis F. Powell.

Wilder defeated Republican J. Marshall Coleman by 6,700 votes. (See also 1/17; 1/26; 11/7; 11/27)

1990— David Duke, former grand dragon of the Ku Klux Klan, failed in his attempt to become the Republican candidate for the U.S. Senate seat held by Sen. J. Bennett Johnston, D-Louisiana. Louisiana voters gave the nod to state Sen. Ben Bagert. Bagert defeated Duke 451 to 52, roughly a 9 to 1 ratio. (See also 1/21; 5/31; 10/8)

1990— In Arizona, recognition of MARTIN LUTHER KING, JR.'s birth date as a state holiday stalled again. In September 1989, Gov. Rose Mofford signed into law a bill that traded Columbus Day for King Day. The prospects looked rosy until Julian Sanders, a supporter of impeached former Gov. Evan Mecham, convinced 80,000 voters to sign a petition that put the King Holiday issue on the November 1990 ballot. Until recently, Arizona, Idaho, Montana and New Hampshire were the only states not recognizing the King Holiday. (See also 1/13; 1/14; 1/15; 1/19; 3/11; 4/4; 4/11; 4/27; 8/28; 8/29; 10/8; 10/14; 12/1; 11/6

15 January

1908— Alpha Kappa Alpha sorority was founded at Howard University by ETHEL HEDGEMAN LYLE. It is the oldest Greek organization for African American college women.

1929— The birthday of the Rev. MARTIN LUTHER KING, JR., who was born in Atlanta, Georgia. King, a civil rights leader often called the "conscience of America," was assassinated April 4, 1968, by career criminal James Earl Ray. (See also 1/13; 1/19; 3/11; 4/4; 4/27; 8/28; 8/29; 10/8; 10/14; 11/6; 12/1)

1990— Jimmy "The Greek" Snyder was fired from CBS after stating in a televised interview that African Americans are better athletes than Whites because they were "bred that way" and "the only thing left for ... Whites is a couple of coaching jobs." Snyder added, in a separate interview also televised, that African American athletes are better than Whites because African Americans have bigger thighs, a genetic feature that allows African Americans to "jump higher and run faster." There was more, but Snyder issued an apology. (See also 2/8, 3/5)

16 January

1918— Alpha Kappa Alpha, the first African American college sorority, was founded on the campus of Howard University. Its founders were ETHEL HEDGEMAN (LYLE), ETHEL ROBINSON, LILLIAN BURKE, BEULAH BURKE, MARGARET FLAGG (HOLMES), MARIE WOOLFOLK (TAYLOR), LAVINIA TAYLOR, ANNA BROWN, LUCY SLOWE and MARGERY HILL.

1920— Zeta Phi Beta sorority, with the help of ROBERT SAMUEL TAYLOR, a Phi Beta Sigma man, was founded at Howard University by ARIZONA STEMMONS, MYRTLE FAITHFUL, PEARL A. NEAL, FANNIE WATTS and VIOLA GOINGS. Its purpose was to "enhance womanhood ... and scholarship." It is open to students majoring in most professions, ranging from engineering to medicine.

17 January

1931— Actor JAMES EARL JONES, a master of delivery and diction, was born in Arkabutla, Tate County, Mississippi. His movie credits include *The Hunt for Red October, Dr. Strangelove, The Man, The Great White Hope* and *Star Wars*. As a child Jones stuttered, but he went on to earn numerous awards for his acting and oratory.

1931— LAWRENCE DOUGLAS WILDER, former lieutenant governor and governor of Virginia, was born in Richmond, Virginia. Wilder graduated from Virginia Union University after earning a degree in chemistry, and Howard University, from which he earned a law degree. (See also 1/14; 1/26; 11/7; 11/27)

18 January

1858— Birthday of Dr. DANIEL HALE WILLIAMS, who performed what is believed to be the first successful open heart surgery at Chicago's Provident Hospital. (See also 7/9)

1942— Former world heavyweight boxing champion MUHAMMAD ALI was born Cassius Marcellus Clay in Louisville, Kentucky. In his professional career, Ali fought 61 times and knocked out 37 of his opponents. (See also 1/22; 4/28; 6/20; 6/28; 9/15; 10/29; 10/30; 11/13)

1990— District of Columbia Mayor MARION BARRY was arrested after a joint sting operation by District police and FBI agents, who charged Barry with possession and use of "crack," a crystalline form of cocaine. Officers and agents videotaped Barry as the mayor smoked crack given to him by Rasheeda Moore, a model and long-time acquaintance. Moore was working for the FBI, which supplied the cocaine Barry was caught smoking, and at the Bureau's insistence, called Barry to her room in the Vista International Hotel. (Authorities said Moore agreed to help in order to solve her own legal problem involving drugs and to help Barry. (See also 3/6)

19 January

1918— Publisher JOHN H. JOHNSON was born in Arkansas City, Arkansas. Johnson publishes *Ebony*, *Negro Digest* and *Jet* magazines. *Ebony*, Johnson's initial publication, was first published in November 1945. It was founded to celebrate African American excellence, while concurrently portraying the experience of Africans in America.

1987— Elements of the Ku Klux Klan protested the new national holiday honoring the Rev. MARTIN LUTHER KING, JR. The holiday was not immediately embraced by all Whites. (See also 1/13; 1/14; 1/15; 3/11; 4/4; 4/27; 8/28; 8/29; 10/8; 10/14; 11/6; 12/1)

20 January

1895— EVA JESSYE was born in Coffey-ville, Kansas. Jessye was choral director for the Eva Jessye Singers, and directed the choral efforts in the initial Broadway production of *Porgy and Bess* in 1935. She also directed choruses for the movie *Hallelujah* and the opera *Four Saints in Three Acts*.

1900— African American Congressman GEORGE H. WHITE, North Carolina, introduced a bill to make lynching of Americans a federal offense. The bill died in committee. In 1900, 105 African Americans were lynched in the United States.

21 January

1773— Poet PHILLIS WHEATLEY, born a slave in 1754, was freed and her first book of poetry, *Poems on Various Subjects, Religious and Moral*, was published. The book of poetry was widely acclaimed in the United States and England. Wheatley, who died in 1814, was once the slave of Boston businessman John Wheatley.

1989— Campaigning as a Republican, David Duke, former Imperial Wizard, Knights of the Ku Klux Klan, found himself running third in the race for a seat in the Louisiana State House of Representatives. Duke is a White supremacy advocate. (See also 1/14; 5/31; 10/8)

22 January

1822— Early Colorado gold miner, hotel magnate and entrepreneur, former slave BARNEY L. FORD was born in Stafford Court House, Virginia. Through a number of business dealings, Ford became a wealthy man but was dogged by a series of tragic accidents. The restaurants and hotels he owned in Denver, Colorado, and Nicaragua were leveled by bombs and fires, and racism periodically forced him out of the gold fields. Despite these setbacks, Ford made and lost several fortunes in his lifetime. (See also 12/14)

1920— Birth date of actor, pianist and singer WILLIAM WARFIELD, who was born in West Helena, Arkansas. Warfield's illustrious career in music spans 54 years. As a young man, Warfield was enrolled in the Eastman School of Music on the University of Rochester (N.Y.) campus. His goal, after earning undergraduate and graduate degrees, was to become a teacher of music and voice. Since 1974, Warfield, whose bass baritone voice is famous for his rendition of "Ol' Man River," has taught at the University of Illinois, Champaign-Urbana. Warfield began performing publicly in 1946 when he joined the touring company of *Call Me Mister*. His career took off four years later when a Canadian offered to finance Warfield's debut with a concert at New York's Town Hall. Review of the concert helped establish Warfield, who was married to Diva Leontyne Price. He starred opposite Price in *Porgy and Bess*. However, nurturing two careers proved difficult and the marriage ended in 1972. Warfield retired from teaching at the University of Illinois, Champaign-Urbana campus in August 1990.

1931— Singer SAM COOK, the son of a minister and believed by many to be the first father of soul music, was born in Chicago. Cook began his singing career with a gospel group known as the Singing Children. He began testing the waters of the entertainment world in 1956, with hit singles "You and Me," "Only 16," "Stand by Me," and "Shake Rattle and Roll." Cook was fatally shot in a Los Angeles motel in 1964 — two weeks before Christmas.

1948— Two-time heavyweight boxing champion GEORGE FOREMAN was born in Marshall, Texas. In a 1973 Kingston, Jamaica, bout, on his 25th birthday, Foreman wrested the heavyweight championship from then champion Joe Frazier with a second round knockout. Foreman kept the title 22 months before losing it to Muhammad Ali in 1974. A gold medalist in the 1968 Olympic Games, Foreman set an unprecedented record by regaining his title 21 years later, at the age of 45. However, he was stripped of his title after he refused to fight the number-one contender, Tony Tucker. Bruce Sheldon later defeated Tucker for the then vacant heavyweight title.

1989— Miami police officer, Colombian William Lozano, was charged with two counts of manslaughter in the fatal shooting of an African American motorcyclist and his passenger. The latter died of injuries suffered when the two-wheeled vehicle crashed after Lozano shot and killed the driver, CLEMENT LLOYD, whom Lozano attempted to stop for a traffic violation. The passenger, ALLAN BLANCHARD, was thrown into a parked car when the motorcycle crashed. The shooting triggered demonstrations and disturbances. In early 1989, the Miami police department was 43 percent Hispanic and about 18 percent African American. (See also 10/23)

1989— CLARENCE WILLIE NORRIS, the last surviving member of the famed Scottsboro Boys, died at age 76 while a patient at Bronx Community Hospital. Norris was one of nine African American teenagers accused of the 1931 rape of two White women in Alabama. The case was tried several times between 1931 and 1937 when one woman recanted her charge. Norris spent 15 years in prison before being paroled. Once freed, Norris left Alabama for New York. He was pardoned by the state of Alabama in 1976, after the Alabama Pardon and Parole Board determined his innocence. (See also 3/25)

23 January

1821— LOTT CARY, minister and pioneer, left the United States leading a contingent of freed slaves, most of whom were members of the American Colonization Society, to colonize that section of West Africa now known as Liberia. The area became the Republic of Liberia in 1847.

1976— Singer and former ex-patriot PAUL ROBESON died in Philadelphia, Pennsylvania.

1988— One of three White teenagers charged with the death of an African American man and the beating of another, was sentenced to state prison for a total of 10 to 30 years. Jon Lester, 18, was the first of three teens convicted of unlawful acts

that led to the death of MICHAEL GRIF-
FITH, 23, and the assault on CEDRIC
SANDIFORD, 37, who was beaten with a
baseball bat. Griffith was chased onto a
New York City freeway where he was
struck by a car. He later died from his injuries. (See also 1/7; 12/21)

1989— In a controversial ruling, the
U.S. Supreme Court severely limited the
ability of cities and states to set aside public works contracts for minority owned and
operated businesses. The vote was 6–3 as
the Justices established a requirement that
cities/states must present clear evidence
of past discrimination before set aside
legislation may be adopted by municipalities.

24 January

1885— Physician, jurist and military
officer MARTIN R. DELANY died in
Charleston, South Carolina.

1987— Segregationists taunted civil
rights marchers passing through Cum-
mings, Forsythe County, Georgia, en route
to the state capital.

1989— Officials of the Episcopal Church,
meeting in Boston, Massachusetts, approved the election of the Rev. BARBARA
HARRIS as the first woman bishop in An-
gelican Church history. Harris was ordained a priest in 1980 at Philadelphia,
after studying theology via correspondence
courses and tutors. Harris was expected to
be consecrated in February. (See also 2/11)

1990— Former Miami police officer
William Lozano was sentenced to seven
years in a Florida state prison. Lozano was
convicted late in 1989 of manslaughter in
the deaths of two African American men
on a motorcycle. Lozano said he believed
the driver, ALLAN BLANCHARD, intended to run him down so he shot and
killed him. CLEMENT LLOYD, a passenger on the motorcycle, later died of injuries suffered when the motorcycle went
out of control and struck a parked car after
Blanchard was shot. Lozano, a Colombian
immigrant, was freed on bail pending an

appeal. He was released into the custody of
his wife and brother, both of whom are
Miami police officers. (See also 1/22;
10/23)

25 January

1966— CONSTANCE BAKER MOT-
LEY was appointed to a federal judgeship
by then President Lyndon B. Johnson. (See
also 9/14)

26 January

1928— Actress/singer EARTHA KITT,
the daughter of William and Anna May
Kitt, was born in North, South Carolina.
Kitt joined the Katherine Dunham Dance
Troupe in 1948, a move that afforded her
an opportunity to see Europe. In Paris,
Kitt left the troupe and took a job in a
popular nightclub. Her following grew and
she soon was one of the most sought after
entertainers in Paris. It was during the
Vietnam War era, while lunching with
Lady Bird Johnson, that Kitt uttered a
comment on the war which created a
media flap. The entertainer soon after discovered opportunities to perform in the
United States had become rarer. She returned to France, where her fans remained
loyal and her popularity was unaffected.

1940— Birthday of Army Brig. Gen.
SHERIAN GRACE CADORIA, in Marks-
ville, Louisiana. A graduate of Southern University, Gen. Cadoria was the
ranking African American woman officer
in the U.S. Armed Forces at the end of
1990.

1944— Year of birth for ANGELA
YVONNE DAVIS, a native of Birmingham, Alabama. Davis graduated magna
cum laude from Brandeis University in
1965, studied at the Sorbonne and later
earned a master's degree from the University of California, San Diego, before joining the University of California, Los Angeles, faculty. Davis, who earned a
philosophy doctorate from UCLA, has
written several books, including her 1974
autobiography, *With Freedom on My Mind.*

Sought in connection with an attempted San Quentin prison break, Davis was a fugitive for a time. After her arrest and subsequent three month trial, Davis was acquitted of all charges. She had been accused of supplying weapons to Jonathan Jackson, brother of San Quentin inmate George Jackson, and others involved in an August 7, 1970, attempt to escape from custody while leaving a San Rafael, California, courtroom for the return trip to San Quentin.

1989— Virginia Lt. Gov. L. DOUGLAS WILDER, at this time the highest elected African American official in the United States, announced his intent to seek the democratic nomination for governor of the state. (See also 1/14, 11/7, 11/27)

1989— RONALD BROWN, former advisor to the Rev. JESSE JACKSON's presidential campaign, announced that he had the necessary votes to win the chairmanship of the Democratic Party. (Brown was elected to replace former party chairman Paul Kirk during a February meeting of the Democratic National Committee.) (See also 2/10)

27 January

1930— Singer BOBBY "Blue" BLAND was born in Rosemark, Tennessee. Bland's soothing baritone voice was a hit in the late 40s and early 50s when rhythm and blues artists laid the foundation for rock and roll. He was inducted into the Rock and Roll Hall of Fame, at age 61, in January 1991.

1973— The Vietnam War cease-fire was negotiated in Paris. The settlement was intended to end the longest war in U.S. history, during which an estimated 47,382 servicemen died in the fighting. African American servicemen and women accounted for 12 percent of combat related fatalities, compared to 19 percent of Civil War combat deaths.

28 January

1818— The birthday of George S.

Boutwell, author of the 13th U.S. Constitutional Amendment, which prohibits slavery.

1934— Baseball outfielder WILLIAM "Bill" WHITE was born in Lakewood, Ohio. Now baseball's National League president, White played in 1,673 games and ended his career with a .286 batting average on 1,706 hits. He won the Golden Glove award in 1960 and 1966. (See also 2/3; 4/1)

1986— African American astronaut RONALD McNAIR was one of seven crew members aboard the ill-fated space shuttle *Challenger*. The shuttle was destroyed by an explosion and fire after 74 seconds of flight following lift-off from Cape Canaveral, Florida.

1989— After 62 years of insensitivity, the Colgate-Palmolive Co. redesigned packaging for its "Darkie" tooth paste, made and sold only in Asia for its subsidiary Hawley & Hazel. Colgate bought Hawley and Hazel in 1985. The logo for Darkie tooth paste, renamed "Darlie," previously was in blackface. In addition to the name change, the logo has been changed to a "non-racially offensive" silhouette.

29 Janaury

1955— Birthday of heavyweight boxer JOHN TATE, who was born in Marion City, Arkansas. Tate won the vacant World Boxing Association title in 1979 from South African Gerrie Coetzee. He lost it less than six months later in a match with Mike Weaver. By 1986, Tate had fought 33 times, winning 66 percent by knockout.

30 January

1880— Units of the 9th Cavalry, posted at Fort Stockton, Texas, met and engaged Apache Indians for the third time in less than three weeks. Three troopers from the 9th Cavalry were wounded. There were no reports of Apache casualties during the fighting in the Caballo Mountains of southwest Texas.

1945— U.S. Rep. FLOYD FLAKE, D-New York, was born in Los Angeles, California. A businessman and minister, Flake established the Allen Christian School and Allen Home Care Agency.

31 January

1914— Boxer JERSEY JOE WALCOTT was born Arnold Raymond Cream in Merchantville, New Jersey. Walcott won the World Heavyweight Championship from Ezzard Charles, whom he knocked out in the 7th round of their 1951 title bout in Pittsburgh, Pennsylvania. Walcott had 69 professional fights. He won 30 of them by knock-out and was elected to the Boxing Hall of Fame in 1969.

1919— In Cairo, Georgia, on this date, baseball great JACKIE ROBINSON was born. The fifth African American to play major league baseball with a White team, Robinson joined the Brooklyn Dodgers in 1947, ending five decades of segregated baseball. At the time of his retirement in October 1972, Robinson is believed to have been the most respected of all baseball players. (See also 10/24)

1931— Baseball great ERNIE BANKS, former Chicago Cub star, was born in Dallas, Texas.

February

In America, Black is a country.—Amiri Baraka

1 February

1865— The 13th Amendment to the U.S. Constitution, which abolished slavery, was adopted by the 38th Congress. Ratification was completed December 6, 1865.

1902— LANGSTON HUGHES, poet, novelist and playwright was born in Joplin, Missouri. He attended Columbia and Lincoln universities, graduating from the latter. Honors and awards won by Hughes include his election to the American Academy and Institute of Arts and Letters, the Spingarn Medal and the Anisfield-Wolfe Award. Hughes died in 1967.

1926— What is now known as African American History Week was first celebrated on this date as Negro History Week by CARTER G. WOODSON. It became a month-long celebration in 1976.

1937— Actor GARRETT MORRIS, formerly of "Saturday Night Live" and the Not Ready for Prime Time Players, was born in New Orleans, Louisiana.

1960— The so-called "Sit-in" became popular in Southern states after African American students first seated themselves at a Woolworth store lunch counter in Charlotte, North Carolina, to protest the practice of serving them only if they stood.

1990— In Greensboro, North Carolina, JOSEPH McNEIL, JIBREEL KHAZAN (given name Ezell Blair, Jr.), FRANKLIN McCAIN and DAVID RICHMOND repeated the original sit-in, of 30 years earlier, by having breakfast at the Greensboro Woolworth store.

1990— House Ethics Committee reported its investigation of a sexual harassment charge against Rep. AUGUSTUS "GUS" SAVAGE, D-Illinois, made in March 1989 by a woman Peace Corp volunteer in Zaire. The investigation revealed that Savage did make improper "sexual advances" to the Peace Corps volunteer he met during a tour of Zaire. The committee deferred action on the complaint because Savage sent a written apology to the woman in November 1989. The committee said Savage had acted "contrary" to a rule demanding the conduct of all members "reflect credibly" on the House of Representatives. No further action was taken since formal charges were never filed against Savage. (See also 10/30)

2 February

1912— HERBERT MILLS, of the original Mills Brothers Quartet, was born in Piqua, Ohio. The highly successful quartet was known for its smooth harmony. (See also 4/14)

1989— In Washington, D.C., the U.S. Senate rejected a request by U.S. District Judge ALCEE HASTINGS that evidence hearings in his impeachment trial be conducted by the full body. The first African American federal judge in Florida, Hastings also was the first African American jurist to face impeachment proceedings. He was tried and acquitted after an earlier trial in a Florida court. However, the efforts of a group of Florida jurists led to formal impeachment proceedings. Hastings was accused of conspiring to obtain a $150,000 pay-off, for which he allegedly agreed to award the defendant a reduced sentence after a trial in his court. (See also 10/20)

1989— In Tampa, Florida, rioting followed the death of EDGAR ALLEN PRICE after he tussled with six uniformed officers and two detectives. No shots were fired during police efforts to subdue the six-foot tall Price who reportedly weighed "more than 300 pounds." A police spokesman said Allen had sold crack cocaine to an undercover officer and was trying to avoid being arrested. The "suspect [Price] hit his head on the ground several times" during the scuffle, according to Tampa Police Chief A. C. McLane. The rioting started after news of Price's death spread through Tampa's African American neighborhoods.

3 February

1964— An estimated 464,000 students stayed home from New York City schools in a one-day protest of de facto segregation. A similar protest was staged March 16. On June 15, the city of New York released a desegregation plan that was accepted by African American parents and students.

1988— In Montgomery, Alabama, THOMAS REED, president of the Alabama chapter of the National Association for the Advancement of Colored People, was arrested after he and 11 others attempted to strike a Confederate flag flying atop the state capitol building. The arrest was ordered by Gov. Guy Hunt, who later asked the State Legislature to decide the issue. The flag remained aloft when Hunt vacated his office in 1994. When Lt. Gov.

Jim Folsum, Jr., took the office, his first action was to remove the flag from the capitol and place it at the state Confederate memorial.

1989— BILL WHITE, a six-time All-Star first baseman and outfielder for the New York Giants, was unanimously named president of the National League. White succeeded A. Bartlett Giamatti, who succeeded Peter Ueberroth as Baseball Commissioner. White began playing baseball with the New York Giants in 1956. He also played for the San Francisco Giants, St. Louis Cardinals and the Philadelphia Phillies ball clubs. He took over the league April 1, 1989, the same day Giamatti became commissioner. (See also 1/28; 2/3; 4/1)

1989— The abortion issue created problems for Dr. LOUIS SULLIVAN. Nominated by President Bush for the post of Health and Human Services Secretary, Sullivan's confirmation hearing was delayed "indefinitely" after Sullivan contradicted himself and became embroiled in the abortion issue. Because of this flap, Sullivan's name was withdrawn.

1989— In Los Angeles, FBI agents investigated the possibility that cross burnings in the county jail by White sheriff's deputies violated the civil rights of inmates belonging to gangs. Two incidents of cross burnings occurred in 1988 in areas of the central jail where members of the Crips and Bloods gang, known arch rivals, were then housed.

1989— Tennis professional LORI McNEIL seeded seventh in the Pan Pacific Open in Tokyo, and defeated Chris Evert, 6–2, 5–7, 6–4.

4 February

1843— "If slavery must go by blood and war, let war come."— President John Quincy Adams

1913— The birthday of ROSA PARKS, who was born in Tuskegee, Alabama. Parks is credited with starting the three-decade-long era of the African American struggle for civil rights that began in the '50s and continues. It began when Parks refused to move to Jim Crow seating at the back of a Montgomery, Alabama, public transit bus. Parks' arrest, on her 42nd birthday, also began an 18-month African American boycott of the Montgomery Transit system. (See also 12/1)

1974— The Symbionese Liberation Army, led by DONALD "Field Marshall Cinque" DE FREEZE and aided by associates, kidnapped University of California, Berkeley, student Patricia Hearst, heir to the Hearst publishing empire, from her off-campus apartment in Berkeley, California.

1990— ANDREW YOUNG, former mayor of Atlanta, Georgia, announced his candidacy (unsuccessful) for the governorship of Georgia. (See also 3/12; 10/13; 11/6)

5 February

1884–1900— U.S. Rep. JEFFERSON LONG, elected from the state of Georgia, died in Washington, D.C. Long was the only candidate interested in running for the 60-day term and he was duly elected. (See also 3/3)

1934— Birthday, in Mobile, Alabama, of HENRY "Hank" AARON, former Atlanta Braves right fielder and all-time home run hitter. In April 1974, Aaron hit his 714th and 715th home runs to break Babe Ruth's long-standing career home run record.

1990— Columbia University graduate and Harvard University law student BARACK OBAMA became the first African American named president of the Harvard Law Review.

6 February

1933— Birthday of WALTER E. FAUNTROY, who was born in Washington, D.C. A District of Columbia delegate to the House of Representatives, Fauntroy was first elected in April 1971.

1950— Birthdate, in Los Angeles, California, of singer NATALIE COLE, daughter of legendary silky-voiced crooner Nat "King" Cole. Cole began singing professionally at age 11, when she appeared on stage at Los Angeles' Greek Theater. Later, as a University of Massachusetts student, Cole worked as a waitress at a club known as "The Pub," and sang on weekends with a band that played at local night clubs. By 1976, Cole had won Grammys for New Artist of the Year and Best Rhythm and Blues Female Vocalist. (See also 3/19)

1989— A White supremacist rally held in California's Napa Valley by the White Aryan Resistance (WAR) fizzled because of bone-chilling cold, rainy weather and a counter demonstration by liberal groups who outnumbered WAR members. WAR is a White supremacist group started by television repairman Tom Metzger of Fallbrook, California, the former grand dragon of the California Knights of the Ku Klux Klan. His White supremacist movement received a boost from a group of youth known as "Skinheads," who say they simply "love the White race." The youngsters have been courted by Metzger and Richard Butler, head of the White Aryan Resistance and titular leader of the Aryan Nations. Despite claims that they are "peace-loving," Skinheads are violence prone. They have been linked to:

Murders of African Americans, or foreigners of African ancestry, in Las Vegas and Reno, Nevada; Portland, Oregon, and San Jose, California; attempted murder in Spokane, Washington; the destruction of a New York City synagogue, and more than 60 percent of racial assaults documented in 1988 by Klanwatch.

Other race-related acts involving Skinheads include the destruction of a church in southern Illinois. After being rebuilt, the church was again destroyed by fire.

7 February

1883— Composer and pianist EUBIE BLAKE was born in Baltimore, Maryland. Blake was a pioneer in African American music and theater. However, Blake's talent was not fully acknowledged until he was nearly 100 years old and still playing concerts and club dates. Blake was awarded the Presidential Medal of Freedom. Blake, who worked with band leader NOBLE SISSLE in writing the music for the 1921 musical *Shuffle Along*, was one month shy of his 99th birthday when his final performance was recorded for television. (See also 2/12)

1990— In Selma, Alabama, NORWARD ROUSSELL, the city's first African American school superintendent, returned to his job. Earlier, African American students, who make up 70 percent of the Deep South school district, boycotted classes to protest Roussell's firing by the Board of Education's White majority. Board members also refused to renew Roussell's contract which expired in June. The student boycott and protests by other African Americans contributed to the decision to reinstate Roussell. (See also 1/4)

8 February

1968— Diminutive actor GARY COLEMAN was born in Zion, Illinois. Although less than four feet tall and beset by frequent medical problems, Coleman achieved fame through roles in television situation comedies.

1986— Figure skater DEBI THOMAS became the first African American to win the Women's Singles of the U.S. National Figure Skating Championship competition. Thomas, who won a bronze medal in the 1988 skating competition, was a pre-med student at Stanford University. (See also 3/25)

1990— Andy Rooney, a CBS "60 Minutes" commentator, received a 90-day suspension from work because of racist remarks about African Americans attributed to him by Chris Bull, a New York–based reporter for *The Advocate*, a weekly homosexual newspaper published in Los Angeles. Bull quoted Rooney as having said during an interview: "I've believed all along that most people are born with equal intelligence, but Blacks have watered down

their genes because the less intelligent ones are the ones that have the children. They drop out of school early, do drugs, and get pregnant." Rooney denied the allegation but David Burke, CBS News president, said Rooney offered his "deepest apologies" to anyone he may have offended.

9 February

1906— Novelist and poet PAUL LAWRENCE DUNBAR, who was born in Dayton, Ohio, died. Dunbar wrote *The Uncalled*, in 1898; *The Love of Landry*, in 1900; and *The Fanatics*, in 1901. (See also 6/27)

1914— Pulitzer Prize winning novelist ALICE WALKER was born in Eatonton, Georgia. Walker's Pulitzer was awarded for *The Color Purple*, her third novel, which was published in 1983.

1952— Author RALPH ELLISON's novel *Invisible Man* won the National Book Award.

10 February

1927— Opera singer MARY LEONTYNE PRICE was born in Laurel, Mississippi. Price majored in music at Wilberforce University, graduating in 1948; she later did graduate work at the Juilliard School of Music while singing professionally to augment her Juilliard scholarship. Price's performance, with William Warfield, in Gershwin's *Porgy and Bess* led to a New York Town Hall concert debut in November 1954, and a role as Countess Leonora in Verdi's *Il Trovatore* with the Metropolitan Opera in 1961. (See also 1/22)

1939— Pop/Soul vocalist ROBERTA FLACK was born in Black Mountain, North Carolina. Flack gained notoriety and prodigy status at age 15 after earning a full music scholarship to Howard University, where she studied music. Until her career began to blossom, Flack taught music and worked the clubs five evenings a week. Later, an interview with Atlantic Records resulted in her first album, "First Take," in 1969. Hits performed by Flack include, "You've Got a Friend," "You've Lost That Loving Feeling," "The First Time Ever I Saw Your Face" and "Killing Me Softly with His Song."

1989— Attorney RONALD BROWN was elected national chairman of the Democratic Party and became the first African American to hold that post. Born August 1, 1941, in Washington, D.C., and raised in New York's Harlem, Brown was appointed Secretary of Commerce by President Bill Clinton in 1994. Brown served in this capacity until April 9, 1996, when he and 32 other Americans died in a plane crash in Croatia. They had been on a mission promoting American trade.

11 February

1920— Air Force Gen. DANIEL "Chappie" JAMES was born in Pensacola, Florida. James, who died of a heart attack in 1978, was the armed forces' first African American four-star general.

1989— In Boston, Massachusetts, the Rev. BARBARA HARRIS, at age 58, was consecrated an Episcopal Bishop, the first woman so elected in the history of the church. Harris, a former Sun Oil Co. public relations executive, serves the Episcopal diocese of Massachusetts. She also took part in the march on Selma, Alabama, with the Rev. Martin Luther King, Jr., in 1965.

1990— Challenger JAMES "Buster" DOUGLAS KO'd heavyweight boxing champion MIKE TYSON with a "left-right-left" combination of punches to the head in the 10th round of a championship fight in Tokyo, Japan. The loss was the first for Tyson, who was 37–0 going into the scheduled 15 round bout. The win was Douglas' 30th for a record of 30–4 and a draw. Tyson was Douglas' 20th knockout.

12 February

1793— Congress enacted the first Fugitive Slave Law. Under the law it was illegal to hide or protect a runaway slave.

1809— President Abraham Lincoln was born in Harding County, Kentucky. Lincoln was assassinated by John Wilkes Booth in Washington, D.C., while attending a performance at Ford's Theatre five days after the Civil War ended. A Republican, Lincoln was elected on an anti-slavery platform. (See also 4/15)

1909— In New York City, the National Association for the Advancement of Colored People was founded to fight racial violence.

1930— In Tuskegee, Alabama, the Rosenwald Fund made grants of $7,750 and $2,250 to the Alabama State Board of Health to help meet the cost of a study of syphilis in African American men living in rural Georgia and Alabama. The grants signalled the beginning of a four-decade long study of syphilis without treatment. Based at Tuskegee Institute, a team of more than a dozen doctors (all but one of whom was an African American) and one African American public health nurse, observed the progress of the then fatal venereal disease carried by 400 African American men. The subjects were never advised that their medical problems were connected with syphilis. Instead they were told they had "bad blood." Participating government agencies included the Federal Public Health Service and Centers for Disease Control, Alabama State Department of Health and the Macon County Alabama Health Department. Others involved were Tuskegee Institute and the Tuskegee Medical Society. The syphilitic subjects were provided "free medical examinations, rides to and from clinics and meals on days they were scheduled for examinations, free treatment for minor illnesses and a guaranteed $50 burial stipend for survivors of the study." The study was kept secret until its disclosure by a newspaper reporter in late July 1972: 40 years and 5½ months after it began.

1934— Birthday of WILLIAM FELTON RUSSELL. Better known as "Bill" Russell, he was player-coach of the Boston Celtics basketball team in 1968 and 1969. He was named coach, vice president and

General Manager of the Sacramento Kings in 1989. After a little more than a year, Russell was sacked and left the Kings organization. Russell was born in Monroe, Louisiana.

1983— Pianist EUBIE BLAKE died in Brooklyn, New York. Blake's death came five days after his 100th birthday. (See also 2/7)

13 February

1635— America's first public school, the Boston Latin School, opened in Boston. African American students were excluded.

1989— The Flo-Jo fashion doll, patterned after its namesake, Olympic track star FLORENCE GRIFFITH-JOYNER, was presented to the public in New York City. Griffith-Joyner won three gold and one silver medal for track competition in the 1988 Olympic Games.

14 February

1760— Birthday of RICHARD ALLEN, co-founder of Bethel A.M.E. Church, the first African Methodist Episcopal Church, in 1794, in Philadelphia. Allen was aided by Absalom Jones who later went his own way and formed the first African Union Methodist Church, in 1807, at Wilmington, Delaware. Ordained a minister in 1814, Allen later became the first African American bishop of any church in the United States. (See also 3/25; 9/1)

1817— Birthday of abolitionist, author and orator FREDERICK DOUGLASS, born Frederick Bailey. Douglass was born a slave on a plantation outside Tuckahoe, Talbot County, Maryland. He purchased his freedom in 1845 and later aided President Lincoln by recruiting troops for the 54th and 55th Massachusetts African American Infantry regiments. Douglass served in the Territorial Legislature, District of Columbia, in 1871, and was a "presidential elector at large" for the state of New York. Douglass later was appointed Minister Resident and Counsel General to the Republic of Haiti and then to Santo Domingo. He died in 1895.

1987— Arson charges were filed against three Whites who set fire to a Philadelphia row house occupied by African Americans.

1946— Actor/dancer GREGORY HINES was born in New York City. His movie credits include *White Nights*, with Mikhail Nikolayevich Baryshnikov, and *Tap*.

15 February

1804— The New Jersey Legislature approved a law calling for "gradual" emancipation of African Americans. In so doing, New Jersey became the last Northern state to outlaw slavery.

16 February

1957— Actor LEVAR BURTON was born in Landsthul, Germany. Burton won fame for his acting in the television movie *Roots*, which was based on the novel by Alex Haley. Prior to the role in *Roots*, Burton had a continuing role in television's *Star Trek* series.

17 February

1902— Opera singer MARIAN ANDERSON was born in Philadelphia, Pennsylvania. Anderson was entered in the New York Philharmonic Competition at age 17 by her music teacher, and placed first over 299 other singers. Awarded a Rosenwald Fellowship in 1930, Anderson went to Europe for a year of study. She returned briefly to the United States but went back to Europe in 1933 to debut in Berlin and again, in 1935, in Austria. In 1933, Anderson performed 142 concerts in Norway, Sweden, Denmark and Finland. On Easter Sunday in 1939, Anderson performed an open air recital at the Lincoln Memorial in Washington, D.C. The performance was scheduled for the concert hall controlled by the Daughters of the American Revolution but was cancelled when the DAR refused to allow Anderson to sing there. In 1955, Anderson signed with New York's Metropolitan Opera Company. (See also 1/7; 4/9)

1918— Birthday of Rep. CHARLES A. HAYES, D-Illinois, who was born in Cairo, Illinois. In 1989, Hayes was re-elected to a fourth term in the House of Representatives. He was first elected Sept. 12, 1983.

1936— JAMES "Jim" BROWN, famed Cleveland Browns running back, was born in St. Simons Island, Georgia. Brown, who has acted in a number of western movies, played college football at Syracuse University.

1938— Birthday of MARY FRANCES BERRY, in Nashville, Tennessee. A former member of the U.S. Civil Rights Commission who was appointed by President James E. Carter, Berry also served in the then U.S. Department of Health, Education and Welfare. After his 1980 presidential inauguration, Ronald Reagan kicked Berry off the Commission. Berry filed a lawsuit and was reinstated to serve until the end of her term. Berry is a graduate of Howard University and earned an advanced degree from the University of Michigan. Formerly chancellor of the University of Colorado, Berry is currently teaching American social thought and history at the University of Pennsylvania in Philadelphia at the end of 1990.

1942— HUEY P. NEWTON, co-founder of the Black Panther Party, was born in Monroe, Louisiana. He also served the party as its chief theoretician and president. A political activist and author, Newton wrote *To Die for the People*, *Revolutionary Suicide*, and co-authored *Insights and Poems* and *In Search of Common Ground*. Newton was shot to death by a drug dealer in the summer of 1989. (See also 8/22)

1973— The Navy frigate USS *Jesse L. Brown* was commissioned. The ship was named for Ensign JESSE L. BROWN, the first African American naval aviator killed in combat over Korea.

18 February

1851— Runaway slave FREDERICK JENKINS was rescued from court custody by Boston residents who later helped him reach safety in Canada.

1913— The Delta Sigma Theta sorority was founded at Howard University.

1931— TONI MORRISON, who won the 1988 Pulitzer Prize for fiction with the novel *Beloved*, was born in Lorain, Ohio. Morrison accepted a professorship in the humanities at Princeton University after leaving a similar position at State University of New York.

1987— Residents of a predominantly White southwest Chicago neighborhood were believed to have hurled Molotov cocktails through the window of the newly purchased home of Dorothy Sturgis, an African American schoolteacher. Sturgis was not hurt in the fire that followed. The Chicago police department's bomb and arson unit investigated the incident as a racially-motivated firebombing, but no arrests were made.

19 February

1940— Pop/Soul singer WILLIAM "Smokey" ROBINSON was born in Detroit, Michigan. Robinson's first singing group was the Miracles, which he formed in 1955 while still a high school student. The Miracles included BOBBY ROGERS, CLAUDETTE ROGERS, PETE MOORE, RONNIE WHITE and Robinson. The group's first success came in 1960 with the hit "Shop Around."

1942— The Army Air Corps' all African American 100th Pursuit Squadron, later designated a fighter squadron, was activated at Tuskegee Institute. The squadron served honorably in England and on the European continent during World War II. (See also 3/22)

20 February

1931— Army Lt. Gen. EMMETT PAIGE, JR. was born in Jacksonville, Florida.

1927— Actor, director and producer SIDNEY POITIER was born in Miami, Florida. His 1950 film debut in *No Way*

Out was successful. Other film credits include *Guess Who's Coming to Dinner*, *Cry Beloved Country*, *To Sir with Love*, *Blackboard Jungle*, *A Raisin in the Sun*, and *Porgy and Bess*.

1936— Jazz singer, actress, NANCY WILSON was born in Chillicothe, Ohio.

1987— California Gov. George Deukmejian refused to fire state Bicentennial Commission members after the group published a book, paid for with public funds, containing racial slurs against African Americans.

1990— In memory of their daughter, Carol DiMaiti Stuart, parents Giusto and Evelyn DiMaiti, along with their son, Carl DiMaiti, announced the creation of a private non-profit foundation to provide scholarships for African American students living in the Mission Hills section of Boston, where police indiscriminantly stopped and questioned African American men about the shooting death of Carol Stuart and her unborn child. Carol's husband, Charles Stuart, committed suicide after learning police considered him a suspect in the fatal shooting of his wife. Stuart lied to police, telling them the man who shot him and his wife Carol was an African American. This was accepted by the authorities when Stuart called for help from his car telephone. The location he gave the 911 operator indicated he and his family were in a predominantly African American neighborhood. Several months later, at a police lineup, Charles Stuart told Boston Police WILLIE BENNETT, who was part of that lineup, was the man who shot him and fatally wounded Carol Stuart. (See also 1/25; 2/18; 10/23)

21 February

1933— Jazz singer NINA SIMONE was born in Tyron, North Carolina. Simone's rendition of "I Loves You Porgy" added a new dimension to the music of George Gershwin.

1936— Lawyer, scholar, educator and member of the House of Representatives and the Texas Legislature, BARBARA JORDAN was born in Houston, Texas. Jordon was a magna cum laude graduate of Texas Southern University and Boston University Law School. She died January 17, 1996. (See also 6/10)

1940— Birthday of Rep. JOHN LEWIS of Georgia, who was born in Troy, Alabama. A former Atlanta city council member, Lewis was elected to the House of Representatives in 1986 following a bitter race against former Georgia state senator Julian Bond.

1965— MALCOLM X, born Malcolm Little, leader of a splinter group from Elijah Muhammad's Nation of Islam (Black Muslims), was assassinated in New York City's Audubon Ballroom, 11 months after breaking with Muhammad. (See also 5/19 and the 1990 entry below)

1987— African Americans in Tampa, Florida, rioted after an African American man was killed by a White police officer while in police custody. The officer reportedly applied the controversial choke hold. Another riot, for identical reasons, followed the death of a second African American at the hands of police in Miami in February 1989. (See also 4/8, 10/23)

1990— On the 25th anniversary of the assassination of MALCOLM X, *Baltimore Sun* reporter Gregory P. Kane wrote that evidence in the case suggested the Nation of Islam, not the FBI or CIA could have been responsible for the death of Malcolm X.

22 February

1888— In West Chester, Pennsylvania, African American painter HORACE PIPPIN was born. Pippin is considered a major American painter. One of his more significant works, "John Brown Going to His Hanging," is owned by the Pennsylvania Academy of Fine Arts.

1911— Novelist and educator FRANCES ELLEN WATKINS HARPER died in Little York, Pennsylvania.

1950— Professional basketball great JULIUS "Dr. J" ERVING, with the

Philadelphia 76er's prior to his retirement, was born in Roosevelt, New York.

23 February

1868— WILLIAM EDWARD BURGHARDT DU BOIS was born in Great Barrington, Massachusetts. A pioneering social scientist, Du Bois earned a bachelor's degree from Fisk University in 1888, graduated cum laude from Harvard University in 1890 and obtained a doctorate from the University of Berlin between 1892 and 1894. Du Bois became a scholar, historian and tactician in the drive to gain racial equality for African Americans in the post-slavery era of the United States. (See also 8/27)

1925— LOUIS STOKES, former mayor of Detroit, Michigan, and member of the U.S. House of Representatives, was born in Cleveland, Ohio. Stokes was the first African American elected to the House from Ohio.

1929— Baseball catcher ELSTON GENE HOWARD was born in St. Louis, Missouri. In 1965, Howard signed a $70,000 contract with the New York Yankees and became the highest paid player in the history of baseball at that time. After 14 years as an active player, being selected as MVP in 1963 and gaining berths on nine All-Star teams, Howard retired and became a coach in the Yankee organization.

24 February

1811— Birth date, in Charleston, South Carolina, of Bishop DANIEL ALEXANDER PAYNE, an educator within the African Methodist Episcopal Church. In 1835, a Charleston school for free African Americans was closed after Nat Turner's revolt triggered laws making it unlawful for anyone to operate a school that accepted or taught African American students.

1940— Former world heavyweight boxing champion Jimmy Ellis was born JAMES ALBERT ELLIS in Louisville, Kentucky. Ellis won the World Boxing Association title after beating Jerry Quarry in April 1968. He lost a 1970 bout with Joe Frazier for the then vacant World Heavyweight crown.

1987— Affirmative action canons were attacked by the U.S. Justice Department, headed by then Attorney General Edwin Meese III. The affirmative action concept was attacked, unsuccessfully, in the U.S. Supreme Court.

1989— CLARENCE WILLIE NORRIS, the last surviving member of the famed Scottsboro Boys, died in Brooklyn, New York. (See also 3/25)

1990— President George Bush picked ARTHUR FLETCHER, a moderate African American Republican, to chair the Civil Rights Commission. Fletcher was an assistant secretary of labor in the Nixon administration; deputy assistant for urban affairs during the Ford presidency, an advisor to Ronald Reagan, and an assistant to President Bush during the latter's United Nations tour.

25 February

1870— Sen. HIRAM R. REVELS, Mississippi, became the first African American to sit in the U.S. Senate. In 1847, Revels graduated from Knox College and became a minister in the African Methodist Episcopal Church. Revels was successful in forming two Baltimore regiments comprised of African Americans when the Civil War began. Revels later moved to St. Louis where he founded a school for freed men. He later joined the Army, became a chaplain, and was posted to Mississippi. Revels remained in Natchez after the war and, concurrently, became the minister of an AME church and active in local politics. In 1870, Revels was appointed to the U.S. Senate seat once held by Jefferson Davis, former president of the Confederacy. He was seated, after a lengthy debate, by a vote of 48–8 and became the first African American to sit in the U.S. Senate. Revels left the Senate in 1871 and was appointed president of Alcorn College. Another governor later appointed Revels secretary of state. After one term, Revels returned to Natchez where he lived until his death in 1901. (See also 9/27)

1978— Air Force Gen. DANIEL "Chappie" JAMES died 24 days after retiring from active duty. (See also 2/11; 9/1)

1987— EDWARD DANIEL NIXON, former president of the Georgia NAACP, died at age 87. Nixon was born in 1900.

1987— A Rand Corporation study reported that, in 1986, African Americans earned 73 percent as much as Whites.

1989— Former U.S. Attorney General Richard Thornburg recommended attorney WILLIAM LUCAS, a former FBI agent and one-time gubernatorial candidate in Michigan, to run the U.S. Justice Department Civil Rights Division. Lucas was not nominated for the post.

1989— Boxer MICHAEL "Mike" TYSON became the undisputed Heavyweight Champion of the World by defeating challenger Frank Bruno of England. (See also 6/30)

26 February

1884— Birthday of Congressman JAMES E. O'HARA of North Carolina. First elected March 4, 1883, O'Hara served two terms, the second ending March 3, 1887.

1928— Singer/songwriter ANTOINE "Fats" DOMINO was born in New Orleans, Louisiana.

1933— GODFREY CAMBRIDGE— Actor and comedian was born in New York City. Cambridge died in 1976.

27 February

1788— PRINCE HALL, Revolutionary War veteran and founder of African American Masonic Lodges, was born in Boston, Massachusetts.

1869— CONGRESS adopted the 15th CONSTITUTIONAL AMENDMENT, making it illegal for the U.S. or any single state government to deny or abridge the right to vote "on account of race, color or previous condition of servitude."

1942— Birth date of print and television journalist CHARLAYNE HUNTER-GAULT, in Atlanta, Georgia. As Charlayne Hunter, Hunter-Gault was one of two students to enroll in the University of Georgia, in 1961, as part of a drive for full civil rights in the 60s. Hunter-Gault has been a national correspondent for the MacNeil/Lehrer News Hour, broadcast weekdays on the Public Broadcasting System television network, for more than a decade.

1990— Racist campaign literature surfaced in the affluent community of Piedmont, nestled in the hills east of Oakland, California. At issue was a ballot initiative known as Measure A, which would ban lighting a soccer field for night games. Campaign flyers, placed surreptitiously on auto windshields, warned Piedmont voters that the lighted playing field would attract "hundreds of disadvantaged African American youth from Oakland, including those from single parent families and drug rehabilitation programs." They were illustrated by a sketch of an African American family of four under the words: "Blacks 4 No on A." The distribution of such campaign literature violates California political practices law and a Piedmont littering ordinance.

1990— A report prepared by the Sentencing Project, using 1989 figures and data from the Bureau of Justice Statistics, disclosed that 25 percent of all young African American men were in prisons or under some form of supervision for felonious acts and or criminal activity. The raw data showed roughly 610,000 African American men, aged 20 to 29, were negatively involved with the criminal justice systems in the 50 states. The annual cost of imprisonment and supervision: $2.5 billion, according to the report.

28 February

1871— The 2nd Force Act is passed, which provides for state and congressional elections to be controlled by federal supervisors.

1989— MARY HATWOOD FUTRELL, president of the National Education Association, warned of the decline in the education of minorities. Futrell called for a commitment to equality and excellence by teachers and other educators.

1990— Rock and Roll Hall of Fame inductee CORNELIUS GUNTER, lead singer for The Coasters, was shot to death in Las Vegas, Nevada. Gunter joined the group in 1957 and was around for a succession of now classic hits, including "Charlie Brown," "Poison Ivy" and "Along Came Jones."

29 February

1940— HATTIE McDANIEL won the award for best supporting actress in her role as "Mammy" in *Gone with the Wind*. McDaniel was the first African American actor to win an Oscar.

1945— The birthday of CHARLES AARON "Bubba" SMITH, football player, who was born in Orange, Texas. Smith began his professional football career with the Baltimore Colts. He later played for the Houston Oilers and Oakland Raiders before retiring and making a name for himself in movies.

March

I am not a perfect servant. I am a public servant. —Jesse Jackson

1 March

1841—Birthday of BLANCHE K. BRUCE, who was born a slave in Farmville, Prince Edward County, Virginia. A graduate of Oberlin College in Ohio, Bruce was the second African American elected to the U.S. Senate and the only African American to serve a full term during Reconstruction. In Mississippi, he was appointed to the Levee Board, was Sergeant-at-Arms of the State Senate, tax assessor and collector and Bolivar County sheriff before his election to the Senate. Bruce died in 1898 at his Washington, D.C., home. (See also 12/2)

1927—Actor, singer and composer HAROLD GEORGE "Harry" BELAFONTE, was born in New York City. Belafonte worked New York night clubs in the 40s and 50s. In 1954 he starred opposite Dorothy Dandridge in the film version of *Carmen Jones*. Belafonte became the first African American to produce a major television program, CBS' "Strolling Twenties," in 1966.

1945—The Liberty Ship *Robert L. Vann*, named for the founder, in 1910, and publisher of the *Pittsburgh Courier* newspaper, sank after hitting a mine in the Atlantic Ocean. The ship was part of a convoy ferrying supplies to Europe during World War II. Vann died in 1940.

1967—For the first time in 46 years, the House of Representatives voted to exclude a colleague, Rep. ADAM CLAYTON POWELL, JR., D–New York. (See also 1/10; 4/4; 4/11; 11/25)

2 March

1932—Lt. Gen. FRANK E. PETERSEN, the first African American officer to reach flag rank in the regular Marine Corps, was born in Topeka, Kansas. Petersen, a fighter pilot, retired in August 1988 after 38 years of active service. His final posting was as commanding general of the sprawling Marine base at Quantico, Virginia.

1943—GEORGE BENSON, jazz guitarist, protégé and student of guitarist extraordinaire Chet Atkins, was born in Pittsburgh, Pennsylvania. Among Benson's hit songs are "Breezin'", "Masquerade," "The Greatest Love of All," and "Love x Love."

1962—WILT CHAMBERLAIN of the Philadelphia Warriors became the first basketball player to score 100 points in one game. Chamberlain made 36 field goals and 28 free throws in the game against the New York Knickerbockers. The score: Philadelphia 169, New York 147.

3 March

1820—The Mason-Dixon Line was established by the Missouri Compromise and based on work accomplished by surveyors Charles Mason and Jeremiah Dixon. The Compromise also barred slavery north of latitude 36 degrees 37 minutes.

1836— JEFFERSON F. LONG, a merchant and tailor and the first African American from Georgia elected to the U.S. House of Representatives, was born in Knoxville, Crawford County, Georgia. A Republican, he served only two months and nine days, the time left by the incumbent, who died in office. Long may have won the election because other potential candidates were not interested in running for such a short term. Long, who worked to ensure enforcement of the 15th Constitutional Amendment, is recognized as the only African American from Georgia in Congress in the 19th Century. (See also 2/25)

1869— The 38th and 41st Infantry regiments were joined and became the 24th Infantry Regiment, the third of four proposed African American regiments in the U.S. Army. The regiment was posted to Texas from 1869 to 1880.

1932— MIRIAM MAKEBA, actress and singer, was born in Johannesburg, South Africa.

1968— A memorandum sent to field offices of the Federal Bureau of Investigation set goals for a new "counter-intelligence program" against African American Nationalist groups. The objective was to block attempts by targeted groups to coalesce. The agency believed unity was the "first step toward a Mau-Mau–style uprising" in the United States and the beginning of an "African American Revolution." The Bureau hierarchy further believed their efforts also would prevent the "rise of a Messiah who could unify and electrify the African American Nationalist movement." Top candidates for this leadership position were Malcolm X and Martin Luther King, Jr., according to then FBI Director J. Edgar Hoover.

1987— Marine Cpl. ARNOLD BRACY, a former guard at the U.S. Embassy in Moscow, became the fourth African American in U.S. history arrested and charged with spying for a foreign government. However, on June 12, 1987, all charges against Bracy were dropped and he was honorably discharged from the Marine Corps.

1989— Howard University students protested the election of Republican National Committee Chairman Lee Atwater to the school's Board of Trustees. Student demonstrations forced the cancellation of Charter Day activities which included a speech by comedian Bill Cosby. Some students said Atwater had been anything but pro–civil rights during his career in politics."

1991— After an alleged high-speed chase by California highway patrol officers, motorist RODNEY KING left the security of his vehicle on a Los Angeles street only to be beaten by four Los Angeles police officers who "took over" the case from a husband and wife highway patrol team. The LAPD officers said King, who was driving a Hyundai Excel import, reached speeds of 115 mph before leaving the freeway. King was shot twice with a Tasaran electric shock pistol — and struck by batons an estimated 70 plus times while the LAPD and highway patrol officers stood by and watched.

4 March

1877— Scientist GARRETT A. MORGAN was born in Paris, Kentucky. Inventor of a belt fastener for sewing machines, the gas mask, and the automatic traffic signal. About 1923, he sold rights to General Electric for $40,000. Morgan died in 1963, at 86, in Cleveland, Ohio, where he moved in 1895. (See also 7/24; Appendix)

1934— Actress BARBARA McNAIR was born in Racine, Wisconsin.

1990— Andy Rooney, commentator for CBS, returned to face network television cameras after serving one-third of a 90-day suspension for making racist remarks about African Americans in an interview with a reporter from *The Advocate*, a gay magazine. The remarks appeared in the February 27, 1990 issue. A CBS official apologized for Rooney, who denied he made the remarks but Rooney only said he "felt terrible" about having offended gays and that "I've learned a lot." (See also 2/28)

5 March

1770, 9 P.M. — The Boston Massacre lasted 20 minutes. CRISPUS ATTUCKS, a run-away slave, was the first person to die for American Independence from Great Britain. Attucks, who ran away from Framingham, Massachusetts, where he was born in 1723, spent his early days of freedom at sea. Attucks returned to the colony in time to take part in the first skirmish of the Revolutionary War.

1920 — The birthday, in Washington, D.C., of LEONTINE T. C. KELLY, the first African American woman to become a bishop within the Methodist denomination. Kelly was elected, in 1984, to lead the United Methodist Church in the San Francisco Bay Area. Her diocese included more than 300 churches whose membership was estimated at 100,000 persons. Bishop Kelly, who retired in 1988, was a visiting instructor at Berkeley's Pacific School of Religion at the end of 1990.

1990 — In California's Castro Valley, the Rev. JESSE DAVIS, SR., and the African American congregation of Shiloh Baptist Church, sponsored New Canyons Community Church. Canyons Community was pastored by the the Rev. Don McEntire, a white Baptist minister from Corpus Christi, Texas. It is the first time, in California, that an African American Church has helped form and develop an all–White church.

6 March

1775 — PRINCE HALL and 14 other persons were inducted into British Army Masonic Lodge No. 441 near Boston. Hall later formed African Lodge 1, which was not recognized by American Masons.

1857 — The *DRED SCOTT vs. SANFORD* case was decided by the U.S. Supreme Court. The Court upheld the exclusion of "Negroes" from the Declaration of Independence. It held that Scott lacked standing to sue for his freedom because he was a slave and therefore without rights unconditionally guaranteed U.S. citizens.

1936 — In Itta Bena, Mississippi, the birthday of MARION SHEPILOV BARRY, JR. Barry, the former mayor of Washington, D.C., entered a Florida substance abuse clinic where he hoped to significantly reduce what publicly was perceived to be an addiction to cocaine and other substances. Barry was the first national chairman of the Student Non-Violence Coordinating Committee. (See also 1/18, 4/8)

1941 — Baseball great WILVER "Willie" DORNELL STARGELL, was born in Earlsboro, Oklahoma.

1989 — Attorney CHARLES S. SCOTT, SR., who caused the desegregation of U.S. public schools by filing the landmark Brown vs. Topeka Board of Education law suit, died at age 67. Scott and his brothers, JOHN J. SCOTT and CHARLES BLEDSOE, both deceased, sued the Topeka, Kansas, School Board on behalf of LINDA BROWN, then an elementary school student. The case was appealed to the U.S. Supreme Court for resolution. The Court declared unconstitutional racial segregation of public schools because separate schools were unequal. (See also 5/17)

7 March

1539 — ESTAVANICO DORANTES, an African Spanish slave, led an expedition to the southwestern United States, which then belonged to Mexico, an unsuccessful search for El Dorado, the lost City of Gold.

1917 — Birthday of ballerina JANET COLLINS, in New Orleans, Louisiana. Collins' 1951 debut in *Aïda* at the Metropolitan Opera was the first on that stage by an African American dancer. Collins' earlier public appearance was for a role in the Broadway musical *Out of this World*.

1943—The U.S. Navy destroyer USS *Dorie Miller*, named for Messman DORIE MILLER, was commissioned. Untrained in the use of anti-aircraft guns and gunnery, Miller, nonetheless, had used such a weapon to shoot down Japanese aircraft during the December 7, 1941, attack on Pearl Harbor. (See also 11/24)

1965—Alabama State Police attacked African Americans marching from Selma to Montgomery, the capital of Alabama, with tear gas, nightsticks and whips.

8 March

1838—DAVID RUGGLES founded *Mirror of Liberty*, the nation's first African American and African American–owned magazine.

1945—PHYLLIS MAE DAILEY became the first African American nurse admitted to the Navy Nurse Corps.

9 March

1871—Birthday, in Florence, Alabama, of OSCAR DE PRIEST, who became a politician after moving to Chicago. Elected in 1928, De Priest was the first African American from Illinois elected to the House of Representatives. He served three consecutive two-year terms beginning March 4, 1929.

1922—In Asheville, North Carolina, civil rights activist FLOYD H. McKISSICK was born. A lawyer, newspaper columnist and business executive, McKissick attended Morehouse College, the University of North Carolina, and North Carolina Central University.

10 March

1820—HARRIET TUBMAN, Underground Railroad conductor, abolitionist, nurse and Union Army spy, was born in Bucktown, Dorchester County, Maryland. In 1849 Tubman escaped from the Maryland plantation where she was born. As part of the Underground Railroad, Tubman helped more than 300 African Amer-

icans escape slavery on Southern plantations. She claimed to have "never lost a passenger" in her years of service.

1928—Birthday of convicted assassin James Earl Ray, also known as Eric Starvo Galt, who was born in Alton, Illinois. Ray reportedly was wanted for his escape, nearly a year earlier, from the Missouri State Penitentiary when he fatally shot the Rev. MARTIN LUTHER KING, JR., as King stood on the balcony of the Lorraine Motel, in Memphis, Tennessee. Ray, who had previously served time in federal and state prisons and jails, including at least one in California, was serving a sentence for armed robbery prior to his escape. Tried and convicted for murder in the King shooting, Ray was sentenced to 99 years in the Tennessee prison system. He was eligible for parole in November 1988. However, parole was denied after a January 1989 hearing at Bledsoe County Regional Prison, near Pikeville, Tennessee, where Ray was imprisoned. He was then transferred several times, once to the prison at Brushy Mountain, Tennessee, where he attempted to escape. He was returned to Bledsoe and in 1991 was moved to the then new prison at Riverbend, Tennessee.

1965—DAISY LAMPKIN, founder of the National Council of Negro Women, died from the effects of a December 1964 heart attack.

1989—A confiscated so-called "The White Man's Bible" was ordered returned to San Quentin prisoner Norman Willhoite by U.S. District Court Judge Fern Smith. The book was taken from Willhoite nearly three years earlier by a prison guard who claimed, at the time, that the book was racist and could provoke racial violence. Judge Smith said the book clearly advocates racial purity but it did not advocate acts of violence.

11 March

1861—Confederate States of America adopted a Constitution; slave trade was outlawed.

1926— The Rev. RALPH DAVID ABERNATHY, aide to the Rev. Martin Luther King, Jr., and Southern Christian Leadership Conference figure, was born in Linden, Alabama.

12 March

1864— Birth date of Army Col. CHARLES YOUNG in Mayslick, Kentucky. Young was the third African American appointed to, and the second to graduate from, the U.S. Military Academy at West Point. After graduation Young was commissioned a second lieutenant and posted to the all–African American 10th Cavalry. After service in the West, Young became a military instructor at Ohio's Wilberforce University. He was transferred to the 9th Ohio Regiment and went with it to Cuba after the Spanish American War broke out. Young also served in Haiti, the Philippine Islands and the Mexican Campaign of 1915 before being forced to retire after being declared unfit, physically, for overseas service at the beginning of World War I. Young died in 1922 while in Nigeria. He was buried in Arlington National Cemetery with full military honors.

1932— ANDREW YOUNG, former U.S. United Nations ambassador, former congressman and former mayor of Atlanta, Georgia, was born in New Orleans, Louisiana. (See also 11/6/90)

1962— New York Mets controversial star outfielder DARRYL STRAWBERRY was born in Los Angeles.

1994— Members of the California State Board of Education reversed themselves and returned stories written by Pulitzer Prize winning authors ALICE WALKER and Annie Dillard. The board decision was preceded by a three hour hearing. Aides to Gov. Pete Wilson say he supported the withdrawal of the stories. Walker read Wilson's published remarks and rejected a literary award from Wilson that was to be conferred March 25. Wilson announced that "his [Wilson's] remarks were fabricated" by his staff.

13 March

1979— In the island Republic of Grenada, the New Jewel Movement, headed by U.S. educated MAURICE BISHOP, ousted the government of Prime Minister Gairy. (See also 10/19)

14 March

1915— LIONEL J. WILSON, former mayor of Oakland, California, was born in New Orleans, Louisiana. A former Oakland Municipal and Alameda County and State Superior court jurist, Wilson was first elected in 1977 and planned to seek a fourth term in 1990. Wilson ran against his protégé California State Assemblyman ELIHU HARRIS and WILSON RILES, JR., son of the former California Superintendent of Public Instruction WILSON RILES. Harris won the 1990 election and was re-elected in 1994.

1933— Jazz composer, arranger and musician QUINCY JONES was born in Chicago, Illinois (See also 12/10)

15 March

1920— The American Legion was formed in Paris at the end of World War II. African American troops were denied membership in what essentially was a veterans' organization.

16 March

1987— The Associated Press wire service reported racial incidents at the University of Chicago, Northern Illinois University, University of Colorado, Purdue University, University of Michigan, Bates College, University of Massachusetts, Philadelphia College of Textiles and The Citadel during 1986 and 1987.

1988— In Rome, Pope John Paul II elevated Bishop EUGENE A. MARINO to Archbishop and appointed him to head the Catholic diocese of Atlanta. The Pope's action made Marino the first African American Roman Catholic Archbishop in the United States. He was ordained in June

1962 at the Shrine of the Immaculate Conception in the District of Columbia. (See also 5/5; 5/29; 8/16; 8/19)

17 March

1806— NORBERT RILLIEUX, chemical engineer, inventor and Egyptologist, was born in New Orleans, Louisiana. The son of an inventor and engineer, Rillieux was educated in Paris schools and, at 24, became an instructor at L'École Centrale and published papers on steam economy. Rillieux is best known for inventing the "multiple evaporation process" used to refine sugar and manufacture paper. The process was widely used in France. In 1934, the sugar industry honored Rillieux with a plaque in the Louisiana State Museum.

1863— Slavery was abolished in Texas but it was June 19th before the Texas citizenry was told. From this delay came JUNETEENTH DAY celebrations among former Texas slaves and their descendents, who consider this their emancipation day.

1944— CLARENCE "Cito" GASTON, manager of the Toronto Blue Jays baseball team was born in San Antonio, Texas. (See also 3/17; 5/31)

18 March

1860— Birthday of RALPH WALDO TYLER, journalist, Auditor-General of the Navy and World War I foreign correspondent. The oldest of 12 children, Tyler is believed to have been born in Ohio. He attended elementary and high schools in Columbus, Ohio, studied a year in Baldwin, Missouri, and began teaching school at age 19. Tyler taught himself shorthand while working as a janitor at the *Columbus Evening Dispatch*. He later was given an opportunity to prove his reporting ability. Tyler worked in circulation, business and news departments of the paper and as an assistant to the manager and secretary to the owner. He became successful as a society reporter. He was the first African American foreign war correspondent and the only accredited African American correspondent in World War I. Both African American and White newspapers carried Tyler's stories. He died in 1921.

1933— Birthday of UNITA BLACKWELL, who was born in Lula, Mississippi. One of the organizing members of the Mississippi Freedom Democratic Party, Blackwell was elected mayor of Meyersville, Mississippi, in 1976. The election made Blackwell the first African American mayor in Mississippi history.

1938— Country and western singer CHARLIE PRIDE was born in Sledge, Mississippi.

1949— In Sanfran, Arkansas, the birthday of BERTHA KNOX GILKEY, organizer of low-income tenant housing management teams in St. Louis, Missouri. Founder and president of Urban Women, Inc., a management consulting firm that provides management training for residents of public housing projects based on Gilkey's St. Louis model.

19 March

1619— Birthday of WILLIAM TUCKER, the first African American child born in the colonies. Tucker was baptized in Jamestown, Virginia. There are unconfirmed reports that Tucker lived to be 108 years old.

1919— NATHANIEL "Nat King" COLE, silky voiced crooner, was born Nathaniel Adams Cole, in Montgomery, Alabama. In his 20s Cole formed a group with Oscar Moore on guitar, Wesley Prince on base and himself on piano and vocals. The group gained fame and later became known as the Nat Cole Trio. The trio stayed together until 1948 when Cole recorded "Nature Boy," which became an instant hit. Cole performed solo thereafter. (See also 2/6)

20 March

1852— Harriet Beecher Stowe's *Uncle Tom's Cabin* was published. The work was based on the life of Maryland slave JOSIAH HENSON, who later escaped to

Canada. Henson, born in Rockville, Maryland, in 1789, frequently helped fugitive slaves and was immortalized in *Uncle Tom's Cabin*.

1934 — California Legislator and attorney WILLIE BROWN was born in Mineola, Texas. First elected to the State Assembly in 1964, Brown was elected Speaker in 1980 and re-elected in 1982, 1984, 1986, 1988 and 1990 and is the first African American Assembly Speaker. He held the post longer than any of his predecessors. Brown is a 1955 graduate of San Francisco State University and earned a law degree from Hastings College of Law in 1958.

21 March

1960 — The first lunch counters were integrated in San Antonio, Texas.

22 March

1941 — The all–African American 99th Pursuit Squadron, U.S. Army Air Corps, was activated at Chanute Field, Illinois. (See also 2/19; 3/22; 4/24; 5/15; 5/22; 12/15)

1972 — Congress proposed the Equal Rights Amendment, essentially banning discrimination on the basis of sex. After nearly two decades of making the rounds of the States for ratification, the measure failed to become law. Of the 50 states, 38 must ratify Constitutional Amendments before they can become law.

23 March

1985 — PATRICIA ROBERTS HARRIS, Housing and Urban Development Secretary and, in 1965, ambassador to Luxembourg during the Carter Administration, died in Washington, D.C.

1954 — National Basketball Association star, MOSES "The Mailman" MALONE was born in Petersburg, Virginia.

24 March

1912 — Birthday of DOROTHY IRENE HEIGHT, in Richmond, Virginia. Height,

president of the National Council of Negro Women for more than three decades, organized a successful drive to place a statue of Mary McLeod Bethune in a District of Columbia park. Once erected, the statue became the first of an African American in a public park in Washington, D.C. Height earned undergraduate and graduate degrees from New York University.

1988 — More than 350 African American men and women, denied jobs by Honda of America, Inc., received a share of a $6 million settlement to be paid by the Japanese auto maker after it was negotiated on their behalf by the federal government. In addition to the settlement, Honda agreed to provide jobs and back pay for the group by the end of February 1989.

25 March

1831 — RICHARD ALLEN, co-founder of the African Methodist Episcopal Church died. (See also 2/14)

1931 — The SCOTTSBORO BOYS, nine young African Americans, were falsely charged with rape and collectively served more than 100 years in prison. The right of African Americans to serve on juries was established by their case. The only member of the group known to be alive in 1978 was CLARENCE WILLIE NORRIS, who lived in Brooklyn, New York. Norris was exonerated October 26, 1976, 90 days after applying for a pardon from then Gov. George Wallace. On April 6, 1977, the Alabama Legislature rejected a bill authorizing $10,000 compensation for Norris. (See also 2/24)

1931 — IDA WELLS-BARNETT, editor of the *Memphis Free Speech and Headlight* newspaper, died in a Chicago hospital. (See also 3/25; 7/16)

1942 — Singer ARETHA FRANKLIN was born in Memphis, Tennessee, to the Rev. Clarence L. Franklin and Barbara Siggers Franklin.

1965 — Outside Montgomery, Alabama, Viola Gregg Liuzzo, a 39-year-old White civil rights advocate from Detroit, was shot to death by four Ku Klux Klansmen as she drove along U.S. Highway 80 with an African American passenger, Leroy Moton, then 19. Liuzzo was in Alabama helping with the five-day march from Selma to Montgomery, the state capitol. At the time of her death Mrs. Liuzzo was returning to Montgomery after having driven a group of marchers from the state capitol to Selma. Four men, Eugene Thomas, William Orville Eaton, Gary Thomas Rowe, Jr., and Collie LeRoy Wilkins, Jr., were charged with Liuzzo's death.

1967 — Birthday of Olympic figure skater DEBI THOMAS in Poughkeepsie, New York. Thomas became the first African American to win acclaim in figure skating after winning the 1988 U.S. Open Championship. The win earned Thomas a berth on the 1988 U.S. Olympic team while she was attending Sanford University as a medical student. Thomas' Olympic performance was good enough for a silver medal.

26 March

1944 — Actress/Singer DIANA ROSS, of the Supremes singing group, was born in Detroit, Michigan.

27 March

1924 — Jazz singer SARAH VAUGHN was born in Newark, New Jersey.

28 March

1949 — Track and field athlete RONNIE RAY SMITH was born in Los Angeles.

1988 — A federal judge barred Attorney General Edwin Meese III from taking part in a civil rights investigation of charges of discrimination and harassment brought by veteran African American special agent DONALD ROCHON. Rochon accused his fellow agents in the Chicago office of making death threats and of the subsequent cover-up of his complaints. (See also 8/10)

29 March

1918 — Singer PEARL BAILEY was born in Newport News, Virginia. (See also 4/16)

1945 — Basketball legend WALT FRAZIER was born in Atlanta, Georgia.

1955 — Football star EARL CAMPBELL was born in Tyler, Texas.

1975 — Major airlift of U.S. troops from Vietnam in the face of a major offensive by North Vietnamese troops. American combat casualties numbered 47,382; African American troops accounted for 5,681 or 15 percent of these deaths.

1990 — Defense lawyers in criminal cases cannot dismiss individuals selected for jury duty because of their race. The ruling, the first of its kind in any state supreme court in the country, was made by the New York State Court of Appeals (equivalent to any state supreme court). It came as the justices upheld the manslaughter convictions of three White defendants in the Howard Beach racial slaying. (See also 1/17; 3/29; 12/21)

1990 — The outspoken Rev. AL SHARPTON of New York, who gained notoriety in the Twana Brawley case, was accused of using a so-called "phantom charity" (the National Youth Movement which Sharpton formed more than a decade ago), to take more than $250,000 for personal use. (See also 7/3)

30 March

1870 — The 15th Amendment to the U.S. Constitution was ratified this date. The amendment made unlawful the act of withholding the right to vote on the basis of race or past servitude.

31 March

1856 — HENRY OSSIAN FLIPPER, the first African American graduate of the U.S. Military Academy at West Point, was born in Thomasville, Georgia. Accounts of Flipper's four years as a cadet indicate that not one of his fellow cadets ever spoke to him during his four years at the Point. After graduation, on June 15, 1877, Flipper was posted to the all–African American 10th Cavalry at Ft. Sill, Oklahoma, then Indian territory. Flipper's military career was stormy and ended when he was falsely accused of embezzling army funds. He was acquitted but the stigma remained and he left the army. Flipper died in Atlanta, Georgia, in 1940.

1878— Birth date, in Galveston, Texas, of JOHN ARTHUR JOHNSON a heavyweight boxer best known as "Jack Johnson." Johnson boxed for the fun of it after he quit school in the fifth grade. He became the first African American world heavyweight boxing champion by defeating Tommy Burns in 12 rounds, in Sydney, Australia. Johnson left the United States in 1912, after becoming involved in several controversies, and traveled in Europe with his wife while lawyers haggled with government prosecutors. In 1915, Johnson fought Jess Willard in Havana. Johnson was 37 and had not trained since his fight with Jim Jeffries in 1910. He lost to Willard in the twenty-sixth round. Johnson fought in 107 bouts, winning 37 percent, or 40, by knockouts. After several years of boxing exhibitions, lecturing and entertaining, Johnson died from injuries suffered in a 1945 auto accident. (See also 4/15; 12/26)

1980— Olympic athlete JAMES CLEVELAND "Jesse" OWENS, died in Tucson, Arizona.

1901— U.S. Navy Seaman ALPHONSE GIRANDY, serving on the *Petrel*, "fearlessly exposed his own life to danger" while saving others when a fire broke out aboard *Petrel*. His Medal of Honor was presented March 22, 1902.

April

Neither slavery nor involuntary servitude, except as punishment for crime whereof the party shall have been duly convicted, shall exist within the United States, or any place subject to their jurisdiction. — Article XIII, the United States Constitution

1 April

1832— An African American man, known only as ROBERT THE HERMIT, died near Seekonk, Massachusetts. Born a slave at Princeton, New Jersey, Robert was one of the nation's most famous hermits.

1905— The birthday of CLARA Mc-BRIDE HALE, in Philadelphia, Pennsylvania. Hale founded Hale House, a home for infant children of drug addicts, located in New York City's Harlem. In 1985, Hale was proclaimed an "American Hero" by President Ronald Reagan.

1989— Former baseball great WILLIAM "Bill" WHITE completed his first day as president of baseball's National League. (See also 2/3)

2 April

1932— World famous African American cowboy WILLIE "Bill" PICKETT died in a Ponca, Oklahoma, hospital of injuries sustained after he was kicked in the head by a horse on the Miller Brothers' Fabulous 101 Ranch. (See also 12/5)

1987— Engineer LENELL GETER was convicted of armed robbery in October 1982, and sentenced to life in prison for a crime by someone else. On this date, Geter filed a lawsuit naming as defendants the po-

lice officers and prosecutors involved in his arrest and subsequent erroneous conviction. Geter served 16 months of the sentence. He was released after authorities determined his innocence and the guilt of another man. Among the documents filed in connection with Geter's suit was an affidavit alleging the recent discovery of electronic listening devices in Geter's Dallas, Texas, apartment.

3 April

1826— Poet JAMES MADISON BELL was born in Ohio. A civil rights advocate, Bell was a friend and aide to abolitionist John Brown. Bell migrated to San Francisco in 1860. In celebration of the Emancipation Proclamation, Bell wrote the poem *The Progress of Liberty.*

1955— JAMES "Bonecrusher" SMITH, a former World Boxing Association heavyweight champion, was born in Magnolia, North Carolina. Smith and the World Boxing Council and International Boxing Federation champions were each defeated by Mike Tyson who once owned all three heavyweight titles.

1961— Actor/comedian EDDIE MUR-PHY was born in the borough of Brooklyn, New York.

1991— The Bush Justice Department dropped charges of conspiracy and income tax evasion against U.S. Rep. FLOYD FLAKE and his wife Elaine. Trial proceedings came to an abrupt end when Asst. U.S. Attorney William J. Muller told the court an earlier court ruling had weakened the government's case considerably and that it would be difficult to prove allegations in the 17-count indictment. Flake is a Democrat and the pastor of an African Methodist Episcopal Church in New York City.

4 April

1928— Writer Maya Angelou was born MARGUERITE JOHNSON in St. Louis, Missouri. Angelou has written five books, each an autobiographical installment about specific periods of her life. The first, *I Know Why the Caged Bird Sings*, was published in 1970.

1939— Former WBA heavyweight champion ERNEST TERRELL was born in Chicago, Illinois. Terrell fought 55 matches and won 21 by knockout.

1968— The Rev. MARTIN LUTHER KING, JR., was assassinated, in Memphis, Tennessee, by James Earl Ray. (See also 1/13; 1/15; 1/19; 3/10; 3/11; 4/4; 4/27; 8/28; 8/29; 10/14; 10/18; 12/1)

1972— Rep. ADAM CLAYTON POWELL, JR., a fixture in the House of Representatives for nearly three decades, died in New York City. (See also 1/10; 3/1; 11/25)

1990— Gannett News Service reported 313 U.S. cities have African American mayors. Six of those lead the country's 20 largest municipalities; an additional 34 head cities with populations of 50,000 or more.

5 April

1839— ROBERT SMALLS was born in Beaufort, South Carolina. He was captain of the Navy ship *Planter* during the Civil War. After the war, Smalls served five terms in the House as the South Carolina representative. When the Civil War began, Smalls was working aboard the *Planter* and immediately began plotting to steal the ship and sail it to freedom. After stealing the *Planter* and turning it over to the Union Navy, Smalls became pilot of the ironclad ship *Keokuk* the following year. The *Keokuk* later was sunk by Confederate gunfire. Smalls, aboard during the attack, jumped overboard and swam to safety. He was reassigned to the *Planter* as its pilot and later as captain.

After the Civil War, southern Democrats falsely accused Smalls of election fraud. He was convicted and sentenced to three years in jail. After a few days in custody, Smalls was released and the charges dropped. However, when Smalls attempted to show he had won the election, Congress voted 142–127 to deny Smalls his House seat. Smalls later was appointed collector of customs for Beaufort, South Carolina. He held this job until 1913, when a Republican controlled Congress failed to confirm his earlier appointment. Smalls died two years later in Beaufort.

1856— Birthday of BOOKER TALIFERRO WASHINGTON, who was born a slave in Franklin County, Virginia. An educator and articulate public speaker, Washington became principal of Tuskegee Normal Institute in June 1881 and opened the school on Independence Day the same year. Washington was the first African American to be honored by having his portrait on a U.S. postage stamp. (See also 11/14)

1937— Army Gen. COLIN LUTHER POWELL, national security advisor to former President Ronald Reagan, was born in New York City. Powell was promoted to four star rank in December 1988. The promotion was the result of his White House service, which ended with the inauguration of George H. W. Bush as president. In August 1989, Bush nominated Powell to be chairman of the Joint Chiefs of Staff when the incumbent chairman, Navy Admiral William C. Crowe, announced his retirement. Powell's Senate confirmation hearing was unanimous and uneventful. (See also 10/1)

1987— In Birmingham, Alabama, LERIA LOWE JORDON was the first African

American member of the 65-year-old Junior League of Birmingham. The League's acceptance of Jordon was a "natural thing" for the service group, according to then President Susan Haskell.

1990— Jazz vocalist SARAH VAUGHN died after a half-century of club dates. Her sultry recording sessions with the Sarah Vaughn Trio and the bands of jazz greats Count Basie, Miles Davis, Earl "Fatha" Hines, Dizzie Gillespie and Charlie Parker, "touched the world with their exceptional talent" (*Ebony* magazine p. 94, November 1990.) Vaughn's singing career began at age 16 with Hines' group. Singer Billy Eckstine, then with Hines' band, encouraged Hines to hire Vaughn. (See also 3/27)

6 April

1909— The North Pole was reached by explorers Admiral Robert Perry, MATTHEW HENSON and four unidentified Eskimos.

1937— Birth date, in New York City, of actor BILLY DEE WILLIAMS. Williams' last major movies were two *Star Wars* sequels and *Mahogany*.

1990— Former Black Panther MICHAEL McGEE, a veteran Milwaukee, Wisconsin, alderman representing one of the city's poorest districts, promised violence for Milwaukee at the hands of a "Black Militia." The alternative: a $100 million job program and the revitalization of African American neighborhoods that had been in decline while other parts of Milwaukee prospered. McGee was first elected in 1984.

7 April

1852— Birthday of Army Lt. Col. ALLEN ALLENSWORTH, Chaplain Corps, who was born in Kentucky and migrated to California after a hitch in the Union Army. After service in the Spanish-American War, Allensworth settled in what is now Tulare County, in California's fertile Central Valley in 1907. He founded the farming community which later was named for him. It is the only settlement in California founded and governed by

African Americans. The small community of Allensworth lives on as a state park and has been partially restored by the California Department of Parks and Recreation. Allensworth the man died in 1914 and a memorial in his honor was placed in San Francisco's Presidio Army Base in 1975; Allensworth the community died in 1918 from severe water shortages and prejudice.

1954— National Football League Hall of Fame running back TONY DORSETT was born in Alaquippa, Pennsylvania. Formerly with the Dallas Cowboys, Dorsett began the 1988 season carrying the pigskin for the Denver Broncos.

8 April

1922— Jazz vocalist CARMEN McRAE was born in New York City.

1960— The Student Non-Violent Coordinating Committee (SNCC) was organized on this date. (See also 3/6)

1974—HENRY "Hank" AARON, Atlanta Braves outfielder, hit his 715th home run to break Babe Ruth's record of 714 which stood 47 years. Aaron's career home run total stood at 755 upon his retirement.

1987— Racial unrest in Tampa, Florida, after an African American man died following a scuffle with the police. It was the second death of an African American in six weeks occurring after an incident that involved Tampa police officers. (See also 2/21)

1989— Although "Colored" and "White" signs, prominently displayed over two drinking fountains along a wall of the Ellisville, Mississippi, Courthouse, were plastered over removal of the fountains (installed on the courthouse lawn in 1907) was delayed while Jones County officials conferred with state historians.

1990— Writing in the *San Francisco Examiner*, columnist Christopher Matthews correctly noted the academic and political success of African Americans immediately after the Civil War. The "well-nurtured myth," Matthews wrote, implied that the election of African Americans to public office had more to do with the presence of Union troops and withholding the right to vote from those loyal to the Confederacy. "Blacks did not stop getting elected to Congress when Reconstruction ended in 1877," Matthews said. Since Reconstruction, fifty-six African Americans have been elected to the House of Representatives and one Republican — former Sen. Edward W. Brooke of Massachusetts — to the Senate.

9 April

1866— Congress passed the first Civil Rights Act over the veto of then President Andrew Jackson.

1898— Birth date, in Princeton, New Jersey, of singer/actor PAUL LEROY ROBESON, who became a devout communist and was black-listed in performing arts circles as a result. The youngest of six children, Robeson was valedictorian for the class of 1919, Rutgers University, from which he graduated with honors. Robeson was a standout in baseball, basketball, football and track and the first African American named All-American in football, which he later played as a professional. Robeson also graduated from Columbia University School of Law. He starred in plays by Eugene O'Neil, including *Emperor Jones*, and Shakespeare's *Othello*. Unable to find work in the 50s because of his politics, Robeson left the United States for the Soviet Union in 1958. After five years in the Soviet Union, Robeson's health began to deteriorate and he returned to the United States in 1963.

1939— The Washington, D.C., chapter of the Daughters of the American Revolution denied contralto MARION ANDERSON the use of Constitution Hall for a concert. Anderson went ahead with her performance, out-of-doors, at the Lincoln Memorial where 75,000 people gathered to hear her sing.

10 April

1877— President Rutherford B. Hayes ordered the withdrawal of occupation forces from the Southern states, thereby signalling the end of Reconstruction and a decline in African American participation in the political process.

1926— Welfare rights advocate JOHNNIE TILLMAN was born in Scott, Arkansas. Formerly a welfare mother, Tillman founded the National Welfare Rights Organization in 1972.

1975— JOSEPHINE BAKER died at age 68.

1986— In the espionage case of former Central Intelligence Agency clerk SHARON SCRANAGE, U.S. District Judge Richard L. Williams slashed three years off the sentence he gave Scranage in November 1985. The action allowed Scranage to be released from prison after having served 18 months. Scranage was convicted of passing classified documents and the names of CIA operatives in Ghana to her Ghanian lover. Judge Williams noted that the "culprit" in the case was her boyfriend who at the government's recommendation, wound up getting nothing. (See also 7/11)

1990— PHILLIP PANNELL, 16, was shot and killed by a Teaneck, New Jersey, police officer. As with most cases involving White officers and African American victims, events as observed by witnesses and police were in conflict. In the Pannell shooting, police said Pannell ran away from them after a body search, during which one officer said he "felt" a pistol inside Pannell's jacket. While he was running away, the officers said Pannell "reached towards his left (jacket) pocket and turned." It was after the youth presumably turned toward the pursuing officers that the first of two shots were fired by police. A second shot was fired as Pannell continued his escape attempt, police claim. Civilian witnesses to the shooting said Pannell was unarmed and was heard pleading for his life when the second fatal shot was fired by police. Officers were called to the neighborhood by a resident who reported a youth brandishing a pistol on a school playground. Pannell was wearing a red jacket, which police said matched the description of the youth with the gun offered by the resident who telephoned police. What is odd about this shooting is that one officer said he "felt a gun" in Pannell's coat while patting the youngster down prior to his alleged escape attempt. Follow-up reports on this incident by New Jersey newspapers indicated that the officers involved did not find or produce the weapon they say Pannell had in the pocket of his jacket. (See also 4/13)

11 April

1899— Chemist PERCY JULIAN was born in Montgomery, Alabama. He attended DePauw University, in Indiana, and later taught chemistry at Fisk University. Julian also studied at Harvard and the University of Vienna. He returned to DePauw to work on research projects and later discovered several synthetic substances, including one that made paint watertight, cortisone, and a fire suppressing foam. (See also Appendix)

1967— Flamboyant minister Rep. ADAM CLAYTON POWELL, JR., D-New York, won a special election in his Harlem district by a margin of six to one. However, Powell, having been censured by Congress for taking his secretary to the Bahamas and charging off the trip as official congressional business, remained in the Bahamas, where he had gone to avoid arrest, for several months. He regained his seat after a second special election. (See also 1/10; 3/1; 4/4; 11/25)

1990— Idaho became the 47th state to recognize Jan. 15 as MARTIN LUTHER KING, JR. Day and as a national holiday. Only the state of New Hampshire does not have an official Martin Luther King, Jr., holiday. There it is celebrated as Civil Rights Day. (See also 4/4)

12 April

1861— The U.S. Civil War began at 4:30 a.m. when Confederate forces fired the first shots on Fort Sumter, South Carolina.

1864— Union troops stationed at Fort Pillow, Tennessee, were wiped out by other Union forces commanded by Gen. Nathan Forrest. The attack on Fort Pillow triggered a congressional investigation. Half of the 500 men who manned the fort were African Americans. Troops under Forrest's command were accused of killing African American troopers after they had surrendered. Forrest's report: "We bust the fort at ninner clock and scatered [sic] the niggers. The men is still killan [sic] 'em in the woods...." (See also 12/24)

1913— Birth date of band leader and vibraphonist LIONEL HAMPTON in Birmingham, Alabama. Hampton, at 76, was still performing publicly and making cameo appearances on "Sesame Street," a children's television show.

1931— Birthday of retired Army Maj. Gen. ROBERT CLARENCE GASKILL in Yonkers, New York.

1940— Contemporary jazz composer and musician HERBIE HANCOCK was born in Chicago, Illinois.

1981— Boxing legend JOSEPH LOUIS "Joe Louis" BARROW died in Las Vegas, Nevada.

1989— Boxer Walker Smith, known as SUGAR RAY ROBINSON, died in Culver City, California. Smith succumbed to the combined effects of Alzheimer's disease, diabetes and hypertension. (See also 5/3)

13 April

1929— Associate California Supreme Court Justice ALLEN E. BROUSSARD was born in Lake Charles, Louisiana. Justice Broussard was appointed by former Gov. Edmund G. Brown, Jr., and seated during the summer of 1981. A veteran of California's Alameda County municipal and superior courts, Justice Broussard is a graduate of Boalt Hall School of Law, University of California, Berkeley.

1946— Blues singer AL GREEN was born in Forest City, Arkansas.

1989— In Ellisville, Mississippi, workmen finally were permitted to cover the words "White" and "Colored" carved into an exterior wall of the courthouse above two drinking fountains. The fountains were installed in 1907.

1989— In Greensburg, Louisiana, African American and Caucasian children, all students at Greensburg Elementary School, shared lunch for the first time ever. The 1989-90 school year also was the first time the children attended the same school since the U.S. Supreme Court's 1954 ruling in Brown vs. Board of Education, Topeka, Kansas.

1990— College students from nearby universities and colleges marched through Teaneck, New Jersey, to diffuse tensions after rioting marred a candlelight memorial service for 16-year-old PHILLIP PANNELL, who was shot and killed by police three days earlier. Police claim Pannell had a gun and was reaching for that weapon when he was shot. (See also 4/10)

1990— Members of the Black Nazarene in the Philippine Islands prepared to celebrate a religious holiday, in Manila.

14 April

1775— The Abolitionist Society was formed in Philadelphia, Pennsylvania.

1865— President Abraham Lincoln was assassinated by John Wilkes Booth. Booth escaped after the shooting but later was captured in a barn in the Virginia countryside. (See also 1/1; 2/12; 4/14; 5/6; 9/22; 10/31)

1989— HERBERT MILLS, one of the original members of the Mills Brothers Quartet, died at age 77 in a Las Vegas hospital. Mills sang with the group for nearly 70 years. (See also 2/2)

15 April

1889— ASA PHILIP RANDOLPH, founder of the Brotherhood of Sleeping Car Porters, was born in Crescent City, Florida.

1850— The California Fugitive Slave Law, introduced earlier by state Senator Henry A. Crabb, a Stockton, California, attorney, was adopted by the State Legislature. It authorized any slave owner claiming a runaway to obtain a warrant for the slave's arrest. Law enforcement officers were required to serve such warrants and make arrests. Owners were required to prove ownership in court hearings and, if successful, could forcefully take the slave out of California. The act was amended in 1854 by anti-slavery senators who rewrote the measure so that it would void itself one year later.

1915— Heavyweight boxer JACK JOHNSON lost a title fight to Jess Willard. (See also 3/31)

1919— Lithographer and sculptor ELIZABETH CATLETT was born in Washington, D.C. Catlett was the first woman to teach sculpture at the School of Fine Arts, National Autonomous University of Mexico.

1922— Chicago's first African American mayor, HAROLD WASHINGTON, was born in the Windy City. Within weeks of his re-election to a second term, Washington was stricken by a fatal heart attack while working in his office. (See also 11/25)

1928— Birthday of architect NORMA MERRICK SKLAREK, in New York City. Sklarek was the first African American woman licensed as an architect in the states of California and New York, and perhaps the nation. Among her notable works is the U.S. embassy in Tokyo.

16 April

1862— Slavery was abolished in the District of Columbia. The federal government set aside $1 million to pay slave holders and any former slave wanting to emigrate to Haiti, Liberia or elsewhere.

1929— Baritone singer ROY HAMILTON was born in Leesburg, Georgia. Hamilton's biggest hits of the 50s were "Unchained Melody" and "You'll Never Walk Alone."

1947— KAREEM ABDUL-JABBAR, who retired from the Los Angeles Lakers basketball team at the end of the 1988-89 season, was born Lewis F. Alcindor, Jr., in New York City.

17 April

1758— Birthday of poet FRANCIS WILLIAMS, whose place of birth is unknown. Williams' first poems were published in Latin. He was the first known African American college graduate in the Western Hemisphere.

1823— Arkansas jurist MIFFLIN WISTAR GIBBS was born in Philadelphia, Pennsylvania. Gibbs became the nation's first African American judge after a successful 1873 election campaign for a judgeship in Little Rock, Arkansas. He is the author of *Shadow and Light*, his autobiography. Gibbs lived in San Francisco from 1850 to 1858 and served as U.S. consul to Madagascar.

1872— WILLIAM MONROE TROTTER, crusader for full equality, publisher of *The Boston Guardian* newspaper and co-founder (with W.E.B. Du Bois) of the Niagara Movement, was born in Boston, Massachusetts. Trotter led a protest against the showing of the film *Birth of a Nation* in a Boston theater. His efforts to have the film banned were unsuccessful. Trotter died on his 62nd birthday after living the last years of his life in poverty. The cause of Trotter's death, like that of abolitionist David Walker, remains a mystery.

1924— ALTHEA T. L. SIMMONS, lead congressional lobbyist for the National Association for the Advancement of Colored People and director of the NAACP's District of Columbia office, was born in Shreveport, Louisiana. Simmons lobbied for the 1982 extension of the Voting Rights Act and legislation that made January 15 — the birthday of the Rev. Martin Luther King, Jr. — a national holiday.

1989— After a bizarre version of show and tell, three students at Bancroft Junior High School in San Leandro, California,

were suspended when each brought a doll to their English class. One doll was decked out in Ku Klux Klan regalia, a second depicted an African American hung in effigy, and the third carried a sign-board with a racial slur. The students' individual apologies did not prevent the suspensions. Because school officials took disciplinary action, they were subjected to criticism from parents, students and teachers.

1990— Playwright AUGUST WILSON won his second Pulitzer Prize for drama with the play *The Piano Lesson*. Wilson's *Fences* won the prestigious Pulitzer in 1987.

1990— The Rev. RALPH DAVID ABERNATHY, keystone of the Southern Christian Leadership Conference and trusted aide to the Rev. MARTIN LUTHER KING, JR., died of heart failure at Crawford Long Hospital on the campus of Atlanta's Emory University. He was 64. (See also 3/11)

18 April

1966— Boston Celtic's basketball team center WILLIAM "Bill" FELTON RUSSELL was named the team's head coach after the retirement of long-time coach Red Auerbach. Russell became the first African American to coach a major league athletic team. (See also 2/12; 11/15)

19 April

1775— African Americans took part in major battles at Concord and Lexington, at the beginning of the American Revolution.

1910— The National Urban League was formed in New York City. The league was born out of a merger of the National League for the Protection of Colored Women, National League on Urban Conditions Among Negroes and the Niagara Movement.

1990— Entertainer JAMES BROWN began taking part in a work release program after serving 15 months of a six-year term in a South Carolina state prison. Brown was convicted of aggravated assault and failure to stop for Georgia police. After a high-speed chase, Brown finally was overtaken and arrested by South Carolina authorities. (See also 4/29; 12/15)

20 April

1871— The 3rd Force act, best known as the Ku Klux Klan Act, gave the president military powers, including the suspension of habeas corpus, to put an end to racial terrorism.

1909— Presidential assistant E. FREDERIC MORROW was born in Hakensack, New Jersey. A graduate of Rutgers Law School, Morrow was a Bank of America vice president for communications and public affairs. He later was appointed an administrative assistant to President Dwight D. Eisenhower. Morrow wrote *Black Man in the White House.*

1926— Birth date of Wyoming state Sen. HARRIET ELIZABETH BYRD, who was born in Cheyenne. A retired elementary school teacher, Byrd became Wyoming's first African American legislator in 11 decades, after a successful 1981 campaign for a seat in the state House of Representatives. Byrd ran a second successful campaign, in 1989, for a state Senate seat she held until 1992.

1962— The New Orleans Citizen's Council, an organization of segregationists, began offering African Americans free, one-way transportation to northern cities. An estimated 9,067 persons accepted over the next six months.

1990— Oakland hosted the first Bay Area "Black Filmworks Festival." Sponsored by the Black Filmmakers Hall of Fame, the three-day event featured 25 films including a documentary entitled "Making 'Do the Right Thing'."

21 April

1898— Volunteer African American army units, including the 3rd Alabama, 3rd North Carolina, 6th Virginia, 9th Ohio, 9th Illinois, 23rd Kansas and 10th Cavalry regiments, some units with African American officers, took part in the Spanish-American War on Cuban soil. African American veterans were difficult for Whites to accept. As a result, some African American veterans were assaulted and lynched after the war while others were met with speeches and parades.

22 April

1692— In Salem, Massachusetts, MARY BLACK, a slave, was convicted of sorcery and jailed after a trial. History did not record Black's ultimate fate. However, her conviction was assured when several witnesses claimed to have felt pin pricks when Black complied with the trial judge's request that she remove a scarf she wore pinned to her blouse.

1989— An estimated 500 anti-racism demonstrators rejected a proposal from Richard Butler, leader of the Hayden Lake, Idaho-based Aryan Nation, that the states of Idaho, Montana, Oregon, Washington and Wyoming secede and join to create a Whites only homeland within the United States. The demonstrators converged on Coeur D'Alene, Idaho, for the Walk for Racial Equality. Cold weather reduced by 75 percent the number of marchers expected from throughout the Pacific Northwest.

1989— The Rev. EVAN E. McDONALD, pastor of Golden Grove Baptist Church, in Meridian, Mississippi, resigned instead of firing former Nesoba County Sheriff Lawrence Rainey as his congregation demanded. Rainey was sheriff in 1964 when civil rights workers James Chaney, Andrew Goodman and Michael Schwerner were murdered. (See also 6/21)

23 April

1856— Birthday, in Columbus, Ohio, of inventor GRANVILLE T. WOODS. Woods received more than 35 patents including those for a steam boiler furnace, an incubator, and an automatic air brake. His electrical devices were sold to American Bell Telephone Company and General

Electric. Westinghouse Air Brake Company ultimately acquired his air brake patent. He also founded the Woods Railway Telegraph Company. (See also Appendix)

1913— The National Urban League was incorporated.

1989— Daniel Johnson, a Glendale, California, attorney and author of a self-styled, so-called Peace Amendment to the United States Constitution — a document that, if adopted by Congress and individual state legislatures, would require all non–Whites to leave the United States — moved from California to Wyoming. Johnson unsuccessfully campaigned for Wyoming's single seat in the House of Representatives, vacated by Rep. Richard "Dick" Cheney. Cheney became George Bush's defense secretary. Johnson felt the nation was in a state of decline. He argued for the preservation of the nation as a White English speaking country.

1990— Harvard University law professor DERRICK BELL, who 20 years before became the school's first African American faculty member, announced his request for a leave of absence without pay until the university added an African American woman to the Law School faculty.

1990— U.S. Food and Drug Administration officials announced the end of an earlier ban on blood donations by Haitians.

1990— The late Rev. RALPH DAVID ABERNATHY was buried following funeral services at Atlanta's West Hunter Street Baptist Church.

24 April

1943— The all–African American 99th Fighter Squadron, Army Air Corps, with training completed, left the United States for combat duty in Europe.

1944— The United Negro College Fund was established.

1990— African American and white physicians began debating the relevance of racism and racial conflicts as significant

factors in high blood pressure, which causes heart and kidney disease and strokes — in African American males.

25 April

1918— Birthday of jazz vocalist ELLA FITZGERALD, who was born in Newport News, Virginia. The song, "A Tisket, a Tasket, a Little Yellow Basket" catapulted Fitzgerald to fame.

1990— Saxophonist DEXTER GORDON, the last of the beboppers, died of kidney failure in Philadelphia. Gordon was 67.

26 April

1785— Naturalist JOHN JAMES AUDUBON was born in Santo Domingo, on the Island of Haiti, in that portion of the Caribbean known as the Dominican Republic. Although his father, a French sea captain, sponsored him in several failed business ventures, Audubon found his calling and embarked on what was to become his major achievement — painting all of the known birds in North America. His work was published in varying lengths as the "Birds of America" between 1927 and 1938. Audubon produced more than 400 hand-colored plates. He died in 1851 and has been memorialized by the Audubon Society.

1798— JAMES PIERSON BECKWOURTH, one of 13 children of a slave woman and a White man, was born in rural Virginia. He became a frontier scout, hunter and trader. Beckwourth's family moved to the area around St. Louis, Missouri, where young Beckwourth was apprenticed to a blacksmith from whom he ran away at age 18. Indians living near the Mississippi River befriended Beckwourth and taught him to trap, hunt and fish. Hired as a blacksmith by the Rocky Mountain Fur Co., Beckwourth made friends with the Indians and soon began trading beaver pelts and horses. After serving as a scout for Gen. Frémont, Beckwourth opened a trading post southeast of Mount Shasta. In the adjacent Sierra Nevada Mountains, Beckwourth discovered a pass — now named for him — that later became the gateway to California for immigrant wagon trains. At age 62, Beckwourth took part in the Cheyenne Indian War. He later left California and settled in Denver, Colorado, where historians believe he died sometime in 1867.

1821— The first performance of an all African American theater group, the African Theater Company, was given in New York City.

1854— Mass movement by abolitionists, with their Kansas Immigrant Aid Society, to support African Americans escaping slavery in Southern states for a home in Kansas.

27 April

1927— CORETTA SCOTT KING, widow of the Rev. Martin Luther King, Jr., was born in Marion, Alabama.

1990— There were 289 instances of racially motivated violence or vandalism in 1989, according to Klanwatch Project, an element of the Southern Poverty Law Center. Forty-five percent of the victims in these incidents were African American families living in predominantly White neighborhoods. Klanwatch reported a steady increase, from 25 percent of prosecutions six and seven years earlier, respectively to 75 percent in 1988 and 1989.

28 April

1967— MUHAMMAD ALI, heavyweight boxing champion of the world, refused induction into the U.S. Army after being denied conscientious objector status and was arrested. Although later reinstated by the courts, Ali was promptly stripped of his title by boxing officials.

1989— Many continue to believe that AUNT JEMIMA was a real person who created the pancake mix that bears her name a century or so ago. Actually, Aunt Jemima's features were created in the mind of an employee of the R. T. Davis Milling Co. of St. Joseph, Missouri, in 1889. Quaker Oats Co. bought out Davis Milling in 1926. Along with the purchase came the rights to Aunt Jemima, whose picture begin aging in July 1989. Aunt Jemima was personified by NANCY GREEN, who was born a slave in Montgomery County, Kentucky, in 1834. Green was used to promote Quaker products marketed with the Aunt Jemima logo.

29 April

1899— Birthday, in Washington, D.C., of EDWARD "Duke" KENNEDY ELLINGTON, composer, conductor, lyricist and pianist. (See also 5/24)

30 April

1931— Rep. WILLIAM "Bill" CLAY, D-Missouri, was born in St. Louis. Prior to his election in 1968, Clay was a St. Louis Alderman from 1959 to 1964.

May

*The right of citizens of the United States to vote shall not be
denied or abridged by the United States or by any state on account
of sex.* — Article XIX of the United States Constitution

This month:

1866 — Forty-six slaves were murdered in Memphis, Tennessee.

The 25th Regiment, Infantry, the fourth African American Army unit, was formed by merging the 39th and 40th regiments and later sent to Louisiana.

1 May

1867 — Post Civil War voter registration began. An estimated 1,363,000 voters registered, including 700,000 African Americans. The figures indicate African American voters were the majority in Alabama, Florida, Louisiana, Mississippi and South Carolina.

1867 — HOWARD UNIVERSITY opened and began accepting students.

2 May

1881 — The last significant battle involving Seminole Indian–African American scouts occurred on this date. It stemmed from an Army action in which a Mescalero Indian raiding party was chased out of Texas, across the Rio Grande and into Mexico. The Indian camp, found in the Sierra del Burro Mountains, was surrounded and attacked at sunrise. The chief, San Da Ve, although seriously wounded, was the only one to escape. The scouts killed four warriors, captured a squaw, a child and 21 animals. The scouts were praised and revered for their tracking skills, i.e., being able to successfully locate and follow old traces of the pursued across open desert and mountain areas and give army troops an advantage. They were described as hard riders, dead shots and fierce hand-to-hand fighters to whom Texas owed a debt of gratitude.

1963 — An established 2,543 African American and White civil rights demonstrators protesting segregation were arrested and jailed in Birmingham, Alabama. (See also 5/7)

3 May

1845 — MACON B. ALLEN became the first African American admitted to the Bar (licensed to practice law) in Maine.

1920 — Welterweight and middleweight boxing champion, SUGAR RAY ROBINSON was born Walker Smith this date in Detroit, Michigan. Robinson was the first boxer to win a title five times. He retired in 1965. (See also 4/12)

4 May

1961 — A baker's dozen of FREEDOM RIDERS left Washington, D.C., to test desegregation of public facilities en route to New Orleans, Louisiana.

5 May

1798— Thaddeus Kosciusko, a Polish citizen who apparently believed in freedom, left the United States to live in France. A brigadier general under George Washington during the Revolutionary War, Kosciusko was exposed to slavery while serving in the South. He found slavery distasteful. In his will, Kosciusko left money to Thomas Jefferson for the purchase and education of Negro slaves. Jefferson accepted the money but failed to honor Kosciusko's wish. Kosciusko, Mississippi, was named for Kosciusko and is the hometown of talk show host OPRAH WINFREY. (See also 1/2)

1801— PIO DE JESUS PICO was born at the San Gabriel Mission. Pico served two terms as governor of California. He was the fifth and last Mexican governor of Alta California, known now as California. Pico was appointed to his first term, in 1832, as the result of a dispute between civil and military factions of the government. He was in office less than a month, from January 27 to February 18. Pico's second term also followed a dispute — the disposition of then Gov. Micheltorena — and began in March 1845. Pico chose Los Angeles as his administrative site and allowed military commander Jose Castro to run the customs and treasury function from Monterey. As governor, Pico was generous with land grants. However, his feud with Castro made each of them vulnerable to an assault by American settlers who sent Pico and Castro packing in July of 1846.

1905— In Chicago, ROBERT SENGSTACKE ABBOTT published the first 300 copies of the *Chicago Defender* newspaper. (See also 11/24)

1988— Bishop EUGENE A. MARINO was installed in Atlanta, Georgia, as the first African American Roman Catholic Archbishop in the United States. Initially, Archbishop Marino was assigned to the Atlanta diocese. (See also 3/16; 5/29; 7/10; 8/16; 8/19)

6 May

1812— MARTIN R. DELANY was born free in Charles Town, West Virginia. Delany became a physician, editor, abolition advocate, scientist and explorer. As a child, Delany could not attend school but he spent time standing beneath open school windows reciting the lessons he overheard. He became a student assistant to a White doctor and learned to sew wounds, set bones and perform some surgery. In 1843 he published *The Mystery*, the only African American–owned and edited newspaper in the country at that time. Accepted at Harvard Medical School, Delany attended only one semester. He was not allowed to return because of student protests. In 1852 Delany published his first book, *The Condition, Elevation, Emigration and Destiny of the Colored People of the United States*. After the Emancipation Proclamation, in 1863, Delany spent two years recruiting men for African American Army regiments. In 1865, he met with President Lincoln and presented a plan to send African American troops, commanded by African American officers, into the Southern states. Delany is believed to be the first African American to hold the rank of major in the armed forces. Delany was sent to Charleston, South Carolina, and honorably discharged in 1868. He stayed in Charleston and became a trial judge. (See also 1/24)

1931— Baseball great WILLIE HOWARD MAYS was born in Westfield, Alabama. Mays played with the New York and San Francisco Giants. He was National League batting champion four times and twice the league's Most Valuable Player.

1985— GLADYS MERRITT ROSS, cofounder of Phi Delta Kappa sorority for African American teachers, died in Stockton, California. (See also 5/6; 5/23; 11/17)

7 May

1963— The arrest of more than 2,000 demonstrators resulted in a negotiated agreement between the Birmingham, Alabama, Chamber of Commerce and demonstrators to end civil rights demonstrations. The chamber agreed to desegregate public facilities within three months, hire African Americans in locally-owned businesses in two months and release all demonstrators without bail in return for an end to the protest demonstrations. (See also 5/2)

8 May

1792— Congress yielded to public pressure to maintain a standing army and passed the National Conscription Act. The law required every "able-bodied White male citizen" to serve a hitch in the armed forces. (See also 7/11)

1932— Heavyweight boxer CHARLES "Sonny" LISTON was born in St. Francis County, Arkansas. Liston had 54 fights, including a 1962 bout in which he knocked out Floyd Patterson to win the World Heavyweight Title. In a rematch with Patterson less than a year later, Liston kept the title only to lose it to Muhammad Ali in 1964. (See also 9/25)

9 May

1800— Abolitionist John Brown was born in Torrington, Connecticut. Brown led the 1859 assault on Harpers Ferry. He also encouraged slaves to attempt escape. Brown was charged with treason, tried, convicted and hung in the same year.

1987— The United States frigate *Rodney M. Davis* was commissioned in Long Beach, California. The *Davis* is named for Marine Sgt. RODNEY M. DAVIS, a Medal of Honor recipient. Davis died in 1967 of injuries he suffered after throwing himself on a grenade in Vietnam's Quang Nam province.

10 May

1837— PICKNEY BENTON STEWART PINCHBACK was born in rural Georgia. A Reconstruction era politician and public servant, Pinchback entered Louisiana politics after the Civil War. A Republican, Pinchback was a delegate to Louisiana's 1867-68 Constitutional Convention. He was elected to the state senate in 1868 and was a delegate to the Republican National Convention. Pinchback was elected lieutenant governor in 1871. Pinchback was never elected governor but acted in that capacity for 43 days, in 1872, following the impeachment of the incumbent. Pinchback completed the ousted governor's term and, at age 37, was immediately elected to the U.S. Senate. Although the Senate debated his seating throughout his term, it did vote to pay Pinchback his full salary. Pinchback lived in Washington, D.C., until his death in 1921.

1854— Professional singer ELIZABETH TAYLOR-GREENFIELD gave a command performance before Queen Victoria in Buckingham Palace. Greenfield later was dubbed "The Black Swan."

1989— JOSEPH BOATNER, a member of the stylish 40s Ink Spots quartet, died at 70 in Laconia, New Hampshire. Boatner joined the group in 1952 — after its popularity had peaked.

11 May

1894— Birth date, in Pittsburg, Pennsylvania, of dancer MARTHA GRAHAM. Graham is considered a pioneer in Afro-Haitian dance.

1924— Baseball pioneer MOSES FLEETWOOD WALKER died in Steubenville, Ohio. (See also 10/7)

12 May

1862— ROBERT SMALLS was left in command of the Confederate ship *Planter* while its officers went ashore for an overnight visit. Smalls took command and with the men who remained aboard, sailed the ship to Fort Sumter and turned it over to Union officers. (See also 4/5)

1926— Rep. MERVYN MALCOLM DYMALLY was born in Cedros on the island of Trinidad, British West Indies. A member of the Phi Kappa Phi Honor Society, Dymally was elected lieutenant governor of

California in 1972, after serving terms in the state assembly and senate. He is a graduate of California State Universities in Los Angeles and Sacramento. He received an honorary law degree from the University of West Los Angeles and earned a doctorate in human behavior from United States International University.

1931 — Retired Army Maj. Gen. ARTHUR HOLMES, JR., was born in Decatur, Alabama.

1940 — Jazz singer AL JARREAU was born in Milwaukee, Wisconsin.

13 May

1914 — Heavyweight boxing champion JOSEPH LOUIS "Joe Louis" BARROW was born in Lafayette, Alabama. Louis, known as the "Brown Bomber," defeated champion James Braddock in the eighth round of their 1937 championship fight in Chicago. He remained undefeated and retired June 25, 1948. Louis had 66 bouts, 49 of which he won by knockouts. Louis was elected to the Boxing Hall of Fame in 1954. (See also 4/12)

1950 — Birth date of Steveland Judkins, later known as Steveland Morris, but best known as STEVIE WONDER, composer, musician, singer and songwriter, in Saginaw, Michigan. Wonder is a graduate of the Michigan School for the Blind.

1989 — DARRYL ROBERTS became the youngest individual and the second African American to stand on the Top of the World, a geographical location known alternately as the North Pole or the Arctic. An outdoor education instructor, Roberts and seven others, who comprised the latest Arctic expeditionary team, made the cross-country trek on skis. Moving at an estimated 8.5 miles per day, they covered the 480 miles between Cape Aldrich, Canada and the Pole in 56 days, braving temperatures that occasionally dropped to 67 degrees below zero. (See also 4/6)

1990 — JAMES RICHARDSON turned 54 this year. He spent 21 of those years in a Florida prison. Richardson was charged and convicted of murdering his seven children by putting poison in their lunch. In a special court hearing in April 1989, retired circuit court Judge Clifton Kelly reviewed the case and found that the prosecutor had withheld evidence that would have been significant in Richardson's defense. Richardson was released and the investigation then shifted to one Betty Reese, the babysitter who served the children lunch. By that time Reese was confined to a nursing home and was considered mentally incompetent and not fit to stand trial. Meanwhile, Richardson waits for the courts to decide the $35 million lawsuit against the prosecutor Frank Schaub.

14 May

1804 — An African American slave, known only as YORK, left St. Louis, Missouri, to explore the northwestern territories with the Meriwether Lewis and William Clark expedition. York, owned by Clark, is believed to have been born in Virginia in 1771; however, no record of his birth has surfaced. York was with Lewis and Clark upon their return to St. Louis in September 1806, and was freed between 1811 and 1813. Clark made a list of the participants in the expedition but York was not among them, according to one account of the post expedition years. Another has it that York left St. Louis and lived out his life as a reclusive trapper in the Rocky Mountains.

1885 — Birth date of JOSEPH "King" OLIVER of New Orleans, Louisiana — jazz musician, coronet player, band leader and composer.

1932 — KENNETH GIBSON, elected mayor of Newark, New Jersey, in 1970, was born in Enterprise, Alabama. An engineer, Gibson earned his degree from the New Jersey Institute of Technology at Newark.

1970 — Police, firing on a dormitory on the campus of Mississippi's Jackson State College, killed two African American students.

1985 — Philadelphia police, with the apparent blessing of Mayor WILSON GOODE, dropped an incendiary or explosive device on the home and headquarters of a cult-like, back-to-nature African American organization known as MOVE. The decision to use the bomb followed a day-long siege during which there was an exchange of gunfire by both sides. Flames from the detonation engulfed the MOVE building and quickly spread to 61 other homes in the block. Eleven people, including five children, were killed in the blast and fire. It was the third major confrontation between Philadelphia police and MOVE. The first, early in 1978, ended after a 50-day standoff during which police denied MOVE members food and water. Police returned to the MOVE residence three months later to enforce a judicial order. Shots also were fired in that confrontation, which ended with the death of a police officer. A Philadelphia grand jury called the incident that city's greatest tragedy and accused Goode and his key advisors of incompetence. However, the grand jury failed to indict city officials. The incident started when police attempted to serve an eviction notice.

1986— African Americans continued to be excluded from the municipal work force in Cicero, Illinois. The town board later agreed to "liberalize" hiring and housing policies after a three-year fight with the U.S. Justice Department. The vote was 3–1 with three board members abstaining.

1990— President George Herbert Walker Bush backed off from a threat to veto the Civil Rights Act of 1990. BENJAMIN HOOKS, executive director of the National Association for the Advancement of Colored People, called the Act a "litmus test" of the president's civil rights commitment. (See also 5/14; 6/18; 7/10; 8/31; 10/23)

15 May

1890— In Arizona, Sgt. WILLIAM McBRYAR, 10th U.S. Calvary, was presented the Congressional Medal of Honor for action against "hostiles" one year earlier.

1942— The 99th and 100th Pursuit squadrons were redesignated Fighter squadrons. (See also 2/19; 3/22; 4/24; 5/22; 12/15)

1975— Eighteen-year-old KELTON RENA TURNER, a Marine from Los Angeles, was the last American military fatality in Vietnam. Turner was killed this date in action. He was the 5,681st African American killed in the Vietnam War.

1990— Governor Rose Mofford called a special session of the Arizona legislature to work out a swap of paid holidays for state workers. Mofford figured to trade Columbus Day for Martin Luther King Day. The proposal to swap was held hostage by a referendum which was put to a November 6, 1990, statewide vote. The King holiday was then celebrated in all states except Arizona and New Hampshire. (See also 11/6)

16 May

1939— The city of Rochester, New York, began what may have been the nation's first food stamp system. It was intended to help the needy who were enrolled in a surplus food distribution program.

1989— The *Los Angeles Times* and its staff writer Nikki Finke discovered Los Angeles' WILLIE BOGAN, a scholar-athlete who could be the best educated individual in the United States. For openers, Bogan played football and was a summa cum laude, dean's list and Phi Beta Kappa graduate of Dartmouth College. Bogan also was named to the All-Ivy, All–New England and All-East football teams. He earned the Academic All-American, National Football Foundation and Hall of Fame Scholar-Athlete awards. Bogan won the National Collegiate Athletic Association's Post-Graduate Scholarship and became a Rhodes Scholar at Oxford University. His education was capped with a Stanford University law degree.

1990— SAMMY DAVIS, JR., actor, dancer, singer and world class entertainer died in Beverly Hills, California, at age 64. Davis was born in New York's Harlem. He was a member of the Hollywood Rat Pack that included singer/actor Frank Sinatra, comedian Joey Bishop, actor Peter Lawford and singer/actor Dean Martin. He had starring roles in the Broadway musicals *Mr. Wonderful*, *Golden Boy* and *Stop the World I Want to Get Off*. Davis was Sportin' Life in the movie *Porgy and Bess*. Other movies included *Oceans 11*, *Sergeants 3*, *Johnny Cool*, *Robin and the Seven Hoods* and *Taps*, which was Davis' last movie. (See also 5/18; 12/8)

17 May

1826— JOHN JAMES AUDUBON, Haitian artist and naturalist left London for the United States after failing to find a publisher for his book of bird sketches. (See also 4/26)

1954— The U.S. Supreme Court ruled, in *Brown vs. Board of Education of Topeka, Kansas*, that segregated schools are illegal.

1956— Boxer SUGAR RAY LEONARD was born in Wilmington, Delaware. The Olympic Light Welterweight champion at the 1976 Games in Montreal, Leonard became the World Boxing Council Welterweight Champion in 1980.

1980— In Miami, the fatal beating of an African American resident by police officers ignited three days of rioting, with racial overtones, in predominantly minority neighborhoods. Authorities reported 14 people killed, more than 300 injured and another 1,000 arrested on various charges. Physical damage to the city of Miami was estimated at $100 million.

1990— A New York City jury convicted Joseph Fama of second degree murder in the fatal August 23, 1989, shooting of YUSUF HAWKINS, 16. Accompanied by three friends, Hawkins went to the Brooklyn community of Bensonhurst to check out a used car advertised for sale. Unknowingly, Hawkins and his friends walked into a dispute between a group of White youths and Gina Feliciano, reportedly a former girlfriend of one of the youths, who told the ex-boyfriend she was dating African American and Hispanic youths. Keith Mondello, the ex-boyfriend, believed Feliciano when she said a group of African American and Hispanic youth were en route to the neighborhood. Mondello and his friends thought Hawkins and his friends were a part of that group. (See also 5/18; 6/11; 8/23)

18 May

1848— San Francisco businessman WILLIAM A. LEIDESDORFF died this date. Born in 1810 on the island of St. Croix in the Virgin Islands, Leidesdorff was a pioneer, merchant, real estate speculator, civic leader and diplomat with U.S. and Mexican citizenship. He arrived in San Francisco in 1841 at age 21 aboard his 106-ton schooner *Julia Ann*. Leidesdorff became active in trade between San Francisco and Hawaii. He became a Mexican citizen and bought land in the center of San Francisco's then business area where he built the city's first hotel. Leidesdorff later became vice consul at Yerba Bena Island and wrote the official report for the "Bear Flag" incident which triggered the annexation of California by the United States. It was Leidesdorff who brought the first steamship to San Francisco Bay. He became the city's first treasurer and later was appointed to oversee the city's first public school in American California. Leidesdorff was buried beneath the floor of Mission Dolores Chapel in San Francisco.

1896— The U.S. Supreme Court upheld Louisiana's segregated railroad car law. The ruling stood for more than half a century before it was reversed by the Warren Supreme Court.

1896— PLESSY vs. FERGUSON case was decided by U.S. Supreme Court. The court declared segregation legal under the U.S. Constitution as long as separate but equal facilities were provided for African Americans.

1946— Birth date, in Wyncote, Pennsylvania, of outfielder REGINALD MARTINEZ "Reggie" JACKSON, now retired, but who is still remembered as baseball's "Mr. October" and for his stellar playing while with the New York Yankees,

California Angels and Oakland Athletics. Jackson hit 563 home runs during his career.

1990 — Keith Mondello, accused of murder in the fatal shooting of African American teen YUSUF HAWKINS, 16, was acquitted by a Brooklyn jury. He was, however, found guilty of rioting, possession of weapons and several other lesser charges. (See also 5/17; 6/11; 8/23)

19 May

1925 — MALCOLM LITTLE, later known as MALCOLM X, was born in Omaha, Nebraska. As a child, he lived in Lansing, Michigan, and Boston before moving to New York. As Little, Malcolm X served time for drug dealing and burglary. While in custody, he educated himself and learned about the Nation of Islam from his family. Until his release from custody, Little wrote to the Muslim leader Elijah Muhammad and studied his teachings. After his release from prison, Little returned to Detroit and joined the Detroit Muslim Temple as Malcolm X. In 1953 he became an assistant to the minister of the Detroit Temple. Malcolm X later established temples in Boston, Philadelphia, Hartford and Springfield. His rise within the Muslims was swift: in 1954 he was appointed minister of the New York Temple and in 1957 began the newspaper *Muhammad Speaks*; he became a national figure in 1959 following a documentary on the Muslims, and in 1961, became the Church of Islam's first national minister. However, there were problems in 1963 and Malcolm X was suspended from the Church. In 1964 Malcolm X made a pilgrimage to Mecca and also visited parts of Africa. He organized the first Muslim Mosque, Inc., and began the Organization for African Unity. His life was threatened and, on February 13, 1965, Malcolm X and his family escaped unharmed after their home was firebombed. (See also 2/21)

1930 — Birth date of playwright LORRAINE HANSBERRY, who was born in Chicago. Hansberry graduated from the University of Wisconsin, where she took courses in literature, art, history and philosophy. After school she moved to New York and worked on *Freedom*, an African American newspaper. Hansberry managed to write only two plays, *A Raisin in the Sun* and *The Sign in Sidney Burstein's Window*, before she died in 1965 of cancer.

1952 — Singer, eccentric, and model GRACE JONES was born in Spanishtown, Jamaica. Jones is known for her eccentricities in dress and hair style.

20 May

1743 — Birthday of PIERRE-DOMINIQUE TOUSSAINT L'OUVERTURE who, in 1791, declared the French colony of Saint Dominique an independent state. L'Ouverture failed, but independence for the colony now known as Haiti came in 1804 under Jean Jacques Dessalines, who gave the island nation its present name.

1945 — Rep. HAROLD E. FORD, D-Tennessee, was born in Memphis. A mortician, Ford served one term in the Tennessee house before his election to the U.S. House of Representatives.

1952 — Actor and entertainment personality LAWRENCE TERO, better known as "Mr. T," was born in Chicago, Illinois.

1959 — Air Force Brig. Gen. BENJAMIN O. DAVIS, JR., was promoted to major general and became the first African American military officer to attain two-star rank. Davis retired as a lieutenant general — three stars — in 1970. A West Point graduate, class of '36, Davis was a pilot. He transferred to the Army Air Corps in May 1942 and was promoted to flag rank in 1954. The younger Davis once commanded the all-Black 99th Fighter Squadron during World War II. (See also 3/22; 4/24; 5/15; 12/15)

1910 — Actor SCATMAN CROTHERS was born in Terre Haute, Indiana. Crothers gained fame as a television and movie actor after 50 years in show business.

1923— Phi Delta Kappa sorority was founded in Jersey City, New Jersey, by GLADYS ROSS, FLORENCE HUNT, JULIA BARNES, MARGARET GROSS, ELLA BUTLER and GLADYS NUNERY.

1952— Boxer MARVIN HAGLER was born in Newark, New Jersey.

24 May

1856— Abolitionist John Brown led the attack on Pottawatomie, Kansas, in a fight between pro- and anti-slavery groups.

1976— EDWARD "Duke" KENNEDY ELLINGTON died. (See also 4/29)

25 May

1878— Tap dancer LUTHER ROBINSON, best known as Bill "Bojangles" Robinson, was born in Richmond, Virginia. Robinson's original goal was to become a jockey; in 1886, he quit school, traveled to Washington, D.C., and took a job as a stable boy. Friends Robinson made among the stable boys taught Robinson the Buck and Wing and several other dance steps. Working as a team the boys occasionally performed on the streets for money.
Robinson's professional dancing career began with minstrel Eddie Leonard. However, it was not until Robinson's 1928 performance in the Broadway shows *Blackbirds* and *Harlem's Heaven* that critics took notice of his abilities. It was not long before Robinson began appearing in movies, and nine years later, he had dazzled movie fans with his fancy footwork in 14 films including *The Little Colonel, The Littlest Rebel, One Mile from Heaven* and *Stormy Weather*.

1926— Composer and trumpeter MILES DEWEY DAVIS of the bebop and cool jazz school was born in Alton, Illinois.

1943— Singer LESLIE UGGAMS, who made her singing debut with the Lawrence Welk Band, was born in New York City.

26 May

1799— Russian poet ALEKSANDR SERGEYEVICH PUSHKIN was born in Moscow. His mother was the granddaughter of Abram Hannibal, famed in the armies of the Czar. Pushkin wrote an unfinished novel about Hannibal called *The Negro of Peter the Great*. Pushkin died in 1837 from a fatal wound suffered at the hands of a cousin in a duel over the honor of Nathalie Goncharova, Pushkin's wife.

1854— Stephen Douglas led Congress in its passing of the Kansas-Nebraska Act. The Act allowed states to vote on the slavery issue and nullified the Missouri Compromise.

27 May

1936— Actor LOUIS GOSSETT, JR., was born in Brooklyn, New York. Gossett won an Academy Award for his role in the movie *An Officer and a Gentleman*.

1975— Former world heavyweight boxing champion EZZARD MACK CHARLES died in Chicago, Illinois.

28 May

1940— BETTY SHABAZZ, widow of Malcolm X and hostess of the New York City radio show "A Forum for Women," was born in Detroit, Michigan.

1944— Singer GLADYS KNIGHT, sparkplug of Gladys Knight and the Pips, was born in Atlanta, Georgia. Knight and the Pips became famous for "Midnight Train to Georgia."

29 May

1917— John Fitzgerald Kennedy, 35th U.S. President, was born in Brookline, Massachusetts. Kennedy's policies were largely responsible for the civil rights legislation of the 60s.

1934— Atlanta Archbishop EUGENE A. MARINO was born in Biloxi, Mississippi. (See also 3/16; 5/5; 7/10; 8/16; 8/19)

1989— The remains of 19 African

American Union soldiers were reburied in the U.S. National Cemetery, Beaufort, South Carolina. The men were members of the 54th and 55th Massachusetts Infantry regiments and the 1st North Carolina Infantry Regiment, each of which fought alongside Union forces in the Civil War. The 54th and 55th were the first Union regiments formed with volunteers. (See also 1/18; 2/14; 7/1)

30 May

1870 — Congress passed the 1st Force Act to prevent violations of the 14th and 15th amendments. The Act set up federal supervision of elections, proscribed state official's use of race as a discriminatory franchise test, and banned use of force, bribery, or threat during federal elections.

1903 — Poet COUNTEE CULLEN was born Countee Porter in Baltimore, Maryland; he became an acclaimed poet at 21, following *Color*, his first book of poetry. Cullen was adopted and raised by the Rev. Frederick Cullen, a Methodist minister. Cullen was a Phi Beta Kappa graduate of New York University and earned a graduate degree from Harvard in 1926.

1940 — Football player GAYLE SAYERS was born in Witchita, Kansas.

31 May

1910 — National Negro Conference organized in New York by concerned African Americans and Whites. In a two-day meeting, they merged with the Niagara Movement and agreed to incorporate as the National Association for the Advancement of Colored People. W. E. B. Du Bois became editor of *Crisis*, the association magazine.

1924 — PATRICIA ROBERTS HARRIS, lawyer and educator, was born in Mattoon,

Illinois. United States Ambassador to Luxembourg, 1965–67, and successively secretary of the U.S. Department of Housing and Urban Development and the Department of Health and Human Services. (See also 3/23)

1931 — Opera soprano SHIRLEY VERRETT was born in New Orleans, Louisiana. Verrett's opera debut was in 1962 with a role in *Carmen* at Spoleto, Italy, and with Bolshoi Opera in Moscow one year later. Verrett studied at Juilliard School of Music.

1989 — CLARENCE "Cito" GASTON, former batting coach for the Toronto Blue Jays baseball team, was named team manager after the firing of former manager James Francis (Jimmy) Williams. Gaston is the fourth African American to manage a baseball team in the 150-year history of the game. The Blue Jays won the American League Eastern Division title by defeating Frank Robinson's Baltimore Orioles. The Blue Jays lost to the Oakland Athletics in the World Series. (See also 3/17)

1990 — In Baton Rouge, Louisiana, the state's House of Representatives passed a bill outlawing affirmative action in the state. The bill was sponsored by State Representative David Duke, former Ku Klux Klan Grand Wizard. Running as a Republican, Duke challenged incumbent U.S. Senator J. Bennett Johnson. The Louisiana Republican Party endorsed Republican State Sen. Ben Bagert. Bagert later threw his support to Johnson to avoid the possibility of Duke winning the election as a Republican. Governor Buddy Roemer said Duke's bill would be vetoed if passed by the State Senate. Duke was not successful; however, in 1996 Governor Mike Foster outlawed affirmative action in the state by executive order.

June

This month:

1945 — California shipyards churned out "Liberty Ships" and "Victory Ships," so-called because construction was swift and inexpensive. Four such ships, *Fisk Victory*, *Howard Victory*, *Lane Victory* and *Tuskegee Victory*, were named for the African American Fisk and Howard universities, Lane College and Tuskegee Institute. Of these ships, only *Tuskegee Victory* may still be in service. It was taken over by the Navy in 1957, renamed *Reverend Dutton*, outfitted as a geological survey ship and used in fleet ballistic missile tests. In April 1971, *Fisk Victory* was scrapped in Kaohshung harbor, off the island republic of Taiwan. *Lane Victory* never saw service and was towed to Suisun Bay to join the Naval Reserve Fleet riding anchors in the waters near Vallejo, California. In July, 1972, *Howard Victory* was scrapped in Campana, Argentina.

1990: A compromise was negotiated to resolve the dispute over who would be valedictorian for Atlanta's Newton County high school seniors of the class of 1991. Earlier, a federal judge had directed an African American and a Caucasian to share valedictorian duties. As a result of the Judge's order, the young men, JOHN HENDERSON and C. Thomas Allgood were co-valedictorians.

1 June

1887 — Birthday in Washington, D.C., of army Brig. Gen. BENJAMIN O. DAVIS, SR., ret. Davis, the first African American military officer promoted to flag rank, who began his military career by enlisting in the Army as a private in the 9th Calvary. He was promoted to brigadier general in 1940 and retired from active duty in 1948. Gen. Davis died in 1970. (See also 7/13; 10/16; 12/18)

1939 — Actor CLEAVON LITTLE, a co-star in Mel Brooks' movie *Blazing Saddles*, was born this date in Chickasha, Oklahoma.

2 June

1854 — Fugitive slave ANTHONY BURNS was returned to the South from Boston. It cost the federal government $100,000 to return Burns, who later was sold to a group of Bostonians who freed him.

1875 — Bishop JAMES AUGUSTINE HEALY, born in Macon, Georgia, in 1830, was installed as first African American Roman Catholic Bishop in the United States. Healy was responsible for the diocese of Maine and New Hampshire, under which his leadership added 68 missions, 18

71

schools and 50 new buildings, some of which were churches.

1991—The Rev. JESSE JACKSON indicated he may sit out the 1992 presidential election. Among the primary candidates was Louisiana's David Duke, former Grand Wizard of the Ku Klux Klan. (On April 22, 1992, Duke, broke and running as a Republican, dropped out of the primary. Jackson did not run.)

1991—DAVID ELI RUFFIN, one of the original members of the Temptations singing group, died in Philadelphia, at 50, of an apparent drug overdose. Ruffin joined the Temptations, first known as the Primes, in Detroit during the 60s.

3 June

1897—Tenor ROLAND HAYES was born in Curryville, Georgia, in 1887. An internationally known tenor, Hayes attended Fisk University and was a member of the famed Fisk Jubilee Singers. Later opting for voice training, Hayes began serious voice training in Boston while supporting himself with odd jobs. He began making concert tours in 1916 with some success. Hayes later abandoned the U.S. tour for Europe and gave a command performance for George V of England. This performance brought Hayes to the attention of concert managers who previously had ignored him. Hayes died in 1976.

1904—Dr. CHARLES DREW was born in Washington, D.C. Drew attended medical schools in Montreal, Canada. After much research and study about human blood, Drew discovered a way to preserve blood in the form of plasma so it could be stored for long periods of time. He also helped the Red Cross establish blood banks.

4 June

1922—Birth date, in Richmond, Virginia, of retired Vice Admiral SAMUEL L. GRAVELY, USN. Gravely, the first African American naval officer to command a U.S. man of war, the frigate *Fal-*

got, in 1962. He also became the first African American admiral in 1971. A graduate of Virginia Union University, he was commander of the naval Communications Command, director of Naval Communications and commandant of the 11th Naval District at San Diego. Gravely was promoted to vice admiral in 1973 and reassigned from San Diego to Hawaii, where he commanded the U.S. 3rd Fleet. He served in this post until his retirement.

1966—JAMES MEREDITH, a military veteran, was shot while trying to enroll in the University of Mississippi. (See also 9/89; 10/1)

5 June

1911—Kappa Alpha Psi fraternity was founded at Indiana University, Bloomington. The founders included BYRON ARMSTRONG, JOHN LEE, EZERA ALEXANDER, HENRY ASHER, MARCUS BLAKEMORE, GUY GRANT, EDWIN IRVIN, PAUL CAINE, GEORGE EDMONDS and ELDER DIGGS.

1945—Olympic track and field star JOHN CARLOS, a bronze medal winner in the 1968 Olympic Summer Games, was born in New York City. In Mexico City, Carlos was the first African American athlete to raise a gloved fist in a silent protest against discrimination.

1968—U.S. Attorney General Robert F. Kennedy was assassinated in Los Angeles' Ambassador Hotel by Middle Easterner Sirhan Sirhan. Sirhan was captured at the hotel. He later was tried and convicted to serve a life sentence in California's Soledad Prison. He was denied freedom after a second parole hearing in 1988. In 1992 he was transferred to the prison in Corcoran, California.

6 June

1790—JEAN BAPTIST POINTE DESABLE, a French speaking Santo Domingo native, was the first permanent resident of Chicago. He became its founder by establishing the first permanent trading post there on this date. DeSable, born in 1745, died in 1814.

1939— Birthday of attorney MARIAN WRIGHT EDELMAN in Bennettsville, South Carolina. A graduate of Spelman College and Yale School of Law, Edelman is founder, president and spokesperson for the Children's Defense Fund, formed in 1973.

1943— National Track and Field Hall of Fame athlete WILLIE DAVENPORT was born in Troy, Alabama. Davenport ran the 110-meter hurdle event in 13.3 seconds during the 1968 Summer Olympic Games in Mexico City.

1987— MAE C. JEMISON, M.D., was selected by the National Aeronautics and Space Administration on this date to begin training as a space shuttle astronaut. Previously, Jemison, 31, was in general practice with Cigma Health Plans in Glendale, California. (See also 10/17)

7 June

1917— Pulitzer Prize winning poet GWENDOLYN BROOKS was born in Topeka, Kansas. One of the nation's most accomplished and learned poets, Brooks' formal education ended after a brief period at Wilson Junior College in Chicago, where Brooks lives. The Pulitzer was awarded for *Annie Allen*, a volume of poetry.

1958— Composer, musician and pop singer Prince was born PRINCE ROGERS NELSON in Minneapolis, Minnesota.

1990— JAMES L. USRY, of Atlantic City, New Jersey, campaigned for a third term as mayor of the Atlantic Seaboard city with a serious handicap. Earlier, Usry was indicted by a federal grand jury that accused him of accepting a $6,000 bribe. The mayor insists the indictment was racially motivated and part of a conspiracy to prevent his re-election. Whether Usry's protests were valid were to be determined by time and the federal government's case against him. Usry, Atlantic City's first African American mayor was first elected in 1984, after a corruption scandal resulted in the recall of the incumbent mayor. More than half of Atlantic City's residents — almost 53 percent — are African Americans. Although the charges were dropped, Usry lost the 1990 election to City Councilman James Whelan.

1991— *Epitaph*, the greatest musical work of renowned bassist CHARLES MINGUS, was performed in San Francisco's Davies Symphony Hall. The manuscript, written in 18 movements for 31 instruments, was found in the home of Mingus' widow, Sue, in 1984 — five years after Mingus' death. Described as "enormous in size," the manuscript was 500 pages in length and weighed 15 pounds.

1991— In Atlanta, Georgia, a federal judge directed an African American and a Caucasian high school senior to share valedictorian duties. African American JOHN HENDERSON declined and media reporters said his Caucasian counterpart, C. Thomas Allgood, 17, could not be found for an interview. Henderson, 18, originally was chosen valedictorian but Caucasian students objected and were supported by two Ku Klux Klan rallies. Henderson finished four years at Newton County High School with a grade point average of 96.96. Allgood claimed a GPA of 97.7 based on grades at Newton High and studies at the private George Walton Academy. Questions about the status of Walton Academy, which is not accredited by the Southern Association of Colleges and Schools, had led the local school board to select Henderson.

1991— Administrators for the Oakland, California, Unified School District rejected a series of social studies texts. According to reports, the books were considered racist by a group of parents and several unidentified community groups. Complainants said the books portrayed Africans as bone eating natives and Chinese immigrants as laborers and ignored major contributions made to California by both groups. Caucasian students account for 8.8 percent of the district student population, African Americans

57.5 percent, Asians 16.1 percent, Hispanics 15 percent, and Native Americans and Pacific Islanders 2.6 percent. William "Bill" Honig, State Superintendent of Education, told the *San Francisco Chronicle* he was "disappointed" with the Oakland district, but agreed the books "don't give the full story."

8 June

1953 — The United States Supreme Court banned segregation in Washington, D.C., restaurants — known to welcome Blacks from other countries, but not African Americans.

1982 — Baseball's legendary pitcher, SATCHEL PAIGE, who labored unrecognized for nearly a decade in the game's so-called Negro Leagues, died in Kansas City, Missouri. Paige, inducted into the Baseball Hall of Fame in 1971, was signed by the Cleveland Indians in 1948 and pitched for the club until 1951, when he was traded to the St. Louis Cardinals. After staying three years with the Cardinals, Paige moved on to the Kansas City Athletics. He pitched three innings and gave up one hit in his only game, in 1965, with the Athletics. (See also 7/7)

1990 — Miami record store owner CHARLES FREEMAN was arrested by Broward County sheriff's deputies for selling a copy of the record album *As Nasty as They Wanna Be*, performed by the rap group 2 Live Crew. The arrest was based on a ruling by Federal District Judge Jose Gonzalez. Gonzalez's ruling held that lyrics of the songs performed by 2 Live Crew were obscene and banned sales of the album in southern Florida. Freeman had spoken out against the ruling as a violation of the constitutional right to free speech, and had continued to sell the album until he was arrested for selling a copy to an undercover officer. (See also 6/12; 10/4; 10/20; 12/12)

9 June

1929 — Rhythm and blues singer Johnny

Ace was born JOHN MARSHALL ALEXANDER, JR., in Memphis, Tennessee. Alexander's major hits were "My Song" and "Pledging My Love," but he never realized his full potential as a recording artist and entertainer. Alexander died of a self-inflicted gunshot wound to the head. The fatal shooting occurred backstage at Houston's City Auditorium. (See also 12/24)

1978 — In Las Vegas, Nevada, boxer LARRY HOLMES won a 15-round decision over challenger KEN NORTON in a match for the World Heavyweight Boxing Championship.

1989 — The Census Bureau and the Population Reference Bureau estimated the U.S. population at 245 million, including 12.2 percent African American, 7.9 percent Hispanic and 2 percent Asian.

1989 — Congressman JOHN CONYERS, D-Michigan, announced that he believed African Americans should receive some form of reparation for slavery and discrimination. Conyers' proposal was triggered by Congress' long-delayed decision to compensate Japanese American citizens interned during World War II. "We've had people ask 'When is it our turn? Why aren't we even considered in terms of injustice and brutality that came out of four million enslaved Africans?'" said Conyers. He was expected to propose a federal commission to study the matter for answers to questions such as who should be eligible and what form reparation should take.

10 June

1760 — Birthday of RICHARD ALLEN, who was born a slave outside Philadelphia. Allen founded and later became bishop of the African Methodist Episcopal Church.

1940 — MARCUS MOZIAH GARVEY, penniless, died in London, England. (See also 6/19; 8/2; 8/17)

1972 — Former Congresswoman BARBARA JORDAN was governor pro tem of Texas for one day. By serving in that capacity, Jordon became the first African

American woman to serve as governor of any U.S. state. (See also 2/21)

1990— The Rev. CHESTER TALTON, then posted to New York City, was named assistant bishop of the Episcopal diocese of Los Angeles. Talton, a native of El Dorado, Arizona, earned an undergraduate degree from California State University, Hayward, and a divinity degree from Berkeley's Episcopal Church Divinity School of the Pacific. He was ordained an Episcopal priest in 1970.

11 June

1930— Birthday of Rep. CHARLES B. RANGEL, D–New York, in New York City. Rangel occupies the House seat held by Rep. Adam Clayton Powell, Jr. First elected to the House of Representatives in 1970, Rangel served one term in the New York State Assembly.

1963— Segregationist Gov. George Wallace of Alabama conceded defeat and admitted African Americans to the University of Alabama.

1987— Sports sociologist Dr. HARRY EDWARDS became a special assistant to Baseball Commissioner Peter Ueberroth. The appointment was intended to help wipe out racism in baseball.

1990— In New York's borough of Brooklyn, Joseph Fama, 19, was sentenced to 32⅔ years to life for shooting to death YUSUF HAWKINS. Hawkins, 16, and three friends had come to Bensonhurst to look at a used car advertised for sale. The quartet of African American young men were attacked by a group of white youth led by Keith Mondello. Fama was convicted to second degree murder, riot, unlawful imprisonment and weapons possession. Mondello was sentenced to 5½ to 16 years in prison and ordered to pay a $2,000 fine. He was convicted of riot, unlawful imprisonment and discrimination. (See also 8/23; 5/17; 5/18)

1991— Comments made by L.A.P.D. officer Laurence Powell, who along with three other defendant officers was charged

in the March 3, 1991, beating of African American motorist RODNEY KING, were ruled relevant by Superior Court Judge Bernard Kamins.

1991— The Recruit Co., a Japanese-owned employment agency, resolved charges that it discriminated against African American job seekers. The company agreed to pay $100,000 to its victims. It also promised to help Japanese businesses understand and comply with United States anti-discrimination statutes. The firm, renamed International Career Information, Inc., discriminated against people on the basis of sex and national origin.

12 June

1963— Mississippi NAACP secretary and civil rights leader MEDGAR WILEY EVERS was assassinated by a sniper in Jackson, Mississippi. Byron de La Beckwith, an avowed segregationist, was charged with Evers' slaying but was acquitted after a trial.

De La Beckwith was arrested, charged and convicted in a second trial.

1990— In Arkansas, African American KENNETH "Muskie" HARRIS convinced more than 15,000 voters — 85 percent of the electorate — that he was the better candidate to serve as the state's lieutenant governor. Ralph Forbes, the other contender for the state's second highest office, is a former member of the American Nazi Party and a Ku Klux Klan sympathizer/supporter.

1990— South Carolina State Sen. THEO MITCHELL won a Democratic primary election for the opportunity to run against Republican Governor Carroll Campbell. Had he been successful, Mitchell would have become South Carolina's first African American governor. Regrettably, Campbell was reelected with almost 70 percent of the vote.

1990— As Rep. WILLIAM H. GRAY III, D–Pennsylvania, campaigned in the House for the post of House Majority Whip, news networks broadcast a Justice Department "leak" alleging that Gray was the subject of a criminal investigation recently opened by the Federal Bureau of Investigation. Over the next two weeks Rep. Gray continued to solicit support for the post of Majority Whip. Just under two days before the House was to vote on Gray's candidacy, Attorney General Richard Thornburgh issued the statement that Gray was not the target of the investigation and that he was cooperating fully. Despite the cloud, Gray continued campaigning among his colleagues and was rewarded. He was elected House Majority Whip. (See also 8/20)

1994—Former NAACP CEO, BENJAMIN CHAVIS, JR., hosted a private three-day meeting of so-called civil rights leaders. Those in attendance included LOUIS FARRAKHAN of the Nation of Islam; the National Urban League; The Southern Christian Leadership Conference; and Jesse Jackson, former head of Operation Push, but now head of the National Rainbow Coalition. Rep. KWEISI MFUME, D-Maryland, chairman of the Congressional African American Caucus, was expected to take part in the discussions. The three-day session was to focus on the "Problems of African Americans." One crisis that might be solved immediately is that Chavis return the $332,000 given to a former employer without seeking approval from NAACP board of directors. It is likely that a considerable portion of that sum came from the less cynical and the elderly, whose contributions are almost always paid on time at each renewal. Without money, the NAACP cannot solve problems of its own, let alone take on those who would benefit from the NAACP's money that is now in the hands of a former NAACP employee.

13 June

1967—THURGOOD MARSHALL, legendary legal counsel for the National Association for the Advancement of Colored People, became the first African American nominated and later confirmed for a seat on the United States Supreme Court. (See also 7/2; 10/2)

14 June

1811—Harriet Beecher Stowe, author of *Uncle Tom's Cabin*, was born in Litchfield, Connecticut.

1952—In Gainesville, Texas, heavyweight boxer MIKE WEAVER was born. Weaver lost to Stan Ward in a bid for the California state heavyweight title in early 1978. He won the vacant U.S. heavyweight title from Ward a year later in Las Vegas. He lost a match for the World Boxing Congress title in June of the same year. Weaver won the California title in September 1983. However, in his bid for the WBC title, Weaver lost by a knockout at the hands of Pinklon Thomas.

1994—"African American leaders" found themselves having to wrestle with Chevron and Monsanto as the two petroleum giants worked on a plan "to eliminate older workers with tenure." A complaint accused the two companies of violating the provisions of the Age Discrimination Employment Act and Americans with Disabilities Act. It later was disclosed that 70 percent of African American sales employees lost their jobs compared to the 43 percent of White sales employees who joined the ranks of the unemployed.

1994—Emerging tennis professional LORI McNEIL defeated Steffi Graf, the defending Wimbledon champion. San Francisco sportswriter Scott Osler decried McNeil's victory as "rude, disrespectful, shocking, stunning ... and beautifully done." McNeil had previously lost all but one of eight games against Graf. However, this time it was McNeil 7-5, 7-6, 7-5.

1994—Dr. LONNIE BRISTOW, a San Pablo internist, was chosen "president-elect of the American Medical Association to insure he became the first African American president of the 147-year-old organization.

1994—In Indianapolis, Indiana, Marion County Judge Patricia Gifford declined to reduce the prison sentence of former heavyweight boxing champion MIKE TYSON. Jude Gifford explained to Tyson that his sentence could not be reduced, adding "I have not heard what I wanted to hear." Tyson's attorneys requested the hearing hoping Judge Gifford would grant Tyson an early release. Tyson had served two years of a six-year sentence. Tyson had other appeals filed by his attorneys. Despite the pending appeals, Judge Gifford's denial indicates Tyson — who celebrated his 28th birthday this month — did not expect to be released until May 1995.

1994— Roughly two days after the slaying of his wife, Nicole Brown-Simpson, 35, and Ronald Goldman, 26, a male friend, Los Angeles police arrested football great ORENTHAL JAMES SIMPSON as the primary suspect in the case. In a preliminary hearing, Simpson told the court that he is "absolutely, positively not guilty of murdering his wife and Goldman." District Attorney Gil Garcetti's office wagered that, if convicted of murder in the deaths of Nicole Brown Simpson and her friend Ronald Goldman, former Bills running back O. J. SIMPSON would not receive the death penalty.

15 June

1755— JOHN MARRANT was born in New York. A writer and religious rover, Marrant often wandered among the Cherokee Indians. He traveled to Nova Scotia as a missionary and was chaplain to the Boston African Lodge of Masons.

1822— In Charleston, South Carolina, a planned slave uprising to be led by former slave DENMARK VESEY was aborted because informants were discovered among the plotters.

1877— 2nd Lt. HENRY OSSIAN FLIPPER, USA, became the first African American to graduate from the army's West Point Military Academy. (See also 3/31)

1966— The USS *George Washington Carver*, a nuclear powered ballistic missile submarine, was commissioned. The ship

was named for scientist GEORGE WASHINGTON CARVER. It was the second naval vessel and first Navy ship named for Carver. (See also 1/5)

1984— An abandoned cemetery, wherein rest the bodies of African American Civil War veterans, was discovered in Greenwich Township in southwestern New Jersey. WILLIAM A. BRYANT, whose great-uncle is one of the veterans buried there, was instrumental in starting a restoration project.

16 June

1987— New York City's so-called "subway vigilante," Bernhardt H. Goetz, was acquitted of attempted murder charges in the shooting of four African American teenagers following an alleged robbery attempt on a subway in December 1984. Goetz was found guilty of illegally carrying a gun. He was sentenced to a year in jail in late 1988.

17 June

1775— African American soldiers in the Union Army distinguished themselves in the Battle of Bunker Hill in Charlestown, Massachusetts. PETER SALEM became one of the heroes after fatally shooting Major Pitcairn, a key officer of the British forces.

1871— Author, lyricist, poet and educator JAMES WELDON JOHNSON, also the first African American executive director of the NAACP, was born in Jacksonville, Florida. Johnson attended Atlanta and Columbia universities and was the first African American to pass Florida's written bar examination. President Theodore Roosevelt admired Johnson's literary work and appointed him consul to Puerto Cabello, Venezuela, to "give him more time for writing." (See also 6/17)

1928— Flamboyant blues singer JAMES BROWN, known as the "Godfather of Soul," was born in Pulaski, Tennessee. Brown was arrested for driving under the influence in South Carolina late in 1988.

Police chased him across two states before taking him into custody. After his trial, Brown was sentenced to six years in a South Carolina prison. (See also 4/19; 12/15)

1937—Journalist ROBERT CLYVE MAYNARD, owner, editor and publisher of *The Oakland Tribune*, was born in the borough of Brooklyn, New York City, New York.

1948—Actress PHYLICIA RASHAD was born in Houston, Texas.

18 June

1939—Retired St. Louis Cardinal baseball star LOUIS CLARK BROCK was born in El Dorado, Louisiana.

1964—The Civil Rights Act of 1990 was adopted by the U.S. Senate but vetoed by President Bush. (See also 5/15; 7/10; 8/31; 10/23)

19 June

1865—Union Army Gen. Granger announced a proclamation that had freed Texas slaves three months earlier. This date is celebrated, generally, by African American descendents of Texas slaves as "JUNTEENTH." Why the information was withheld from Texas African Americans is unknown.

20 June

1858—Novelist CHARLES WADDELL CHESNUTT was born in Cleveland, Ohio. The first of his four works, *The House Behind the Cedars* (1900), addressed the problem of a passing oneself off as being White. A commercial and legal stenographer, Chesnutt became a lawyer after passing the Ohio bar in 1887. Other books by Chesnutt were published in 1901 and 1905.

1943—Rioting broke out in Detroit after it was rumored, in the White sections of the city, that an African American male had killed a White woman and thrown her baby into a local river. The same rumor, alleging the slaying of an African American woman by a White man who threw the victim's baby into a local river raced through African American neighborhoods. The truth was no one had been killed. An estimated 25 African Americans and nine Whites died in the resulting riots.

1967—MUHAMMAD ALI, stripped of his title by boxing authorities, was sentenced to five years in prison and fined $10,000 for his refusal to be drafted into military service. Selective Service officials rejected Ali's petition for an exemption from military service because of Ali's role as a minister in the Nation of Islam.

21 June

1821—The African Methodist Episcopal Zion (AMEZ) Church was formed in New York City.

1859—Painter HENRY OSSAWA TANNER, who specialized in religious subjects, was born in Pittsburgh, Pennsylvania. Tanner is believed to be the first major African American artist. He attended the Pennsylvania Academy of Fine Arts and held several showings of his work yet made very little money. Tanner planned the "grand tour" for himself in the latter part of the 19th century but stopped in Paris where he remained for five years. Tanner finally gained recognition in 1896 and won major honors almost annually thereafter. He died in 1937.

1916—Elements of the 10th Cavalry Regiment were ambushed by Mexican troops near Carrizal, Mexico. PETER BIGERSTAFF, fought alongside his commanding officer until their position was overrun and both men were killed.

1964—JAMES E. CHANEY, Andrew Goodman and Michael H. Schwerner, volunteers working in the Southern voter registration drive were murdered in Philadelphia, Mississippi, by members of the Ku Klux Klan. On the 25th anniversary of the slayings, an estimated 1,000 people met in Philadelphia to remember the trio who came to Mississippi to register African

Americans to vote in local and national elections. Those who killed Chaney, Goodman and Schwerner never faced trial in the Mississippi courts. Seven were convicted of civil rights violations, and one pled guilty. Not one of the defendants spent more than six years in prison.

22 June

1898— Twenty thousand men of the 24th Infantry Regiment, famed as the Army's best unit in the Indian wars, then commanded by Gen. William R. Shafter, landed at Daiquiri, Cuba, east of Santiago.

1909— Choreographer and dancer KATHERINE DUNHAM was born in Joliet, Illinois.

1937— In Chicago, boxer JOE LOUIS BARROW became Heavyweight Champion of the World. Louis defeated Jim Braddock with an eighth round knockout. (See also 5/13; 4/12)

23 June

1899— Pvt. FITZ LEE, 10th U.S. Cavalry was awarded the Congressional Medal of Honor for bravery at Tayabacoa, Cuba. Lee was decorated for voluntarily going ashore to rescue wounded troops after others' unsuccessful attempts.

1904— The birthday of gospel singer WILLIE MAE FORD SMITH in Rolling Fork, Mississippi. Smith appeared in the film *Say Amen Somebody*.

1929— Navy Rear Admiral GERALD E. THOMAS, ret., was born at Natick, Massachusetts. Thomas was U.S. ambassador in Kenya during the Reagan presidency. Commissioned an ensign in 1951, Thomas was promoted to rear admiral in 1975. He retired from active service in 1981 and became ambassador to Guyana the same year.

1940— WILMA GLODEAN RUDOLPH WARD was born in Clarksville, Tennessee. Winner of three gold medals in the 1960 Olympics in Rome, Ward was named Athlete of the Year in 1960 and 1961.

24 June

1936— MARY McLEOD BETHUNE was named director of Negro Affairs within the National Youth Administration and became the first African American appointed to a significant federal position since Reconstruction.

25 June

1773— Massachusetts slaves petitioned the state legislature for freedom. Eight similar petitions were offered during the Revolutionary War. A bill was drawn and passed by the Massachusetts legislature. However, the governor withheld approval and the measure never became law.

1876— Interpreter ISAIAH DORMAN, whom the Army paid $75 a month for his ability to speak the Sioux language, joined Brevet Maj. Gen. George Armstrong Custer for the Battle of the Little Bighorn. Dorman died with Custer and other members of Custer's command. Dorman was married to a Santee Sioux Indian. Reports indicate troopers found Dorman's mutilated body with more than a dozen arrows in his chest.

1941— The U.S. Armed Forces were desegregated by a presidential executive order signed by President Harry S Truman.

1942— Star basketball player and coach WILLIS REED was born in Hico, Louisiana.

26 June

1938— JAMES WELDON JOHNSON, author, poet, lyricist and educator, died of injuries received in an auto accident near his home in Maine. (See also 6/17)

1956— Astronaut candidate BERNARD A. HARRIS, JR., M.D., was born in Temple, Texas. Harris began his association with the National Aeronautics and Space Administration as a flight surgeon at the Johnson Space Center. He is a graduate of the University of Houston, from which he earned a bachelor of science degree in biology, and Texas Technical University's School of Medicine, from which he earned a doctorate in medicine. He was a resident in internal medicine at the Mayo Clinic and a 1987 National Research Council Fellow. His astronaut training in 1990 qualified him as a mission specialist on future shuttle flights.

1987—The U.S. Census Bureau reported half of all African American children were born out of wedlock compared to one in five among White women in the 18–24 age group.

1990—A New York Times/CBS News Poll disclosed that most New Yorkers believe race relations in the Big Apple are "bad" and "worsening." The deaths of African Americans MICHAEL GRIFFITH, in Howard Beach just before Christmas of 1986, and YUSUF HAWKINS, in Bensonhurst in 1989, were senseless. In both cases the victims were unaware they were unwelcome in the mostly White neighborhoods. Other incidents included the gang rape and savage beating by a group of African American teenagers of a White woman jogger in Central Park and the report of an assault of a Haitian female immigrant by a Korean merchant. This confrontation set the stage for boycotts of Korean-owned stores in predominantly African American neighborhoods.

27 June

1872—Birthday of poet PAUL LAWRENCE DUNBAR who was born in Dayton, Ohio. Dunbar published his first volume of poems, *Oak and Ivy*, in 1893. (See also 2/9)

1917—Birthday of WILSON C. RILES in Alexandria, Louisiana. In 1971, Riles became the first African American elected to a constitutional office in California after defeating a Republican opponent for the office of superintendent of public instruction. Riles withdrew from public life after losing the 1982 election.

1990—Reportedly because of their relatively small numbers, the Census Bureau announced that it will count Asians as "Whites" in a post-census survey. Census officials said they could not produce a sample of Asians large enough to correct possible errors in the 1990 census. Asians will find themselves lumped into a category inappropriately named "Others," that includes Native Americans not living on reservations and Pacific Islanders.

1991—House Majority Whip, Rep. WILLIAM GRAY, D-Pennsylvania, resigned from the House of Representatives. He was positioned to have become the first African American Speaker of the House. Gray announced that the directors of the United Negro College Fund had selected him as their president. There were rumors that a Justice Department investigation of his finances was to be held. Gray did not comment on the rumors.

1991—*Washington Times* reporter Paul Rodriguez accused Rep. GUS SAVAGE, D-Illinois, of swearing at him following an attempt to interview the crusty and occasionally sharp-tongued Savage.

28 June

1839—JOSEPH CINQUE, the son of a Mendi chief, along with several other Africans, was kidnapped and sold into slavery in Cuba. Cinque and several of his colleagues planned an escape by enacting a mutiny aboard the ship *Amistad*, with the intent of returning the Africans to their homeland. But the navigators tricked the Africans and they remained at sea for 63 days. The ship sailed for the United States, where it was intercepted by the U.S. Navy off Long Island and escorted to the New London, Connecticut, Naval Base. After a trial for mutiny and murder, then President Martin Van Buren ignored a plea to free the Africans. However, the U.S. Supreme Court ordered the men freed because they were kidnapped and had the right of free men to make every effort to regain their freedom. After receiving an education in the United States, Cinque and his colleagues returned to Africa in 1842.

1971— Former heavyweight boxing champion MUHAMMAD ALI won the four year fight over his draft status when, on this date, the U.S. Supreme Court overturned his 1967 conviction on charges of draft evasion. The Court also found that Ali qualified for conscientious objector status.

1990— Police in St. Charles, Missouri, raided the estate of rock and roll legend CHARLES EDWARD "Chuck" BERRY west of St. Louis. A spokesman for the raiding party said they were looking for cocaine but admitted there was no trace of the drug. United Press International reported the seizure of hashish, marijuana, weapons and $122,000 in cash. The raid was the result of information from an informant who told officers where cocaine might be found once they gained entrance to Berry's home. Berry told authorities he never used cocaine or liquor.

1991— U.S. Supreme Court Justice THURGOOD MARSHALL, citing ill health, announced his retirement from the nation's highest court after 24 years of service. Marshall was appointed in 1967 by then President Lyndon B. Johnson.

1991— Until this date, Roger Lee Kelly, grand dragon of the Maryland State Invisible Empire, Knights of the Ku Klux Klan, was a member of the Rock Ridge, Maryland, chapter of the National Association for the Advancement of Colored People. "I joined them so I could know the enemy," Kelly said. His membership expired in February and was not renewed by NAACP officials.

29 June

1926— Army Lt. Gen. JULIUS WESTLEY BECTON, ret., was born in Bryn Mawr, Pennsylvania.

1987— Folk singer, composer, storyteller and musician ELIZABETH COTTEN died in Syracuse, New York. Cotten, a 1984 Grammy Award winner in 1984, was born in 1892, in Chapel Hill, North Carolina.

1991— Miami police officer William

Lozano, convicted of manslaughter in the January 1989 fatal shooting of an unarmed African American motorcyclist, was granted a new trial following his appeal of the manslaughter conviction.

1991— Walter Leroy Moody, Jr., was convicted of charges against him in the mailbomb deaths of Federal Judge Robert Vance at his Mountain Brook, Alabama, home, and African American Alderman Robert Robinson at his Savannah, Georgia, office. Moody blamed the Ku Klux Klan for the bombings. Of the four convictions in Vance's murder, two call for mandatory life sentences without parole and two could possibly result in life sentences without parole.

30 June

1917— Jazz singer LENA HORNE was born in Brooklyn, New York.

1936— U.S. Rep. MAJOR OWENS, D–New York, was born in Memphis, Tennessee. Owens served two four-year terms in the New York State Senate before being elected to Congress in 1982.

1966— Former world heavyweight boxing champion MICHAEL GERALD TYSON was born in Brooklyn, New York. Tyson won the undisputed championship by defeating World Boxing Association, World Boxing Council and International Boxing Federation champions Tim Witherspoon, Trevor Berbick and Michael Spinks in bouts held from 1986 through 1988. In late Feb. 1989, Tyson easily handled challenger Frank Bruno of England to retain his championship. (See also 2/11)

1967— Air Force Maj. ROBERT H. LAWRENCE, a native of Chicago, was selected for training as an astronaut. Lawrence holds undergraduate and graduate degrees in chemistry from Bradley and Ohio State universities, respectively. He has participated in the Air Force's Manned Orbiting Laboratory Program. (See also 12/9)

1974— ALBERTA WILLIAMS KING, mother of Martin Luther King, Jr., was shot to death while playing the organ in her Atlanta church.

1980— The New York City Police Department formed a "Bias Crime Unit" when a study indicated an increase in racial attacks. What began as a detail headed by a police captain and seven investigators grew to 21 investigators supervised by a higher ranked inspector by 1989. The unit's log showed officers had investigated 1,300 crimes prior to MICHAEL GRIFFITH's death. Baltimore, Boston, Chicago, and Miami have similar units.

1991— In New Orleans, U.S. District Judge ROBERT F. COLLINS, an African American, became the first federal judge convicted of bribery. Collins was caught with $16,500 in marked FBI money. He was the first African American appointed to the federal bench in the South.

1991— The unrest surrounding the summary firing of Selma, Alabama, school superintendent NORWARD ROUSSELL, ended when school district trustees refused to renew Roussell's three-year contract. Roussell was replaced by long-time Selma District employee JAMES CARTER. Earlier, Selma students boycotted classes in a show of support for Roussell.

July

We hold these truths to be self-evident, that all men are created equal; that they are endowed by their creator with certain inalienable rights; that among these, are life, liberty, and the pursuit of happiness. — The Declaration of Independence, July 4, 1776

This month:

1863—Army Sgt. WILLIAM H. CARNEY accepted the first Medal of Honor awarded to an African American serviceman. Carney, a member of the 54th Massachusetts Infantry (Colored), was among Union troops who took part in the attack on Fort Wagner, South Carolina. When the unit's color bearer was wounded, Carney snatched away the U.S. flag before it could touch the ground, made his way to the front of the column and, although under heavy fire, led the advance to the walls of the fort. He was wounded twice but did not give up the flag in two return trips to Union lines.

1991—In San Pablo, the Rev. Douglas and Marcia Drumright filed a $1.5 million lawsuit against their neighbor, Brent Case. Case, 33, chased the Drumright's seven-year-old daughter to school while threatening her life and those of the child's interracial parents. Case, who claims to be a member of the Ku Klux Klan, moved into a house next door to the Drumrights in 1987. He began harassing the Drumrights almost immediately after moving into the neighborhood. Marcia Drumright is a pediatric nurse and her husband is a minister and a Marin County employment developer. Case is alleged to have poured motor oil in the Drumright's swimming pool and scratched the paint on a car owned by the Drumright's elder son.

1 July

1753— Birth date of LEMUEL HAYNES, a Minuteman who took part in the Battle of Ticonderoga and later became pastor to the White congregation of a New England church. (See also 7/18)

1926— GEORGE L. BROWN, who was elected lieutenant governor of Colorado in 1974 and served one term, was born in Lawrence, Kansas. He earned degrees from Kansas and Colorado universities.

1961— Olympic track and field star CARL LEWIS was born in Willingboro, New Jersey.

1991— Freddie George Helms, 20, a passenger in the car driven by RODNEY KING and a witness to the beating King received at the hands of four Los Angeles Police officers, was killed in an auto accident. The car in which Helms was riding slammed into a utility pole in Pasadena, California. The car was reported traveling at 75 mph when the accident occurred.

1991— President Bush, members of his administration and Washington-based

83

lobbyists claimed the Civil Rights Act of 1991 would result in hiring quotas for minorities. Meanwhile, senior executives from nine of the nation's ten major corporate entities disagreed. Spokesman Mark Holcomb for IBM told the *Los Angeles Times*: "We're not opposed to any of the legislation. It's not good business to be against affirmative action."

1 July

1994— Republican senators, led by Sen. Strom Thurmond of South Carolina, promised the death of the new crime bill. "If race is in it, I think the bill will be dead, and they [Democrats] know it," according to Utah's Sen. Orrin Hatch. In the meantime, as the Southern senators plan their takeover of the federal government, it seemed right and proper that voters reconsider the source for the money the GOP planned to spend on new prisons. Taxes appear to be simplest. The GOP asked for $28.3 billion for prisons over five years.

2 July

1692— CANDY, a slave, was acquitted following her trial in Salem, Massachusetts, on charges that she "wickedly, malliciously [sic] and felloniously [sic]" practiced acts of sorcery in Salem.

1777— Vermont abolished slavery. It was the first state to do so.

1908— U.S. Supreme Court JUSTICE THURGOOD MARSHALL was born in Baltimore, Maryland. Marshall attended Lincoln University, studied law at Howard University, and was chief counsel to the National Association for the Advancement of Colored People from 1938 to 1962. Marshall won 29 of the 32 cases he argued before the Supreme Court for the NAACP.

1925— Civil rights leader MEDGAR WILEY EVERS was born in Decatur, Mississippi. (See also 6/12)

1990— LEANDER SHAW became the first African American chief justice of Florida's State Supreme Court, and the second African American in the nation to hold the post. (The first was ROBERT NIX, chief justice of the Pennsylvania Supreme Court.) After Shaw's first day on the bench, anti-abortionists wanted him off the bench (November 1991) because of an abortion related decision he wrote in October 1990. His written ruling overturned a state law prohibiting single minors from obtaining abortions without permission from parents, legal guardians or a judge. The ruling held that "the [state's] recent right-to-privacy amendment to its Constitution prevented government from interfering in abortion decisions."

1991— President Bush nominated CLARENCE THOMAS, a judge on the U.S. Circuit Court of Appeals, to replace retiring Justice Thurgood Marshall. Thomas, a native of Savannah, Georgia, was born June 23, 1948. He earned a law degree from Yale University after completing undergraduate work at Holy Cross College. A former chairman of the Equal Employment Opportunity Commission, Thomas was appointed by Bush to the Court of Appeals in 1990. When Thomas was nominated, President Bush denied that he had selected Thomas because of his race. The president stated that Thomas was the best candidate for the job. Thomas' Senate confirmation hearings were highlighted by testimony from his former subordinate, Oklahoma law school professor Anita Hill. Under oath, she described several instances when Thomas had sexually harassed her. In spite of her testimony, and because of his denials, Thomas was confirmed and appointed as the 106th Justice of the United States Supreme Court.

1991— Denver's District Attorney WELLINGTON WEBB, 50, was sworn in as the city's first African American mayor.

3 July

1775— PRINCE HALL founded Africa Lodge No. 1. It was the first African American Lodge of Free Masons.

1990— The self-styled, flamboyant

African American activist Rev. AL SHARPTON was acquitted of charges that he stole money from a civil rights group he had founded when still in his teens. Jurors in the case discussed Sharpton's fate for six hours before they found him innocent of multiple counts of fraud and larceny. (See also 3/29)

4 July

1881— Tuskegee Normal School opened with BOOKER T. WASHINGTON, then 25, as its first president.

1892— Birthday, in Demopolis, Alabama, of ARTHUR G. GASTON, SR., business executive. Graduate of Tuggle Institute, Gaston was awarded six honorary degrees and founded the Booker T. Washington Insurance Co. and other enterprises headquartered in Birmingham, Alabama.

1900— LOUIS "Satchmo" ARMSTRONG was born in New Orleans. Armstrong borrowed a pistol for the 1913 New Year's celebration but was arrested while firing it. He was sent to the Colored Waif's Home for Boys to think about his deed. Armstrong learned to play the coronet while in custody and became the leader of the Home's Brass Band until he was released at age 14. Armstrong's career covered 55 years and included movies, numerous world tours, working with JOE "King" OLIVER, KID ORY and FATE MARBLE's band — and becoming the first African American musician to play aboard the riverboats and the small towns in which they often docked. Armstrong, believed to be the most influential musician in the jazz era, was a goodwill ambassador for the U.S. State Department, which periodically sponsored world tours by his band.

1910— JACK JOHNSON successfully defended his heavyweight boxing championship against Jim Jeffries. Congress later adopted federal laws banning interstate transportation of prizefight films after learning that such films triggered race riots in several cities.

1991— A National Collegiate study of graduating athletes disclosed that 26.6 percent, of African American athletes, compared to 52.2 percent of whites, complete their studies and leave universities with degrees. Most African Americans do not, according to data offered to the Associated Press by Kevin Messenger, a sports publicist for the University of the Pacific in Stockton, California. Among basketball players who enrolled at UOP between the 1980-81 and 1984-85 academic years, three of nine minority students graduated, compared to 19 of 20 Whites.

1991— Of the reported 54 incidents of brutality and or excessive force used in the period 1986 to 1989 by Los Angeles police officers, only one officer was prosecuted by District Attorney Ira Reiner, according to the Los Angeles *Daily News*. The remaining 53 cases were passed on to Reiner by Police internal affairs investigators. They were spurned by District Attorney Reiner's investigators.

1991— In Memphis, Tennessee, veteran African American civil rights leaders gathered to dedicate the museum established in the former Lorraine Motel to honor the Rev. MARTIN LUTHER KING, JR. The civil rights leader was fatally wounded by assassin James Earl Ray as King stood on the balcony outside his second floor room at the Lorraine. King was in Memphis to help city sanitation workers organize a strike.

5 July

1910— A number of U.S. cities banned movies of the July 4 heavyweight fight between then champion JACK JOHNSON and challenger Jim Jeffries because of civil disturbances in seven cities that resulted in ten deaths. The fight film was banned previously in Atlanta, Georgia; Baltimore, Maryland; Cincinnati, Ohio,; St. Louis, Missouri, and the District of Columbia.

1990— Fifth-seed tennis professional ZINA GARRISON defeated Steffi Graf, 6-3, 3-6, 6-4, winning the right to play

Martina Navratilova in the women's finals of the 1989 Wimbledon tournament. Garrison lost to Navratilova.

6 July

1854—"Republican Party" was the name officially chosen for the new "anti-slavery" political party.

1931— Jazz vocalist DELLA REESE was born Delorese Patricia Early in Detroit, Michigan.

1990— Former presidential candidate JESSE L. JACKSON put aside high aspirations and opted to run for the office of "shadow senator" for the District of Columbia. The term is a euphemism for "lobbyist," which is what Jackson became since he planned to pressure Congress to sanction statehood for the District. The District would be known as the State of New Columbia if granted statehood. While several attempts have been made to have Congress consider the formation of New Columbia, none have been successful.

1991— According to figures released by the U.S. Census Bureau, African Americans are abandoning northern states, where winters are generally severe, for states in the so-called Sun Belt. However, the number of African Americans in New York and northern New Jersey rose 16.4 percent; Philadelphia up 6.5 percent; Los Angeles 16.1 percent; 17.8 percent in Houston; 32.4 percent in Dallas and 14.8 percent in San Francisco, Oakland and San Jose. In Sacramento, San Diego, Miami–Ft. Lauderdale, Atlanta and Seattle, African American populations also increased significantly.

7 July

1906— Baseball legend SATCHEL PAIGE was born in Mobile, Alabama. Sports authorities and historians feel Paige could be the best moundsman ever even if he were only half as good as record books indicate. There are those who insist Paige won 104 of the 105 games he pitched in 1934 and that he completed 55 no-hit games during his tenure in the old Negro Leagues before signing with the Cleveland Indians and later with the St. Louis Browns and the Kansas City Athletics. Paige was the first African American elected (in 1971) to the Baseball Hall of Fame in the category for Negro League players. (See also 6/8)

8 July

1914— BILLY ECKSTEIN, vocalist, was born in Pittsburgh, Pennsylvania.

1921— Former heavyweight boxing champion of the world, EZZARD MACK CHARLES, best known as Ezzard Charles, was born in Lawrenceville, Georgia. Charles fought 122 times professionally, winning 58 by knockouts. He defeated Jersey Joe Walcott for the vacant title in June 1949. Walcott regained the title in their second 1951 rematch. Charles was elected to the Boxing Hall of Fame in 1970. (See also 5/27)

1990— Singer JAMES BROWN was allowed to complete his prison sentence at home. In September 1989, Brown was arrested on suspicion of aggravated assault after leading Alabama authorities on a chase into South Carolina. He had been in a limited work-release program at the Lower Savannah (North Carolina) Work Release Center since April. (See also 4/18; 6/17; 12/15)

1990— U.S. District Judge Thomas Penfield Jackson relented and rescinded an earlier order barring Bishop GEORGE STALLINGS, JR., and LOUIS FARRAKHAN, respectively a renegade catholic Bishop and the leader of the Nation of Islam, from the trial of District of Columbia Mayor MARION BARRY. Jackson said the presence of Stallings and Farrakhan would be a probable source of intimidation in the court. Barry, who campaigned unsuccessfully during his trial for a seat on the District City Council, was charged with possession and use of cocaine.

8 July

1805— BILL RICHMOND, son of a

slave, became the first African American to distinguish himself as a prizefighter. On this date, Richmond knocked out Jack Holmes, also known as Tom Tough, after 26 rounds at Cricklewood Green, England.

1943— FAYE WATTLETON, a registered nurse and New York activist, was born in St. Louis, Missouri. Wattleton served as president of the Planned Parenthood Federation of America from 1978 to 1992.

1971— Jazz trumpeter and musical ambassador LOUIS "Satchmo" ARMSTRONG died in New York City, four days after his 71st birthday. (See also 7/4)

1990— The Rev. BENJAMIN HOOKS, executive director of the National Association for the Advancement of Colored People, urged the federal government to stop harassing elected African American officials.

"At no time since Reconstruction has there been a comparable period of incessant harassment of [African American] officials," Hooks told United Press International. "Something is wrong with the system when millions of dollars are spent and over 70 FBI agents assigned to trail and monitor [Washington, D.C., Mayor Marion] Barry, while [the Justice Department complains there are insufficient resources to thoroughly investigate the savings and loan association scandal."

9 July

1893— Dr. DANIEL HALE WILLIAMS performed what is believed to be the first open heart surgery at Chicago's Provident Hospital. The patient was James Cornish, who was brought to the hospital emergency room with a stab wound near the heart. Williams first determined the heart was not damaged until Cornish complained of pain around his heart. Williams hesitated only seconds before deciding to perform a surgical exploration of the heart and found the pericardium was torn. Williams sutured the pericardium and the

patient survived. A similar operation, performed December 6, 1891, by a Dr. H. C. Dalton, was unknown to Williams. The determination of who was first, Williams or Dalton, can only be resolved if both operations were identical.

1990— In New York City, police charged Korean grocery clerk Pong Ok Jang, who managed the Family Red Apple Grocery, with assault. The charges stemmed from his alleged attack on a Haitian woman accused of shoplifting. The incident led to a bitter six-month boycott, by African Americans, of Family Red Apply Grocery and the Church Avenue Market, both Korean-owned stores in a predominantly African American community in the borough of Brooklyn. The victim in the case, GISELAINE FELISAINT, said Jang and two other employees slapped, punched and kicked her during an argument at the Church Avenue Market.

1991— In Las Vegas, Nevada, comedian REDD FOXX, born Fred Sanford, 68, married Ka Ha Cho in the Little Church of the West at the southern end of the Las Vegas Strip.

1991— Elected officials and civil leaders in Atlanta, Georgia, were forced to consider hosting the 1996 Olympic Summer Games against a backdrop of apartments in Techwood, a low-income housing project. Some of the Techwood units were home to dealers of crack cocaine and other drugs. The problem of how to clean up and beautify the city, which was rumored to be broke, caused Atlanta to turn to its boosters for help.

10 July

1775— African Americans were excluded from service in the Continental Army by Horatio Gates, adjutant general to Gen. George Washington. Gates' order was rescinded by Washington.

1875— MARY McLEOD BETHUNE was born in Mayesville, South Carolina. An educator, Bethune taught school in Georgia and South Carolina. In 1904, she opened a school for African American girls at Sumter, South Carolina. The first students were five girls and her son. On the first day of classes, they sat on orange crates under a tree. In 1923 Bethune's Daytona Educational Industrial Training School for Negro Girls merged with the Cookman Institute for Boys and the new school became Bethune-Cookman College. She opened McLeod Hospital in 1911. (See also 10/3)

1933— Air Force Lt. Gen. BERNARD P. RANDOLPH was born in New Orleans, Louisiana.

1941— Pianist FERDINAND "Jelly Roll" MORTON died in Los Angeles.

1943— Once topseeded ARTHUR ASHE, tennis ace, was born in Richmond, Virginia. Ashe, his activities restricted by heart problems, coached the U.S. Davis Cup Tennis Team. He graduated from the University of California, Los Angeles. After an outstanding amateur career, as a professional Ashe went on to become the first African American to win the U.S. Open (1968), the Australian Open (1978), and the men's singles championship at Wimbledon (1975). As his playing career diminished, Ashe wrote several inspirational books about his life. In 1992, when he announced that he had contracted AIDS from a previous blood transfusion, the world was shocked. He died in New York City, February 6, 1993, and the country lost a world class athlete and an international civil rights spokesman.

1990— Atlanta Archbishop EUGENA A. MARINO submitted his resignation, citing health problems. The nation's first African American archbishop, Marino headed the Atlanta diocese. He temporarily relinquished his duties for a brief period in May, claiming severe stress and a close brush with a heart attack. (See also 3/16; 5/5; 5/29; 7/10; 8/16; 8/19)

1991— Louisiana State Assemblyman David Duke, former Ku Klux Klan grand dragon, and gubernatorial candidate, accepted an invitation to speak at Memphis'

Savior's Temple of the Penecostal Holiness Church. The curious handed over $22 for each ticket.

11 July

1863— Working class Irish in New York City, angered by the Conscription Act that allowed exemptions from military service for $300, burned a provost marshal's office and the Colored Orphan Asylum. The act triggered a three-day race riot against the "niggers" whom the Irish believed were responsible for the Civil War. (See also 7/13)

1953— Olympic boxing champion LEON SPINKS was born in St. Louis, Missouri. Spinks won the heavyweight championship from MUHAMMAD ALI in February 1978. His championship was brief— seven months and one day. Ali regained the title in a September rematch.

1985— SHARON SCRANAGE, a Central Intelligence Agency clerk, became the second African American arrested on espionage charges. Scranage, posted to Ghana before her arrest, later was convicted of having given classified papers and the names of agency operatives in Ghana to her Ghanian lover, Michael Soussoudis. Soussoudis is a cousin of Jeffrey Rawlings, head of the Ghanian government. Scranage was convicted and sentenced to five years in a federal prison. Soussoudis was sentenced to 20 years in federal prison but was exchanged in a spy swap and returned to Ghana 24 hours after his sentencing. (See also 4/10)

12 July

1926— Birthday of actress BEAH RICHARDS, in Vicksburg, Mississippi. Richards appeared in *Guess Who's Coming to Dinner* and won an Emmy for her work in "Frank's Place," a short-lived television series that starred Tim Reid.

1937— Actor, comedian, writer, WILLIAM "Bill" COSBY was born in Philadelphia, Pennsylvania. Cosby was the first African American to play a starring role in a television series, "I Spy."

13 July

1863—The New York Draft Riot became a race riot during which innocent African Americans were hung in the streets and arsonists destroyed an African American orphanage.

1898—Brig. Gen. BENJAMIN O. DAVIS, SR., enlisted as a private in the 9th Cavalry. Davis was promoted to brigadier general 42 years later. (See also 6/1; 7/13; 10/16; 12/18)

1954—DAVID THOMPSON, Basketball Hall of Fame honoree, was born in Shelby, North Carolina. Thompson began his career with the Denver Nuggets in 1975. He was ABA Rookie of the year in 1975-76, ABA All-Star in 1976 and NBA All-Star from 1977 to 1979. He was one of only two players named MVP in both the ABA and the NBA. He scored his 10,000th point in 1981 and was elected to the Hall of Fame in 1996.

1956—Middleweight boxing champion MICHAEL SPINKS, brother of Leon, was born in St. Louis, Missouri. Spinks won the world heavyweight title in September 1985 from Larry Holmes, and retained it in an April 1986 rematch. Spinks lost the title to Mike Tyson in the summer of 1988. Tyson unified the title by defeating the WBA and WBC champions and Spinks in the summer of 1988.

1989—At the Saluda Swim and Tennis Club, Saluda, South Carolina, three African American youngsters on an outing with a religious group were barred from swimming in the club pool with their White companions.

14 July

1892—All Civil War veterans, African American and White, who were wounded in service, received a $50 monthly pension. Congress later awarded $12 monthly pensions to women who served in the war as nurses.

1934—Professional golfer LEE ELDER was born in Dallas, Texas.

15 July

1980—Racial disorders lasting three days began in Miami, Florida. Some claimed the exceptionally heavy influx of immigrants from Cuba, and the resultant competition African Americans faced for lower level jobs, were the causes of the riots. The final bit of unrest that ignited the riots might have been the acquittal of four white police officers who had been accused of beating an African American businessman to death.

16 July

1862—Journalist and publisher IDA WELLS-BARNETT was born in Holly Springs, Mississippi. A Memphis schoolteacher, Wells attended Fisk University and Lemoyne Institute. In 1883, Wells published an article she had written about a lawsuit filed in her behalf against a railroad that denied Wells a seat in the first class section of a train. (The railroad was not identified.)

Wells later bought an interest in the *Free Speech and Headlight*, a Memphis weekly newspaper. The ultimate cost of that investment was Wells' teaching job after the pager published a series of articles critical of the Memphis schools. Between 1893 and 1895, Wells toured the United States and England speaking against lynching. Wells, known as Ida Wells-Barnett after her marriage to lawyer Ferdinand Barnett, died in 1931 at Chicago Hospital.

1934—Rep. DONALD M. PAYNE, D-New Jersey, was born in Newark. Payne was elected in 1988 after serving seven years on the Newark City Council.

1990—An honor guard of veterans gathered at the site of the Navy's old Port Chicago Ammunition Station to remember the massive explosion that killed 320 men, more than two-thirds of whom were African Americans, and to dedicate a granite and concrete memorial to their fallen shipmates. (See also 7/17)

1990—Eviction was imminent for

JACQUELINE SMITH, who in March 1988 took up residence in a tent outside the Lorraine Motel in Memphis, Tennessee, where the assassination of Martin Luther King, Jr., had occurred 26 years earlier. Smith's 16-month vigil was an attempt to derail state plans to turn the historic site into the Lorraine National Civil Rights Museum. Smith believed King would be better honored if the site were used as a medical clinic or shelter for the homeless.

1991—In Paris, jazz trumpeter MILES DAVIS was named a Knight in the (French) Legion of Honor, one of that nation's highest cultural awards.

17 July

1862—Congress approved arming African Americans as soldiers in the Union Army.

1935—The birth date of singer and actress DIAHANN CARROLL, who was born in the borough of the Bronx, New York City, New York.

1944—In the late evening hours of this day, 202 African American sailors were killed when the ammunition transport ships *E.A. BRYAN* and *QUINALT VICTORY* exploded while taking on munitions at the Port Chicago Ammunition Station, California. The explosion occurred about 10 P.M. It had sufficient force to nearly destroy the city of Port Chicago and throw sailors based at the naval magazine out of their bunks. Both ships disappeared in the blast, along with the pier at which they were berthed and the surrounding munitions holding area. Many buildings on the base simply collapsed—beaten down by the force of the explosion. (See also 7/16; 8/25)

18 July

1753—LEMUEL HAYNES, New England minister, was born. Haynes' congregation was almost entirely White. (See also 7/1)

1897—STEPHEN GILL SPOTTS-

WOOD, social activist religious leader and civil rights lobbyist, was born in Boston, Massachusetts. He attended Albright College and Gordon Divinity School. He was ordained a minister in the African Methodist Episcopal Zion Church in 1920.

1943—Professional golfer CALVIN PEETE was born in Detroit, Michigan.

19 July

1941—The U.S. Army Air Corps began fighter pilot training—for African Americans—at Tuskegee Institute.

1848—FREDERICK DOUGLASS joined Elizabeth Cady Stanton at the first women's rights convention in New York. Douglass declared that all men and women were created equal.

1932—Footballer ROOSEVELT "Rosie" GREER was born in Linden, New Jersey. Greer was present when Attorney General Robert F. Kennedy, then a presidential candidate, was fatally shot at Los Angeles' Ambassador Hotel. Greer captured Sirhan Sirhan who later was convicted of shooting Kennedy. Sirhan was denied parole after a hearing early in 1988 and in 1992 was transferred to the prison in Corcoran, California. (See also 6/5)

1987—According to the U.S. Census Bureau, wealth of White U.S. households is 12 times that of the typical African American household and 8 times the typical net worth of Hispanics.

20 July

1950—The *New York Times* reported the defeat of North Korean troops and the recapture of Yech'on, identified as an "important railhead" lost earlier by South Korean troops. Victorious after a 16-hour firefight were members of the African American 24th Infantry Regiment, which had been in Korea only eight days. A decade later, a book by Lt. Col. Roy E. Appleman, U.S. Army Reserve, went to press. An army historian, Appleman challenged the heroism of the 24th, attacked its capabilities as a combat unit and raised doubts about the battle. Although flawed, Appleman's book, which was sponsored by the Army, was officially adopted by the Army Department's Office of Military History. Members of the 101st Congress took up the fight by the 100th Congress to have Appleman's work, believed to be a fictional account of the action, replace the official reports on the battle for Yech'on.

21 July

1864— The *New Orleans Tribune*, the nation's first African American daily newspaper began publication.

1896— The National Association of Colored Women was formed.

1934— The birthday of U.S. Rep. EDOLPHUS TOWNS, D–New York, in Chadbourn, North Carolina.

1950— U.S. Army Capt. CHARLIE BUSSEY sought refuge behind two machine guns which he used to kill an estimated 258 North Korean soldiers wearing peasant dress instead of their uniforms. After gunning down the Korean troops, Bussey said he ordered his men to dig a 75-yard-long grave for the Korean troops. The combat veteran, now 73, has a photograph of the grave. Bussey expected to be awarded the Congressional Medal of Honor but was disappointed largely because Army brass failed to record Bussey's heroism. According to Bussey, his White commanding officer told him he would not recommend him for the Medal of Honor because "African Americans can't have heroes."

1991— It was disclosed that Alabama's Chambers County continues to follow a so-called pre–Civil War policy of recording the marriages of county residents in separate books. One book bears the label "Colored" and the other "White." In the event of an interracial marriage, the couple's names appear in separate record books, according to the Associated Press.

1991— Actor THEODORE WILSON, who appeared in the television sitcom *That's My Mama*, died at age 57, in Los Angeles.

22 July

1750— JAMES VARICK, born in Orange County near Newburgh, New York, was the first bishop of the African Methodist Episcopal (AME) Church. In 1848 the church became known as the African Methodist Episcopal Zion Church. Varick dedicated his life to the development of the AME church. He died on his birthday in 1827.

1980— Three days of racial disorder and rioting in African American neighborhoods began in Chattanooga, Tennessee, after two Ku Klux Klan members were acquitted of shooting at and wounding four African American women. A third Klansman, also tried in the case, was convicted of assault.

1989— The installation of indoor plumbing began in the 125-year-old African American community of Blue Hill, Mississippi. The work began with a $155,000 grant from the Farmers Home Administration but stalled when it was discovered that Blue Hill residents had enough sinks but lacked the $2,800 needed to run pipes to roadside spigots in front of their homes.

23 July

1868— The 14th Amendment to the U.S. Constitution, which defines U.S. citizenship and the privileges thereof, officially was ratified by a proclamation from the U.S. secretary of state. It gave men the right to vote but deliberately excluded women.

1962— Baseball giant JACKIE ROBINSON was inducted into the Baseball Hall of Fame.

1991— West Coast journalists reported from Capitol Hill that minorities continue their quest for top federal jobs. Minorities hold 28 percent of all federal jobs but only 7.5 percent of all senior positions.

24 July

1651— ANTHONY JOHNSON, a former African American indentured servant, was granted 250 acres of farmland in North Hampton County, Virginia. Johnson later established an African American community on the shores of the Pungoteague River.

1802— Novelist and playwright ALEXANDRE DUMAS (père) was born Alexandre Davy De La Pailleterie, at Villers-Correts, France. Better known under his pen name, Dumas moved to Paris at age 25 and began working as a clerk. It was not long before he and a friend were writing skits for vaudeville performers. As a playwright, Dumas gained notoriety with his *Henri III et sa coeur*, which he wrote in 1829. Dumas' best known works are *The Three Musketeers* and the *Count of Monte Cristo*. Dumas wrote more than 200 plays and historical romances and also was a newspaper journalist. He started *Le Mousquetaire* and wrote most of its articles and features. Dumas later built a theater where his plays were performed. (See also 7/24; 7/27; 12/5)

1804— Shakespearean actor IRA ALDRIDGE is believed to have been born in Africa. Aldridge was an apprentice carpenter in Maryland, where he learned German and became interested in the theater. Edmund Kean, himself a celebrated Shakespearean actor of the period, was an influence on Aldridge who, during his career, performed mostly in Europe. He once played Othello to Kean's Iago. Aldridge died in 1867, at , ódź, Poland.

1916— In Cleveland, Ohio, the gas mask, invented by GARRETT A. MORGAN, was first used successfully in a rescue. (See also 3/4)

1991— Congress received a bill intended to end police brutality and to be the House's response to the March 3, 1991, beating of RODNEY ALLEN KING. King was struck more than 60 times by four baton wielding officers of the Los Angeles Police Department. The officers also shot King twice with an electric charge from a stun gun. There have been 79,000 reports of police misconduct since 1981, but only 537 were investigated by federal

grand juries, according to the *Baltimore Sun*.

25 July

1943— The Navy destroyer escort, USS *Harmon*, was commissioned. The ship was named for Mess Attendent First Class LEONARD R. HARMON, who was awarded the Navy Cross in 1942. (See also 8/31)

1980— Order was restored in Chattanooga, Tennessee, after police patrols in African American neighborhoods were replaced with "volunteer peace patrols" comprised of African American leaders.

26 July

1847— Liberia became a Republic under an agreement with the United States for repatriating African Americans in Africa.

27 July

1847— Birthday of ALEXANDRE PIERRE DUMAS, author of *Camille* and son of novelist Alexandre Dumas. (See also 7/24)

1990— During the trial of District of Columbia Mayor MARION BARRY, Barry's attorney, R. KENNETH MUNDY, accused the Federal Bureau of Investigation of having a team of agents that targeted JULIAN BOND, recent Georgia gubernatorial candidate ANDREW YOUNG and other prominent African Americans for sting operations. According to Mundy, the agents set up shop in Chicago, Atlanta and several California cities at about the same time District agents arranged Barry's arrest. Bureau spokesman Gregory Jones later told the Associated Press that it would be "inappropriate" to comment on a continuing trial.

1991— Los Angeles teenager BOBBY SNYDER, 19, was sentenced to one year in federal prison for sending hate letters to an African American student and the White principal and an African American assistant principal at the city's Grant High

School. In sentencing Snyder, U.S. District Judge Mariana R. Pfaelzer said the offenses were "too serious" for probation. Snyder, who pleaded guilty, could have received an additional six months.

1991— In spite of allegations that Boston, Massachusetts, police "leaned on" so-called witnesses to the fatal shooting of expectant mother Carol Stuart and her unborn child to say the shooter was an African American, area U.S. Attorney Wayne Budd found no reason to prosecute the Boston Police Department for violating the civil rights of African American males who were subjected to impromptu body searches, arrests and a warrantless search of African American neighborhoods. Charles Stuart, the husband of Carol, had told police he and his wife were shot by an African American during a robbery attempt as the couple drove through an African American neighborhood. In fact, Charles Stuart, who later committed suicide by diving off a Boston bridge, had killed his wife and collected insurance money while recovering from a self-inflicted gunshot wound. In a police lineup Charles Stuart identified African American WILLIE BENNETT as the man who had shot Stuart and his wife.

28 July

1866— With the act to "increase and fix" military peace, Congress authorized four new cavalry regiments to augment the existing six, indicating that two "shall be composed of colored men, having the same organization as is now provided by law" for cavalry regiments. The act created the U.S. Army's 9th and 10th Cavalry regiments, which, except for their officers, were comprised entirely of African American men. They were nicknamed "buffalo soldiers" by the Indians. Members of the regiments made up 20 percent of all cavalry units west of the Mississippi in the period of warfare with Indians. The Congressional Medal of Honor was awarded to 14 buffalo soldiers, whose desertion rate was one-third that of Whites. The regiments served in the Philippines during World War I, North Africa in World War II and, in later years, Korea and Vietnam.

1949— Former baseball pitcher VIDA BLUE was born in Mansfield, Louisiana.

1977— ROY WILKINS handed off the leadership in the National Association for the Advancement of Colored People to the Rev. BENJAMIN L. HOOKS

1990— The *Los Angeles Times* reported that Army Gen. COLIN L. POWELL, Chairman of the Joint Chiefs of Staff, returned to Fort Leavenworth, Kansas, to break ground for what he called "a memorial to honor all [African American] soldiers who had served this nation over its long history." During an earlier tour at the Midwestern army base, Powell discovered two gravel alleys named for the 9th and 10th Cavalry units, called buffalo soldiers by the Indians with whom they frequently clashed. The memorial was built on a hillside beside a lake, where men of the 9th and 10th cavalry were once quartered. (See also 1/9; 1/30; 3/12; 4/21; 5/15; 6/21; 6/23; 8/3; 8/22; 8/27; 9/17; 11/12; 11/27)

29 July

1914— Civil rights activist DOVIE HUDSON was born in Carthage, Mississippi. Hudson and her sister, WINSON HUDSON, were the first to file a segregation suit on behalf of their children against the state of Mississippi. The Hudson sisters also helped bring Mississippi voter registration procedures into the 20th century. (See also 11/17)

1980— Three days of racial disorder and rioting began in Orlando, Florida. This was the second Florida riot in two weeks. A contributing factor in both was the increase in job competition African Americans experienced as a result of a high influx of Cuban refugees.

1987— In San Jose, a 54-year-old African American woman walking her dog was accosted by four White youths who threatened to lynch her. The youths, who claimed to be members of the Aryan Youth Movement–White Student Union, grabbed the woman and demanded money, telling her: "Niggers pay toll!" and "We're going to string you up in that tree!" One youth, an 18-year-old, later was arrested in San Francisco and held for investigation of property destruction and possession of a syringe.

30 July

1854 — The Immigrant Aid Society, an abolitionist organization founded in Lawrence, Kansas, tried to have Kansas enter the Union as a "free state." Their efforts were valiant but unsuccessful — Kansas joined the Union as a slave state.

31 July

1874 — PATRICK FRANCIS HEALY, a Jesuit priest, became the first African American president of Georgetown University, which was established in 1789.

1988 — The first NATIONAL BLACK ARTS FESTIVAL, lasting over nine days, opened in Atlanta, Georgia. The festival provided exposure for artists in visual arts, literature and performing arts.

1991 — The Susanville School District, located in California's Lassen County, suspended a Lasson Union high school football coach for five years. Coach Edward Murin had been the target of parental complaints for calling Native and African American members of the school football team "wagon burners" and "niggers." One set of parents spent the past five years trying to have Murin removed from his coaching position. By withholding an estimated $2 million in state financial aid, the California State Department of Education was successful in leveraging Murin's suspension. Previously, Susanville officials had refused to take any action against Murin despite the complaints.

1991 — In Los Angeles, ten police officers, who "stood around" while other officers beat RODNEY ALLEN KING following an alleged March 3 high-speed chase along a Los Angeles freeway and onto city streets, were suspended up to 22 days without pay pending an administrative hearing regarding the incident.

1991 — Opposition to the Supreme Court nomination of Federal Appeals Court Judge CLARENCE THOMAS was declared by the leadership of the NAACP and the AFL-CIO.

August

If there is no struggle, there is no progress ... power concedes nothing without a demand. — Frederick Douglass

This month:

1990 — Marine Lance Corp RONNIE CURTIS was convicted of murder in the slayings of Marine Lt. James Lotz and his wife. Curtis may be the first Marine to be executed in 29 years. Curtis' attorneys, one civilian and one naval officer argued that, in 1984, President Ronald Reagan abused his executive privilege by signing an executive order outlining whom the military may sentence to death.

Navy Lt. Cdr. John B. Holtz, one of the two attorneys representing Curtis, advised the military court that sections of the military death penalty are unconstitutional. Congress has not decided nor has Congress delegated this power to the president. The slaying took place at Camp Lejeune, North Carolina, on April 13, 1987.

Curtis, an African American, told the court that Lotz's racial taunts drove him to kill the lieutenant and his wife. Meanwhile, Curtis resides on death row at the military prison in Ft. Leavenworth, Kansas, pending a final decision on who has the right, courage and or power to call for the young Marine's execution.

1 August

1793 — The city of Philadelphia, at this time the nation's capital, experienced the first of an estimated 5,000 deaths from a yellow fever epidemic. Long since eradicated by the results of medical research, the disease ravaged Philadelphia for 100 days during which African Americans — nurses and laypersons not initially affected — cared for Whites of all stations. They buried the dead and learned the two treatment techniques from Dr. Benjamin Russell. Russell taught them how to administer doses of concoctions intended to purge the digestive system and how to let blood.

Philadelphia's African American residents, organized and led by Richard Allen and Absalom Jones, often worked without compensation, although many were paid voluntarily by their patients. In spite of the honesty and integrity of those who helped, there were reports that some African Americans took advantage of the plague victims. But most of those who helped were members of the Free African Society, which compensated them from the organization's limited financial resources. (See also 2/14; 4/11; 6/10; 11/6)

1874 — CHARLES CLINTON SPAULDING, business executive, president of the first African American–owned multimillion-dollar corporation, was born on a farm in Whitesville, Columbus County, North Carolina. After an education in Durham, North Carolina, public schools, Spaulding and two Durham businessmen, JOHN MERRICK, a barber, and Dr. A. M. Moore organized and opened North Carolina Mutual Life Insurance Company for African Americans. Spaulding advanced

95

within the company from janitor to salesman to office boy and, later, to general manager. In August 1919, Spaulding became secretary-treasurer with the death of John Merrick. He became president three years later when Dr. Moore died. Spaulding died in 1952.

1895— BENJAMIN E. MAYS was born in Epworth, Greenwood County, South Carolina, and died in 1984. Mays was an educator and civil rights pioneer. He attended Virginia Union University, and was a graduate of South Carolina State College High School, Bates College (Phi Beta Kappa) in Maine and the University of Chicago where he earned a master's and a doctorate degree. Mays was ordained a Baptist minister in 1922. He later taught mathematics at Morehouse College and became Dean of Howard University's School of Divinity. Mays wrote or coauthored five books and contributed to more than a dozen others.

1930— Actor GEOFFREY HOLDER was born on the island of Trinidad, British West Indies.

1935— Track and field star RAFER JOHNSON was born in Hillboro, Texas.

1941— Democratic Party chairman RONALD BROWN was born in Washington, D.C. Brown later was appointed secretary of commerce within the Clinton administration.

1952— Former heavyweight boxing champion TREVOR BERBICK was born in Port Anthony, Jamaica. Berbick lost his World Boxing Council heavyweight title on Nov. 22, 1986, to Mike Tyson. Berbick has had 37 fights, winning 23 by knockout, since his professional career began in 1976.

1990— Birmingham, Alabama, resident LOUIS J. WILLIE, president of Booker T. Washington Insurance Co., was made an honorary member of the Shoak Creek Golf Club. Willie's membership was an eleventh hour action taken by club directors to avoid cancellation of a PGA Championship Tournament scheduled Aug. 9–12

at Shoal Creek. The Rev. JOSEPH LOWERY of the Southern Christian Leadership Conference put off plans for a protest demonstration. Two things are significant about Willie's membership: he was not asked to pay the $35,000 entry fee and his membership did not require approval by the full Shoal Creek membership.

1991— The Secretary of the Navy was given authority to review the 1944 court-martials of 258 African American sailors, who were retained at the Port Chicago Ammunition Station as untrained ammunition handlers, rather than being assigned to combatant and resupply ships. Previously, Navy Secretary H. Lawrence Garrett had refused to investigate what many call "a mass example of racial prejudice prevalent within the Navy during World War II." At the time, Lawrence said he lacked proper legal authority to review the case.

Although charged with mutiny — any attempt to wrest command from the commanding officer of any military ship — the ammo handlers told Navy officials they would not go back to work without improved safety conditions. For that refusal, the 258 were charged with mutiny and court-martialed. Of the total, 50 were given sentences of eight to 15 years in military prisons. The refusal to return to work without safety precautions followed a massive explosion at the ammunition depot on July 17, 1944. The blast killed 320 sailors, of whom 202 were African Americans.

1992— A claim against the Long Beach, California, police by DONALD JACKSON, a former member of the Huntington Beach police force continues in limbo. A Long Beach officer stopped Jackson on a city street and slammed his head into a plate glass window while an NBC film crew recorded the incident. Jackson named as defendants the arresting officer, that officer's partner, and the city of Long Beach.

2 August

1920— African American nationalist MARCUS GARVEY told those attending a Universal Improvement Association rally at Madison Square Garden that African Americans should work for economic self sufficiency and a return to Africa.

1946— Olympic long jumper BOB BEAMAN, winner of the gold in the 1968 Mexico City Olympic Games, was born in New York City, New York.

1990— Rep. FLOYD FLAKE, D–New York, was indicted and charged with conspiracy and fraud, which authorities say stemmed from Flake's alleged embezzlement of thousands of dollars, between 1983 and 1989. An African Methodist Episcopalian minister and leader of 6,000-member Allen AMC church, Flake faced a 17-count indictment. There were nine counts in the indictment of his wife, Margarett. Flake is believed to be the third African American government/political official charged with crimes during 1990.

3 August

1492— Navigator ALONSO PEDRO NINO, aboard the *Nina*, and Christopher Columbus, in command of the *Nina*, *Pinta* and *Santa Maria*, left Palos, Spain, in search of a new route to the Orient. Two months and nine days later, after landing in the Bahamas, Columbus and his expedition discovered what is now America.

1866— Men for the first of two "all-colored" cavalry units, the Ninth Regiment, U.S. Cavalry, were recruited from the New Orleans, Louisiana, area.

1986— African Americans comprised 6.2 percent of the 4,023 full-time, career, U.S. State Department employees.

1990— New Jersey's attorney general announced that a grand jury did not indict the Teaneck, New Jersey, police officer in the fatal shooting, April 12, of PHILLIP C. PANNELL. Attorney General Robert J. Del Tufo did, however, note that the case was "contaminated" by major errors committed by the Bergen County medical examiner and that the evidence would be heard by a second grand jury. Errors of "major significance" in the examination

and autopsy of Pannell were disclosed after "all evidence" had been presented to the grand jury. That evidence, Del Tufo added, led to an incorrect conclusion about Pannell's action before he was shot by Officer Gary Spath. (See also 4/12; 4/13; 8/23)

1990— Rep. HAROLD E. FORD, D–Tennessee, rolled over two challengers in the second re-election campaign he ran after a 1987 indictment for bank and mail fraud. After an 11-week trial, jurors deadlocked on a verdict in April. Prosecuting attorneys said they would seek a second trial but one was never held.

4 August

1932— Retired Army Maj. Gen. HUGH GRANVILLE ROBINSON was born in Washington, D.C.

5 August

1954— Boxers HENRY ARMSTRONG, JACK JOHNSON and JOE LOUIS were among the first 24 men elected to the Boxing Hall of Fame.

1992— The Confederate flag continued to fly atop the capitol building in Montgomery, Alabama, in spite of complaints of divisiveness from the NAACP and others. The Confederacy, having died with its heroes, has more properly become a part of the nation's history.

1994— BENJAMIN CHAVIS, JR., former NAACP CEO, failed to avoid being dismissed by the organization's board of directors. At issue was Chavis' handling of a promise to find an $80,000-a-year-job for attorney Mary Stansel, a former NAACP legal assistant.

CHAVIS had refused to quit, but was fired after a special August 5, 1994, board meeting. It was during or after this meeting that Chavis admitted having given Stansel $322,400, which he had taken from NAACP accounts without board knowledge and or consent. Chavis claimed he had noticed that organizational funds were low when he took over from the Rev. BENJAMIN HOOKS, adding that Hooks was responsible for the shortage. Hooks' poetic response: "It's the books, not Hooks!" Board members are now aware of an estimated $3 million shortage, most of which apparently was given to Stansel.

The NAACP board appointed EARL SHINHOSTER interim director.

6 August

1973— ROBERTO CLEMENTE and MONTE IRVIN were inducted into the Baseball Hall of Fame.

7 August

1904— RALPH JOHNSON BUNCHE was born in Detroit and reared in Los Angeles, where he attended Jefferson High School and the University of California–Los Angeles. Bunche also attended Harvard, Howard and Northwestern universities, the London School of Economics and the University of Capetown, South Africa. A statesman, Bunche served the United States in the State Department and, in 1967, as United Nations undersecretary general. He earned the Nobel Peace Prize in 1950 for negotiating the 1949 armistice ending the Arab-Israeli dispute over Palestine. Bunche was the first African American so recognized internationally.

8 August

1934— Birth date of Rep. JULIAN DIXON, D-California, who was born in Washington, D.C. Dixon was elected to the House of Representatives in 1978. He won the seat formerly held by Yvonne Braithwaite Burke. Dixon served three two-year terms in the California Assembly from 1972 and 1978. His major House assignment was Chairman of Ethics panel, officially the House Committee on Standards of Official Conduct. It was this committee that held hearings on the impeachment of U.S. District Judge ALCEE HASTINGS of Florida. (See also 2/2; 10/20; 10/23)

1977— MARTIN DIHIGO and JOHN HENRY "Pop" LLOYD of the Negro Leagues and ERNIE BANKS were inducted into the Baseball Hall of Fame.

1990— Former Atlanta mayor ANDREW YOUNG lost his and the Democratic party's race for the gubernatorial nomination to incumbent Lt. Gov. Zell Miller. Had he been successful Young, also a former member of Congress and ambassador to the United Nations during the Carter years, would have been Georgia's first African American governor.

9 August

1866— Men for the 10th Regiment, U.S. Cavalry, were recruited from the St. Louis, Missouri, area.

1883— Birth date in Washington, D.C., of DAISY LAMPKIN, vice president of *The Pittsburgh Courier* newspaper. A founder of the National Council of Negro Women and long-time president of the Lucy Stone League, Lampkin was also an adept fund-raiser for the NAACP. (See also 3/10)

1936— In this year, JESSE OWENS won four gold medals in track and field during the Summer Games in Berlin. Owens' feat was a blow to White supremacy in what was then Adolf Hitler's Germany. Not surprisingly, Owens was snubbed by Hitler. Owens was the 1936 U.S. Athlete of the Year in Track and Field. His gold medals were in the 100 meter run, 200 meter run, 400 meter relay and the long jump. Owens was born in Danville, Alabama, and was a graduate of Ohio State University.

1943— Heavyweight boxing champion KENNETH HOWARD NORTONwas born in Jacksonville, Illinois. Norton began fighting professionally in 1967 but did not win a title until 1973 when he defeated MUHAMMAD ALI, in 12 rounds, for the North American Boxing Federation title. Ali recaptured the title in September, 1973, six months after the initial fight. Norton was proclaimed World Boxing

Council heavyweight champion in March 1978 but lost the title to LARRY HOLMES less than three months later.

1990— Lawyers representing FBI agent DONALD ROCHON against the Federal Bureau of Investigation were given the ok to a settlement agreement effectively ending a three-year court war. The war began when Rochon accused the FBI of failing to act when two White agents harassed Rochon while he was assigned to the Bureau's Chicago office. The settlement could be worth $1 million or more to Rochon who had been on disability leave for emotional stress since April. Rochon will receive full compensation, back pay for a promotion he was denied and full pension benefits. He also will remain on disability leave until 2001, when he is eligible for retirement. In his suit, Rochon said that his family received threatening phone calls and letters, including one with a picture of the dismembered body of an African American male. (See also 3/28; 8/21)

1990— Georgia's run-off election procedures came under U.S. Justice Department scrutiny this year. Department lawyers said the system discriminates against African Americans. The federal government had sued, alleging the procedures water down African American voting strength. There are nine other Southern states that stage comparable run-off elections. Under the rules, a candidate must win a majority of the vote in races where there are several candidates or undergo a run-off with the second best vote-getter. The legal action against Georgia marked the first time the Justice Department has used elements in the 1965 federal Voting Rights Act to challenge a majority run-off system. John R. Dunne, assistant attorney general for civil rights, said the department had no "immediate plans" to bring action against other states that use the run-off method. Alabama, Arizona, Arkansas, California, Florida, Louisiana, Oklahoma, Mississippi, South Carolina and Texas conduct run-off elections.

10 August

1835— In Canaan, New Hampshire, an unruly White mob set fire to the Noyes Academy after 14 African American students were enrolled there.

1909— Rep. GEORGE W. CROCKETT, JR., D-Michigan, was born in Jacksonville, Florida. Crockett was a judge on the Michigan Court of Appeals and worked as a corporate attorney before his 1980 election to the House of Representatives.

11 August

1842— ROBERT BROWN ELLIOTT, who became a major general in the South Carolina National Guard, was born in Boston. Owner of the largest private library in South Carolina, Elliott was a scholar, lawyer and politician. Elliott was admitted to the South Carolina Bar and practiced law in that state. He was a member of the South Carolina Constitutional Convention in 1868, the South Carolina House of Representatives, 1868–71 and 1874–76, and was elected to one term in the U.S. House of Representatives, 1871–74. After losing a bid to become South Carolina's attorney general, Elliott moved to New Orleans where he practiced law until his death in 1884.

1925— *Washington Post* columnist CARL THOMAS ROWAN was born in Ravenscroft, Tennessee. A former director of the U.S. Information Agency and ambassador to Finland, Rowan was charged and convicted of unlawfully shooting a trespasser in 1986. Rowan took a handgun, registered to his son, a former FBI agent, to investigate noises in his back yard. He admitted shooting a White youth whom he found near the Rowan's swimming pool.

1965— First day of the so-called "Watts Riot," which began in South Central Los Angeles and areas adjacent to the city of Compton. The rioting was triggered by the arrest of an African American motorist accused of drunken driving. It lasted five days, ending on the 16th of August.

12 August

1974— JAMES "Cool Papa" BELL, a star baseball player in the Negro League, was inducted into the Baseball Hall of Fame.

13 August

1948— Opera soprano KATHLEEN BATTLE was born in Portsmouth, Ohio.

1990— Rhythm and blues musician CURTIS MAYFIELD was paralyzed after his neck was broken in a "freak accident." Mayfield recovered and left Shephard Spinal Center in Atlanta after a scaffold fell on him from behind during a New York concert. His father is paralyzed from the chest down, according to his son Todd. Mayfield is learning to operate a wheelchair by breathing and puffing through a straw. "Mayfield gets frustrated sometimes but still laughs and jokes," said Todd. "He's not moping around nor [is he] depressed."

14 August

1908— A White woman resident of Springfield, Illinois, triggered a race riot by claiming to have been raped by African American GEORGE RICHARDSON, who was spirited out of town. Whites subsequently began destroying African American homes. After two days of rioting, two African Americans were lynched, six others were killed by gunfire or beaten to death and more than 70 people, African Americans and Whites, were injured. An estimated 2,000 African Americans left town. The rioters were arrested and indicted, but escaped punishment. Before a special grand jury, the woman later admitted she had been raped by a White man whom she refused to identify.

1936— In Owensboro, Kentucky, RAINEY BETHEA, then 22 and convicted of murdering an elderly White woman, was the last person publicly executed in the United States.

1938— Birthday of NIARA SUDARK-ASA, in Ft. Lauderdale, Florida. Sudark-asa was the first woman appointed president of Lincoln University, the nation's oldest African American college which began as a school for men.

1959— NBA superstar EARVIN "Magic" JOHNSON, of the Los Angeles Lakers basketball team, was born in East Lansing, Michigan.

1990— MARION BARRY, the embattled District of Columbia mayor, announced his candidacy for a seat on the District city council. Barry was convicted earlier this year on a single charge of cocaine possession after a 2½-month-long trial. Barry failed in his bid for a city council seat. (See also 1/18; 1/20; 3/6; 7/7/ 7/27; 8/15)

15 August

1815— Birth date of BIDDY MASON, born a slave in Georgia and taken overland to Utah in 1848 and to San Bernardino, California, in 1851. Mason remained in California after a judge ruled Robert Smith, Mason's "owner," lost his "property rights" because Mason and another slave woman, Hannah, and their 12 children and grandchildren, had lived in California three years, during which time the state adopted legislation banning slavery. The belief was that Mason and the others could not be taken to Texas as slaves.

Hannah vanished after the slaves were freed in a Los Angeles courtroom late in 1855. Mason moved into Los Angeles and supported herself by doing housework and nursing. Mason soon owned property and would become one of Los Angeles' wealthiest African Americans and a role model for others.

1817— GEORGE WASHINGTON was born in Frederick County, Virginia, of a White mother and slave father. George was four when his father was sold and his mother allowed a White family (the Washingtons) moving west to adopt her son. Despite the lack of normal schooling, Washington learned arithmetic, reading and writing after the family moved to

Missouri. He also became skilled as a miller, tanner, distiller, cook, weaver and spinner, all of which would later serve him well. Discrimination forced the Washingtons farther west — into that portion of Oregon territory that is now the state of Washington. While in his 30s, Washington staked out a 640-acre claim, which was put in his father's name. (Early Oregon law kept African Americans from settling in the territory.) Young Washington grew a variety of crops and, with his father, raised cattle and operated a hotel and a ferry on land along the shores of the Chehalis River, where Centralia, Washington, would later stand. Washington originally named his settlement Centerville. Although in good health in 1905, Washington died of injuries received when he was thrown from his horse-drawn buggy.

1938— Former California State Assemblywoman MAXINE WATERS was born in St. Louis, Missouri. Waters was elected in November 1990 to the House seat vacated by retiring Rep. AUGUSTUS HAWKINS, D–Los Angeles. (See also 11/6)

16 August

1987— CHARLES HARRIS WESLEY died. Born in 1892, in Louisville, Kentucky, Wesley was an African American scholar, historian, author and former president of Central State College, Wilberforce, Ohio.

1990— Vicki Long, whose intimate relationship with Atlanta Archbishop EUGENE MARINO forced the archbishop's resignation in July of this year, announced that she and Marino had "exchanged vows" in December 1988 and that that is enough to consider herself married to Marino. As a Roman Catholic archbishop, one of Marino's vows was celibacy. There were earlier reports that Marino had attempted to take his own life. These reports have been denied by acting Archbishop James Lyke. Marino has remained mute. (See also 3/16; 5/5; 5/29; 7/10; 8/19)

17 August

1887— Birth date of MARCUS MOZIAH GARVEY, a master printer, who was born in St. Ann's Bay, Jamaica. In 1915, he founded a New York City chapter of the United Negro Improvement Association. Garvey later organized the Black Star Steamship Line, a fleet of three ships, to promote trade among African Americans. The steamship line failed when Garvey was unable to raise money to sustain its operation. Other Garvey enterprises included the Universal Black Cross Nurses, Universal African Motor Corps and the Black Eagle Flying Corps. Around 1920, Garvey petitioned the League of Nations for permission to establish an African colony and began negotiations with Liberia. In 1921, Garvey announced the formation of the Empire of Africa with himself as president. He served two years in prison for mail fraud in connection with a complex plan to fund the struggling steamship line. Garvey was pardoned in 1927 by President Calvin Coolidge. After a string of setbacks, Garvey left the United States for Jamaica and later moved to London, where he unsuccessfully tried to revive UNIA. Garvey died a pauper in 1940.

1990— Jazz vocalist PEARL BAILEY, 72, died while a patient at Philadelphia's Thomas Jefferson University Hospital. Miss Bailey was a U.S. delegate to the United Nations in the Ford, Reagan and Bush administrations. Services for Miss Bailey, who was married to drummer Louis Bellson for 38 years, was held at Deliverance Evangelistic Church, and preceded burial in West Chester, Pennsylvania. Miss Bailey starred as Dolly in the All African-American Broadway production of *Hello Dolly!*, and won a Tony for her work. She also will be remembered for her role in the film version of *Porgy and Bess*. (See also 3/29)

18 August

1987— EATONVILLE, Florida, now the oldest incorporated African American city in the United States, was founded 100 years ago on this date. The city's centennial was celebrated August 16, 1987, with a parade, street festival and an unscheduled appearance by the Ku Klux Klan. Eatonville was founded by 27 African Americans who bought lots from Josiah Eaton, a White landowner for whom the city was named. (See also 1/7)

1934—ROBERTO CLEMENTE was born in Carolina, a suburb of San Juan, on the island of Puerto Rico. Clemente began his baseball career with a Santurce (Puerto Rico) professional baseball team. He received a $600 signing bonus, $60 a month and a glove while still in high school. In 1955, Clemente signed with the Pittsburgh Pirates. He died in 1972, when the plane he had chartered crashed while carrying food and medical supplies to Nicaragua earthquake victims.

1990—Three African American teenagers, two 16 and one 15, were convicted for their individual roles in the rape and vicious beating of a woman, a 30-year-old investment banker, jogging alone in New York's Central Park in mid–April 1989. The teens each received sentences of from five to ten years in prison only for the rape charge. The jurors deliberated ten days before rendering guilty verdicts.

1990—At a Washington, D.C., summit of African American organizations, journalist TONY BROWN called for representatives of some 150 African American organizations to cancel $3 billion worth of conventions booked into White-owned hotels in 1992. Brown said the $3 billion savings could be used to buy or build an African American hotel/convention complex where conventions sponsored by African American organizations could be held by 1993. Led by former U.S. Rep. SHIRLEY CHISHOLM, who offered $25,000 toward the project, 20 other summit attendees pledged $1,000 to $10,000 each. There are no major hotels in the United States that are African American-owned. The summit, held at Howard University, was called by BENJAMIN HOOKS, executive director of the Na-

tional Association for the Advancement of Colored People.

1991—A proposed New York City redistricting plan has pitted African Americans, 12 percent of the U.S. population, against Hispanics, who make up 8 percent. Population forecasters claim Hispanics will be the dominant minority by the year 2010, when African Americans are expected to slip to the second position. New York is home to an estimated 7,370 African Americans who hold elected offices, compared to 3,783 elected Hispanic officials, according to the *Chicago Tribune*.

1992—The retrial of Colombian-born Miami police officer William Lozano, accused of the fatal shooting of an African American motorcyclist and the death of the cyclist's passenger, has been rejected by Dade County Judge Thomas W. Spencer. Judge Spencer ordered the case out of his jurisdiction. According to the Associated Press, Spencer had earlier ruled that Lozano should be tried in Tallahassee, Florida, where the racial mix would be "similar" to Miami's. Lozano was convicted in an earlier trial of the 1989 shooting, but the verdict was reversed by an appellate court.

1992—The Sons of Confederate Veterans, an organization of people whose ancestors fought for the Confederacy 130 years ago, formerly voted to "thank African Americans who fought for the Southern cause and to renounce the White supremacist Ku Klux Klan."

19 August

1814—Birthday of MARY ELLEN "Mammy" PLEASANT in Philadelphia, Pennsylvania. Pleasant migrated to San Francisco in 1849. Historians offer conflicting information about Pleasant. One claims Pleasant ran a boarding house and another insists it was a "bawdy" house. In any event, the money Pleasant made from her business was used to help runaway slaves and other African Americans who needed it. Pleasant later accepted a job as the housekeeper for San Francisco banker Thomas Bell. The site of Pleasant's San Francisco home was converted to a small park that is now surrounded on two sides by a San Francisco hospital. A plaque set into the sidewalk identifies the park as the site of Pleasant's former residence.

1875— JEREMIAH BURKE SANDERSON died in Oakland, California. A native of New Bedford, Massachusetts, where he was born in 1821, Sanderson moved to California in 1854. He spent eight years as principal of a San Francisco school for African American children before moving in 1868 to a similar post in Stockton, 80 miles east of San Francisco. In 1872, Sanderson was ordained an elder in the Stockton African Methodist Episcopal Church. He later left Stockton to lead an Oakland church.

1946— Marine Corps Col. CHARLES F. BOLDEN, JR., assigned to the National Aeronautics and Space Administration as a shuttle pilot, was born in Columbia, South Carolina. A 1968 graduate of the U.S. Naval Academy, Bolden earned a degree in electrical science and later acquired a master of science in systems management from the University of Southern California. He is also a graduate of Naval Test Pilot School. On his first space flight, Bolden piloted the shuttle *Columbia* following its January 12, 1986, launch from Kennedy Space Center. Bolden was selected for astronaut training in 1981 and was officially designated an astronaut in the following year.

1990— A *Chicago Tribune* update on the reported affair and marriage of Atlanta Archbishop EUGENE MARINO, 56, and an attractive parishioner, VICKIE LONG, 27, disclosed Long's history of intimate relationships with priests in and around Atlanta. Still unsettled, according to the *Tribune*, is a 1987 paternity suit that names the Rev. Donal Keohane as the defendant. Keohane, supported by blood tests, denies fathering Long's four-year-old daughter. (See also 8/16)

20 August

1619— The first ship carrying 20 African indentured servants from England arrived in Jamestown. Those most affected by their arrival were free Africans already living in the Jamestown area.

1941— Birthday of Rep. WILLIAM H. GRAY, III, who was born in Baton Rouge, Louisiana. Gray became the House Majority Whip after the 1989 resignations of former House Speaker James Wright and former U.S. Rep. Tony Coehlo.

1942— Composer, songwriter, musician and singer ISAAC HAYES was born in Covington, Tennessee.

1990— From Nashville, Tennessee, came word of an invitation from the Progressive Baptists, whose membership is largely African American, to dissident members of the mostly White Southern Baptist Convention. The invitation was extended by the Rev. FRED LOFTON, pastor of an African American Baptist Church in Memphis. "We especially invite moderates, who are disillusioned with the far right in the SBC, to come and join us as representatives of the New South, with an agenda for a new region with new possibilities and potentialities for the Christian Church to become an inclusive community of faith, hope and love," Loften said in an interview reported by United Press International.

1990— The Catholic Church exhumed the remains of former slave PIERRE TOUSSAINT, who was born in Haiti in 1766. The Roman Catholic archdiocese of New York is considering Toussaint's canonization as the first African American saint. Exhumation of Toussaint's remains was one step in that process, according to church officials. Toussaint was known for his generous work with the poor; he raised money to build orphanages and churches for neglected children. He died in 1863 at New York City after becoming a freedman. Toussaint was buried in Old St. Patrick's Cathedral Cemetery in the Little Italy section of Lower Manhattan.

1992— Voters in Fulton County, Georgia, which includes the city of Atlanta, could score another first in November with the election of JACKIE BARRETT as Fulton County sheriff. Barrett joined a small group of women sheriffs in the United States.

1994— House Rep. MEL (Melvin) REYNOLDS, D-Illinois, was charged with statutory rape. The charge stemmed from Reynolds' alleged sexual relationship with a 16-year-old who helped with his 1992 election campaign, in June 1992. Reynolds reportedly began having sex with the young woman five months before she celebrated her 17th birthday. Under Illinois law, teens may consent to having sexual relations at age 17.

1994— White residents of Battleboro, North Carolina (population 524), dominate this rural city in which 45 percent of the residents are African Americans. During the summer there were complaints of police brutality and needless traffic stops during which the officers (all White) checked for properly fastened seatbelts and licenses. Battleboro's African Americans have asked for an African American police chief, but the request has fallen on deaf ears. In an effort to underscore their point, African Americans living in Battleboro formed Concerned Citizens of Battleboro. On July 30, Battleboro's largest retail store and second-level taxpayer (the Red and White Super Market) went out of business following a boycott by African Americans. The boycott cost supermarket owners 25 percent of their business.

21 August

1831— NAT TURNER, a slave, led the "Southampton (Virginia) Insurrection," in which 54 Whites were killed. African Americans killed in the aftermath numbered about 100. Turner avoided capture for six weeks by fleeing, but he was caught two days after his 31st birthday. Turner was tried, convicted and sentenced to death. He was hung later in the year.

1904— Musician, composer, arranger and band leader WILLIAM "Count"

BASIE, was born in Red Bank, New Jersey.

1936— Professional basketball player WILTON "Wilt the Stilt" CHAMBERLAIN was born in Philadelphia, Pennsylvania. Chamberlain began play for the Philadelphia Warriors team, which later became the Golden State Warriors.

1990— Navy Secretary H. Lawrence Garrett, III, announced the Navy's refusal to reverse the conviction of 258 African American sailors who, in 1944, declined to resume loading ammunition onto ships after a July 17 explosion demolished ammunition piers at the Port Chicago Ammunition Station.

The base is known now as the Concord Naval Weapons Station. According to the Navy, the refusal to work constituted a mutiny and the men were summarily charged, court-martialed, found guilty, discharged from active duty and imprisoned for varying periods. Mutiny, defined as "an open rebellion against authority," generally applies to attempts by crews to take over ships or stations. In this case, the sailors had asked for training and the installation of safety features before resuming the hazardous work. Meanwhile, the cause of the explosion, which destroyed and damaged parts of the city of Port Chicago, has never been determined. (See also 7/16; 7/17; 8/23)

1990— FBI Special Agent PAUL R. PHILIP, formerly agent in charge of the Bureau's San Juan, Puerto Rico, office, was named to investigate charges that White supervisory agents covered up evidence of "widespread" racial discrimination within the Bureau. The charges were made by agent DONALD ROCHON, who reached a settlement with the Bureau earlier this month. According to Rochon, an "honest investigation" showed the destruction of evidence that linked White agents to death threats (made against Rochon and his family) and revealed that senior Bureau officials committed perjury when questioned during the initial investigation, according to a *New York Times* report. (See also 8/10)

1991—Walter Leroy Moody, Jr., was convicted of using mail bombs to kill Federal Appeals Court Judge Robert S. Vance and Savannah, Georgia, City Councilman ROBERT E. ROBINSON in December 1989. Judge Vance died in his Mountain Brook, Alabama, home after opening a letter Moody sent him. Robinson, also an official of the National Association for the Advancement of Colored People, was killed from a blast set off when he opened a letter addressed to the organization at his office address. Moody was sentenced to seven life terms in federal prison without the possibility of parole, plus an additional 400 years.

1991—In New York City, racial clashes between African Americans and Jews continued for the third day in the city's Crown Heights area. The violence began August 18 when a seven-year-old African American boy died after being hit by a car. The vehicle was driven by a Hasidic Jew. African American residents of the area were concerned that the driver of the car that struck and killed GAVIN CATO was not arrested by police. Jews in the neighborhood said that their African American neighbors were responsible for crime in the area, while African Americans said that their Jewish neighbors, most members of the Hasidic Jews of the Lubavitcher sect, had too much power and benefited from "preferential treatment" by city officials. An estimated 300,000 people lived in the neighborhood at the time, including some 30,000 members of the Lubavitcher sect, according to the Associated Press.

1992—A federal grand jury has indicted ERLAINE M. RICHARDSON and former U.S. Sen. EDWARD BROOKE, R-Massachusetts. The nine-count indictment charges that Brooke and Richardson arranged—with the help of Housing and Urban Development officials—to hold (for Brooke) 150 housing units valued at $14.7 million.

22 August

1787—In New York City, members of the Constitutional Convention argued whether the United States should permit slavery and slave trade. The vote was for slavery.

1917—Legendary blues singer, songwriter and guitarist JOHN LEE HOOKER was born in Clarkdale, Mississippi. Hooker began his 50 years as a musician at age 14, when he sang with religious groups and studied guitar with Will Moore. By age 73, Hooker had received the 1968-69 Best Blues Album award from *Jazz and Pop* magazine, the 1975 Blues Hall of Fame Award from *Ebony* magazine and the 1983 Folk Heritage award from the Smithsonian Institution. Hooker said: "Blues is the root of all music, jazz, spirituals, pop, rock, all of it ... a good blues singer can really tell the story of my life, your life, everybody's life; it's got something in there to fit everybody, what everybody's been through ... that's what I live for ... I love playing for the people."

1989—In the false light before dawn in a shoddy, drug plagued neighborhood of Oakland, California, Black Panther Party co-founder HUEY P. NEWTON, 47, was gunned down by Tyrone Robinson, a minor functionary in the Black Guerrilla Family drug hierarchy. Robinson, who reportedly told Oakland police that he shot Newton three times in the head, claimed Newton was armed and that he, Robinson, killed Newton in self defense. Oakland police reported finding no evidence to support Robinson's claim of self defense. (See also 2/17; 9/8)

1992—Harvard Law School Professor DERRICK BELL said there was no hard evidence that his two-year leave of absence, in protest of the schools' discriminatory hiring practices, had been effective. Bell, who has taught at Harvard for 20 years, took the leave to protest Harvard's failure to recruit a female minority for the faculty.

1994—GEORGE WEST, an Atlanta, Georgia, security guard, filed a lawsuit against Equifax Credit Information Services, Inc., and a used car dealership where West once worked. When West requested a copy of his credit report in May 1993, he found the word "nigger" listed as his former employment.

23 August

1796—The African Methodist Episcopal Church was incorporated.

1932—In Oakly, South Carolina, Army Maj. Gen. HENRY DOCTOR, JR., was born.

1994—In Los Angeles, House Rep. WALTER TUCKER, D-California, was arraigned on eight counts of extortion and two counts of filing false income tax returns. Tucker also has been charged with extortion. FBI officials, who staged the sting, say Tucker extorted bribes from individuals he thought represented a business that wanted to build and operate a solid waste incinerator in the city of Compton, California. The men who met with Tucker were FBI agents.

24 August

1924—Birthday of novelist JAMES BALDWIN in New York City. Baldwin, a former teenage Pentacostal minister, moved to Europe, where he died in 1987. Baldwin's books include *The Fire Next Time, Go Tell It on the Mountain, If Beale Street Could Talk* and *Another Country*. (See also 12/2)

1987—BAYARD RUSTIN died in Washington, D.C. A pacificist and civil rights advocate, Rustin was born in 1910 at West Chester, Pennsylvania. He organized the New York City branch of the Congress of Racial Equality, best known as CORE.

1988—CURTIS TERRELL, JR., 22, was fatally shot in Vallejo, California, by Marine Corps PFC Alexander Osinski. Osinski admitted killing Terrell, but more than a year after the shooting he had not been charged in the case. Terrell was shot seven times with a semi-automatic handgun. His family filed a $15 million lawsuit. Osinski reportedly told police that Terrell had tried to sell him (Osinski) cocaine and then tried to take the Marine's gun. Osin-

ski claimed he was afraid to walk through tough neighborhoods and had carried the gun for protection. Police later found an unloaded AR-15 assault rifle and a shotgun in Osinski's car.

1991—Two years and two days after shooting HUEY P. NEWTON, a founder of the 60's Black Panther Party, Tyrone Robinson, alleged drug dealer and once convicted bank robber, went before a jury of his peers. The prosecution presented testimony of witnesses who claimed they saw Robinson shoot Newton in the early morning of August 22, 1989. Their testimony convinced the jury that Robinson was guilty of murder.

25 August

1905—Birthday of ETHEL HILDA KEELER, who gained fame as a dancer and an actress. RUBY KEELER was known for her performance in Harlem's famed Cotton Club during the 30s.

1927—Tennis great ALTHEA GIBSON DARBEN was born in Silver, South Carolina. She was the first African American to win the U.S. Women's Tennis Championship at Wimbledon, in 1957. Gibson retired from competition in 1958. She was selected for the International Tennis Hall of Fame in 1971.

1994—Richard Campos, an 18-year-old White separatist from Sacramento, has been held to answer for a dozen felonies, including firebombings of the Sacramento offices of the NAACP, Japanese American Citizens League and the home of Sacramento City Councilman Jimmie Yee, who is Chinese. Campos' attorney Michael Brady did not call any witnesses to testify on behalf of his client. "Don't be stampeded into convicting this young man on the basis of his beliefs ... even racists are entitled to justice," Brady said according to the *San Francisco Chronicle* (August 25, 1994).

1994—A federal appeals court reopened the RODNEY KING beating case, saying the two officers, Sgt. Stacey Koon and Laurence Powell, were convicted of using excessive force. With the turnabout ordered by the federal appeals court, it is likely that sentences for both Koon and Powell will be extended to 70 to 80 months or somewhere between. Both officers are now serving prison terms of 2.5 years each at a federal prison in Pleasanton, California.

1994— The State Board of Prison Terms today rejected, for the thirteenth time, ELMER GERONIMO PRATT's request for parole. Pratt, formerly the deputy defense minister for the Black Panther Party, was sentenced to life in prison for the murder of an Oakland schoolteacher, Caroline Olsen. Pratt, 46, is a decorated Vietnam War veteran. He will have another parole hearing next year. Three days before the most recent hearing, demonstrators filled the office of Los Angeles District Attorney Gil Garcetti, seeking parole for Pratt. Pratt is serving his sentence at Mule Creek State Prison in the Sierra Foothills.

26 August

1920— The 19th Constitutional Amendment, which gave women the right to vote, officially was ratified.

1991— In Tokyo's World Track and Field Championships, sprinter CARL LEWIS ran the 100-meter race in 9.86 seconds. He set a new world record and was given the title of the "world's fastest human." Lewis regained the title after losing it to Leroy Burrell in June.

1994— Rep. MEL REYNOLDS, indicted earlier for the 1992 sexual assault of a 16-year-old campaign worker, faced new charges. Federal Election Commission investigators claimed Reynolds neglected to report all campaign contributions given him during the 1992 election. Authorities said more than half the contributions— $242,209 — to Reynolds' campaign came from PACs (Political Action Committees). A review of Reynolds records— by the FEC— indicated the disappearance of $76,000, which represented money given to Reynolds by 72 PACs. Officials of each PAC were able to present canceled checks,

which indicated the money had been deposited in a bank. Some of the checks were deposited in banks not "registered" for that purpose.

1994— African Americans and Jews continue to work towards resolving their relations following a speech given in Dallas by KHALID ABDUL MUHAMMAD. Muhammad was invited by the city's Junior Black Academy of Arts and Letters. The group was formed to enhance the awareness of African American art, culture and history. The group rented a space to a group honoring Muhammad.

In his speech, Muhammad offended Jewish City Councilman Paul Fielding. Fielding, in response, threatened to cut off funding for the academy, which owed the city more than $140,000 on a four-year-old loan. He repeated the threat at Monday's city council meeting. Fielding's threat immediately strained relations between African Americans and Jews.

African Americans comprise 16 percent of the 2.5 million people who live in the Dallas area, which includes 45,000 Jews. According to Mark Briskman, regional director of the Anti-Defamation League, the communities had not meshed for a long time.

Al Lipscom, an African American city council member, said the problems between African Americans and Jews run deep and have been growing for years.

27 August

1918— Shortly after 4 P.M. on this date, in Nogales, Sonora, Mexico, units of the 10th U.S. Cavalry responded when a customs officer fired a shot at a Mexican National who failed to stop for questioning at the border checkpoint. A Mexican customs officer then shot at the U.S. customs officer. This shot went wild and fatally struck Army Pvt. W. H. KLINT, who had followed the customs officer to offer protection. Cpl. WILLIAM A. TUCKER shot the Mexican officer and the battle was enjoined. 1st Sgt. THOMAS JORDAN was commended for taking command of his troops (platoon) in the absence of a commanding officer. A white flag went up over the Mexican customs station and U.S. Army officers ordered a cease-fire at about 7:45 P.M., three hours and 35 minutes after the shooting began. Sniping at U.S. troops and customs officers from the Mexican side of the border had long been a problem, including shots fired at U.S. officers en route to negotiate a truce. Casualty reports indicate that at least three officers and five enlisted men were killed and about a dozen more wounded.

1928— Retired Army Maj. Gen. FRED CLIFTON SHEFFEY, JR., was born in McKeesport, Pennsylvania.

1963— Orator, scholar and writer WILLIAM EDWARD BURGHARDT DU BOIS died.

1990— A communication failure pitted one African American organization against another in the waning days of an Oregon summer. Members of the Chicago-based organization PUSH (People United to Save Humanity) arrived in the Portland suburb of Beaverton to continue their boycott of the Nike Corp. and Nike products. There was one problem: members of the Portland chapters of the NAACP or Urban League knew nothing about the boycott. The Chicago delegation was led by the Rev. TYRONE CRIDER, the current executive director of the organization founded by the Rev. Jesse Jackson. Officials of PUSH failed to notify any of the Portland organizations about the boycott. (PUSH does not maintain offices in Portland.) Meanwhile, PUSH continued with its Portland agenda, demanding Nike establish accounts at African American–owned banks and hire African American–owned ad agencies. The group also took issue with Nike's two-year table for hiring a minority vice president.

28 August

1821— Birthday, in Gloucester County, Virginia, of Pony Express rider WILLIAM

M. ROBISON. Although born a slave, Robison obtained his freedom by taking part — at age 15 — in the Seminole Indian War of 1836. Ten years later he left the East for California on the USS *Ohio*, which reached Monterey in January 1847. Robison returned to the eastern U.S. after taking part in the Mexican-American War, but came back to California in 1850. He worked briefly as a miner but later was employed at various times by the express companies of Page, Bacon & Co., Adams & Co., and Wells Fargo & Co.

1955— EMMITT TILL was kidnapped from his uncle's home in Money, LeFlore County, Mississippi, by two White men. Till's body was found four days later, bound with barbed wire, in the Tallahatchie River. An all–White, all-male jury acquitted the two suspects after a trial.

1963— More than 200,000 African Americans and Whites marched on Washington, D.C., in a civil rights demonstration. It was at this gathering that the Rev. MARTIN LUTHER KING, JR., delivered his famous "I have a dream" speech to the marchers who gathered at the Washington Monument.

1991— White supremacist Tom Metzger, also former grand dragon of the California Ku Klux Klan, was not present when his Fallbrook, California, home was sold to Jim McElroy for the minimum bid of $121,500. Metzger will receive $45,000 from the sale. He is working to reduce the $12.5 million judgment an Oregon court ordered him to pay to the family of MULUGETA SERAW, an Ethiopian immigrant beaten to death by skinheads in Portland. The Oregon jury found that the skinheads were encouraged to assault Seraw because of a racial hatred campaign waged by the Metzgers and their White Aryan Resistance organization.

29 August

1924— The birthday of jazz and blues vocalist Dinah Washington, born RUTH JONES, in Tuscaloosa, Alabama. Washington was best known for her ability to smoothly shift from a soulful offering of

"This Bitter Earth" to the torchy "What a Difference a Day Makes," two of her biggest hits. She set the standard for other female jazz and blues singers.

1933 — Army Maj. Gen. ROBERT BRADSHAW ADAMS was born in Buffalo, New York.

1945 — Track and field athlete WYOMIA TYUS was born in Griffin, Georgia.

1988 — In Chicago, Ku Klux Klan members and their supporters threw rocks, bottles and racial slurs at an unidentified African American man wearing headphones, who accidently walked through a Klan rally in Marquette Park. The African American was rescued by mounted police. At the other end of the park, African Americans celebrated "Dream Day," the 25th anniversary of the Rev. MARTIN LUTHER KING, JR.'s famous 1963 address in Washington, D.C.

1990 — The *San Francisco Chronicle* published an article about The Ark, an 11-month-old, six-bedroom residential shelter for those suffering from AIDS (acquired immune deficiency syndrome). Until 1995 the Ark was run by the Love Center Church of Oakland, California, an arm of the Pentecostal faith. When the church began this endeavor, it had a congregation of about 1,100 and was led by the Rev. WALTER HAWKINS, founder and pastor, and the Rev. Yvette Flunder, associate pastor and executive director of An Ark of Love, the church's non-profit subsidiary that ran the Ark.

1991 — The conservative California Supreme Court slashed $89,000 from a $90,000 damage award to ROBERT CANNON, 67, who prevailed in a housing discrimination case. The court set the damage award at $1,000 and ordered the defendants to reimburse Cannon for out-of-pocket attorney fees and court costs totaling $2,724.50.

1994 — According to staff reporters for the *San Francisco Chronicle*, African Americans are dusting off old tomes and rethinking what the newspaper calls "The

New Black Panther Philosophy." "It's coming back," say *Chronicle* reporters.

According to reporters, the New Panther Philosophy is under wraps by day when African Americans work as lawyers, nurses, physicians, electricians and other skilled professions. After dark, the "New Panthers" switch to black berets, black ankle boots and dark gray fatigues worn by the New Panthers as they patrol Dallas. Texas' neighborhoods. The New Panthers are well known in Texas for their '90s revolutionary philosophy, fiery rhetoric and "bold display" of weapons. It is regrettable that HUEY P. NEWTON, a co-founder of the original Black Panthers, will not witness the link-up between Panthers past and Panthers present.

Founded in Oakland, California, during the '60s, the New Black Panther Party resurfaced in 11 major U.S. cities during the '90s. The group once was tagged by the FBI as "the greatest threat to U.S. internal security." It will be interesting to track the activities of the New Panther group, barely four years old, and their plan for the 21st century and the next decade.

30 August

1901 — Birthday in St. Louis, Missouri, of ROY WILKINS, former executive secretary of the NAACP. Wilkins, the grandson of a slave, graduated from the University of Minnesota and joined the staff of the *Kansas City Call* newspaper where he became managing editor before joining the NAACP.

1931 — CARRIE SAXON PERRY was born in Hartford, Connecticut. A former three-term state assemblywoman, Perry was elected mayor of her hometown in 1987. Winning the election made Perry the first African American woman mayor of a major U.S. city.

1990 — The family of the late Rev. RALPH DAVID ABERNATHY announced the establishment of the Abernathy Foundation. (See also 1/10; 3/11; 4/17; 4/24)

1990— Marine Corps L/Cpl. RONNIE CURTIS sat on death row at Ft. Leavenworth, Kansas, awaiting the outcome of appeals to military courts of review. When these failed, his lawyers appealed his death sentence to the U.S. Supreme Court. His appeal process continued, still unsettled, for more than six years. Curtis earlier was convicted of the April 13, 1987, murders of Marine 1st/Lt. James Lotz and his wife Joan at Camp Lejeune, North Carolina. Curtis was convicted of fatally stabbing Lotz, who was Curtis' platoon leader, and then Lotz's wife. The Lotzs were White. According to Curtis' lawyers, Lotz needled Curtis by calling the then 21-year-old Marine "Bebop" and "Shoo-be-do." The last military execution, the hanging of a soldier for rape and attempted murder, was carried out in 1961. Since then the military has built a death chamber at Ft. Leavenworth to handle executions by lethal injection. Should his appeal to the Supreme Court be denied, Curtis would be the first person to die in the new chamber.

31 August

1907— Birthday of Rep. AUGUSTUS F. HAWKINS, D-California. A Democrat, Hawkins defeated Frederick M. Roberts, California's first African American legislator, in the 1934 campaign for the California Assembly seat Roberts held for 16 years. Early in 1990, Hawkins announced his intention to retire from Congress later in the year.

1935— Former Baltimore Orioles manager, baseball legend and Hall of Famer FRANK ROBINSON, was born in Beaumont, Texas. Robinson was named Manager of the Year for the 1989 season. Raised in Oakland, California, Robinson played with the Cincinnati Reds, the Orioles, the Los Angeles Dodgers, the California Angels and the Cleveland Indians. He became baseball's first African American manager after agreeing to manage the Indians in 1975. Robinson was the National League's Most Valuable Player in 1961 and won the same honor in the American League five years later. He is the only Major League player to be so honored in the history of baseball.

1935— Birthday of ELDRIDGE CLEAVER, former Black Panther Party minister of information, ex-convict, ex-patriot and presidential candidate for the Peace and Freedom Party in the 1968 elections. Paroled from Soledad Prison in 1966, Cleaver left the United States after violating terms of his parole. Then 40, Cleaver and his wife Kathleen lived in several countries, including Mexico, Cuba, Algeria, and France. He returned to the United States voluntarily in 1975. Cleaver also was subpoenaed by a Senate subcommittee to testify on terrorism and other subversive activities in the United States. He was freed after spending several months in prison.

1943— The Navy destroyer escort USS *Harmon*, named for Mess Attendant LEONARD R. HARMON, who won the Navy Cross for bravery in 1942, was launched. (See also 7/25)

1958— Track and field star EDWIN CORLEY MOSES was born in Dayton, Ohio.

1991— California Supreme Court Justice ALLEN BROUSSARD retired after 10 years. Broussard was appointed to the court in 1981 by then Gov. Jerry Brown and elected to a 12-year term the following year. Broussard pointed out that he spent 27 years on the bench, including his stint on the state Supreme Court.

1994— A group of Latino elected officials endorsed the Rev. AL SHARPTON in his campaign to defeat incumbent Senator Daniel Patrick Moynihan, D–New York. Sharpton said the "endorsements illustrate the growing appeal his candidacy has among Latino New Yorkers."

September

We have to keep in mind at all times that we are not fighting for integration, nor are we fighting for separation. We are fighting for recognition as free humans in this society. — Malcolm X

This month:

1790 — The first census posed only six questions:

*Name of the head of household
*Number of free White males 16 years of age or older
*Number of free White males under 16
*Number of free White females
*Number of other free persons
*Number of slaves

1963 — Schools of the South were integrated without further incident, except those in Alabama, where the National Guard kept them open after then Gov. George Wallace used state troopers to close them.

1966 — National Guardsmen were used to quell African American rioting in Dayton, Ohio, and San Francisco, California.

In Granada, Mississippi, 30 African American students and their parents, while integrating the local high school, were beaten by 200 Whites armed with pipes, chains and ax handles.

1989 — JAMES MEREDITH, the first African American to enroll in the University of Mississippi — with help from the National Association for the Advancement of Colored People and 16,000 soldiers and National Guardsmen — applied for, and won, a job on the staff of North Carolina Sen. Jesse Helms. Meredith works as a democratic policy advisor.

1 September

1975 — Air Force Lt. Gen. DANIEL "Chappie" JAMES was promoted to general and assumed command of the North American Air Defense Command at Peterson Air Force Base, Colorado. James was the first African American military officer to achieve four-star rank.

1994 — ROSA PARKS is often thought of as the person who literally kick-started the civil rights movement (in 1955) by refusing to allow a Montgomery, Alabama, bus driver to force her to give her seat on the city bus to a White male passenger. Parks refused to move, and her continued refusal to do so marked the beginning of the civil rights movement in Alabama. Parks at 81 was herself a victim of crime when a young man broke into her Detroit home, struck her in the face twice and emptied her purse of $566. The robber stopped before leaving Parks' home to ask if she was, in fact, ROSA PARKS. The thief kept Parks' money nonetheless. (See also 9/3)

2 September

1943 — The Liberty Ship *Frederick Douglass*, then part of a naval convoy carrying supplies to Europe during World War II, was torpedoed and sank in the Atlantic Ocean.

111

1947— Elementary schoolteacher WIL-HELMINA JOHNSON SMITH began her career as the first African American to teach in the Stockton, California, public school system. Smith, who continued to teach and mold young minds for more than 40 years was assigned to the first grade.

1956— The Tennessee National Guard was dispatched to Clinton, Tennessee, to handle demonstrations against school integration.

3 September

1838— FREDERICK DOUGLASS disguised himself as a sailor and escaped to freedom in the North. (See also 2/14; 2/23; 7/19; 8/2; 8/11; 9/2)

1990— Kenyan scientists report success in their use of the drug alpha interferon, sold under the brand name "Kemron," in treating AIDS and AIDS-related infections. The Kenyan researchers say the drug is an inexpensive cure for AIDS, while scientists in the United States decline to be impressed by Kenyan's research. African Americans and African researchers have suggested that the Western media have "under-reported" the findings on Kemron, for two reasons: to protect the status quo of more expensive drugs prescribed for AIDS patients and racially motivated disbelief in the validity of work done by African scientists. Despite the debate, Kemron/Alpha Interferon costs an estimated $1 per day and is now popular in the clandestine network that offers a variety of drugs AIDS sufferers believe will cure or slow the development of the disease.

1994— Police later arrested Joseph Skipper and charged him with robbing and assaulting Rosa Parks. Skipper was booked into the Wayne County Jail, but separated from other inmates. "They tried to beat him up on the streets," an escorting police officer said. Parks moved to Detroit in 1957 and has lived there since.

4 September

1781— The Pueblo of Our Lady Queen of the Angels was established by 11 families, divided almost evenly between African Americans, Spanish and Native Americans. That pueblo is known now as Los Angeles, California.

1848— Birth date, in Chelsea, Massachusetts, of LEWIS HOWARD LATIMER, inventor and pioneer in uses of electric power. Latimer joined the Navy at age 16 and served aboard the USS *Massasoit* during the Civil War. Honorably discharged after the war, Latimer took a job as an office boy for a company of patent attorneys and later became their chief draftsman. He met Alexander Graham Bell about 1876, and was employed to make the drawings and help prepare patent applications for Bell's then recently invented telephone.

Latimer also worked for Hiram S. Maxim, owner of the U.S. Electric Lighting Company, of Connecticut. While with U.S. Electric, Latimer invented and patented a carbon filament for the Maxim incandescent lamp. He was granted the patent in 1881. In 1884, Latimer joined the firm of Thomas Alva Edison after working for several other companies. He wrote one of the first books explaining the principle of electric light. In September 1988, the New York borough of Queens and General Electric Foundation agreed to pay for relocating and preserving the house in which Latimer lived the last 20 years of his life. The house had been scheduled for demolition. (See also 12/11)

1989— In Virginia City, Virginia, things got out of hand at the so-called Greek Fest, a Labor Day celebration by fraternities from predominantly African American colleges and universities along the Atlantic Seaboard. According to reports from this resort city, thousands of college students rambled down the main street firing handguns, looting stores and setting fires. The students numbered roughly 100,000, city officials said, and were considered responsible for sacking 100 stores. An estimated 43 people were injured, including two struck by random gunfire, two others who received injuries that authorities did not describe, and others who were hit by thrown bottles. Authorities said they were not sure what triggered the disturbance. Local police, backed by 150 National Guardsmen, arrested 260 people, half of whom were residents of Virginia City.

1990— During a trip to Kuwait following the invasion of that nation by neighboring Iraq, the Rev. JESSE L. JACKSON concluded his visit to the occupied oil-rich sheikdom by securing the release of 26 ill or ailing Americans detained by Iraqi invasion forces. Jackson traveled to Kuwait to interview Iraqi President Saddam Hussein for "Inside Edition" a program produced by the Fox Television Network. Jackson also interviewed the U.S. ambassador to Kuwait and people who sought refuge in the U.S. Embassy after the invasion. He returned to the U.S. with 47 Americans, including 21 others who had been detained in Iraq.

1990— In Adairville, Kentucky, four Whites who torched the Smith Glover AME Zion Church, which was founded by freed slaves, returned to the site of the arson and delivered court-ordered apologies to the congregation. The arsonists ranged in age from 19 to 22. There were two men and two women and each made a statement. One of the men said he was sorry, yet he knew an apology was not enough.

5 September

1916— Author FRANK YERBY, writer of swashbuckling adventure and romance novels set in the 18th and 19th centuries, was born in Augusta, Georgia.

1987— It was disclosed, more than three decades after the U.S. Supreme Court overturned laws legalizing segregated schools, that the Constitution of the State of West Virginia continues to bar African Americans from attending schools with their White counterparts. The reason: state legislators have been "afraid" to permit a pubic vote on repealing the offensive section. Officials of the state school system claim past attempts to update the Constitution did not succeed because some legislators are afraid voters would balk at more conformative language. The Mississippi Constitution, which had a similar section, was not changed until 1978.

6 September

1853— In New York City, the World Temperence Conference met with the Women's Rights Convention but refused to seat an African American minister who was a part of the conference.

7 September

1932— Retired Army Maj. Gen. JERRY RALPH CURRY, was born in McKeesport, Pennsylvania.

8 September

SAMUEL R. PIERCE, Secretary of Housing and Urban Development during the Reagan era in Washington, was born this date in Glen Cove, Long Island, New York. Pierce, attempting to ride out a major scandal at HUD that began during his tenure, earned a law degree from New York University in 1942. Pierce was volunteered little information about the enormous profits made by Republican insiders through government financed housing projects ostensibly planned for the elderly and the underprivileged.

1968— HUEY NEWTON, Black Panther Party leader, was convicted of manslaughter in the death of a Northern California police officer.

1990— In Atlanta, the Ku Klux Klan presented a petition to the Georgia Supreme Court asking the justices to overturn a four-decade-old state law prohibiting masks. Klansmen called the law "discriminatory," adding that its continued existence "restricted" their right to associate freely.

1994— Thirty-three years ago the 114-year-old National Baptist Convention U.S.A. spurned an opportunity to draw African American religious leaders, mostly

Baptists, into the revised civil rights movement. The Rev. Timothy Mitchell of New York City felt the time was critical because many criticized the church as being powerless in times of trouble.

In 1961, the Rev. Martin Luther King, Jr., invited the largest African American religious denomination to lead the civil rights movement. The Baptist Convention declined and King (along with other civil rights leaders) abandoned the Convention. Since then the Convention has been criticized for its lack of social activism in the face of drug abuse, AIDS, African American versus African American violence, and the crumbling of Black family life.

9 September

1739— A slave known as JENNY led a band of slaves in an attempted march to freedom in Spanish Florida. About 25 Whites were killed and the escaping slaves were either slain or captured and returned to their owners.

1908— Novelist RICHARD WRIGHT was born on a plantation near Natchez, Mississippi. Wright published a collection of stories in 1938 based on the memories of his childhood. The novel *Native Son* was published two years later.

1957— President Dwight D. Eisenhower signed the first civil rights bill adopted by Congress since Reconstruction.

10 September

1965— FATHER DIVINE, born George Baker, died in Philadelphia of lung congestion brought on by arteriosclerosis and diabetes. The founder of the Kingdom of Peace religious cult, Divine is believed to have been born in Maryland. He took his more widely known name after claiming divinity in 1912. Once a gardener and part-time minister, Divine may have been born in 1874 on Hutchinson's Island, near Savannah, Georgia. However, the files of historians and legal records contributed to by Baker himself are vague on when and where he was born. In May 1932, Divine

reportedly told a New York judge he believed he was born in Providence, Rhode Island, and believed himself to be 55 years of age. In 1933, Divine moved his followers from Long Island to Harlem. He later organized places of worship established by his followers into what became known as the Peace Mission. Divine's age was estimated to be between 88 and 100, at the time of his death.

1974— LOU BROCK of the St. Louis Cardinals baseball team stole 105 bases to break the record held by Maury Wills. Brock finished the year with 118 stolen bases and a record 938 for his career when he retired in 1979. RICKEY HENDERSON later broke both of Brock's stolen base records.

11 September

1851— African Americans routed a band of slavecatchers bent on sweeping Christiana, Pennsylvania. One White was killed and one wounded.

1922— CHARLES EVERS was born in Decatur, Mississippi. In 1969, Evers was elected mayor of his hometown. Evers is the brother of assassinated civil rights leader Medgar Evers.

12 September

1913— Birthday of Olympic athlete JESSE OWENS, who was born James Cleveland Owens in Decatur, Alabama. Owens won four gold medals in the 1936 Summer Olympics in Berlin. (See also 3/31; 8/9)

1935— Birth date in Chicago, Illinois, of artist and sculptor RICHARD H. HUNT, known for artwork fashioned from metal. Hunt attended the University of Chicago and the Art Institute of Chicago. He taught at his alma mater, the University of Illinois, and Chouinard Art School in Los Angeles. Hunt's works are part of the permanent collections of museums in Chicago, Cleveland, New York, Buffalo, Milwaukee and Israel.

1990— RON TOWNSEND, president of Gannett Television, became the first African American member of the Augusta National Golf Club, home of the Masters Tournament each year. (See also 8/1; 9/13)

1990— In Mount Clemens, Michigan, three White youths were charged with murder and "ethnic intimidation" in the death of an African American Detroit teenager, 19-year-old CHARLES GIBSON. He was riding in a car driven by a White friend who pulled even with a group of Whites in a pickup truck. Those in the pickup yelled racial insults at Gibson, after which the vehicles were brought to a halt and the two groups began fighting. Witnesses told authorities Gibson was struck on the head with a wooden stick more than two dozen times.

1990— The number of African American owned businesses rose 38 percent in a five year period — from 308,000 in 1982 to 424,000 in 1987. Gross revenues for the businesses, including those run by African Americans, increased 106 percent during the same period, while rising 105 percent for African American owned businesses, according to a U.S. Census Bureau report.

13 September

1926— Economist ANDREW FELTON BRIMMER was born in Newellton, Louisiana. Brimmer was the first African American to serve on the Federal Reserve Board (1966–74). Brimmer was educated at the University of Washington, where he earned a bachelor's degree. Brimmer was a Fullbright Fellow at the University of Bombay, India, from which he earned a master's degree, and he attended Harvard University, where he earned a doctorate. Brimmer also earned a law degree from Nebraska Wesleyan University.

1948— Television actress NELL CARTER was born in Birmingham, Alabama.

1990— Shoal Creek Country Club, near Birmingham, Alabama, became the third formerly all-white golf club to admit an African American member. The admission

followed a threat to remove a major tournament from Shoal Creek. The club offered full membership status to HENRY KING. (See also 8/1; 9/12; 9/13)

1990— Aided by special agents of the Federal Bureau of Investigation, police in Union City, California, investigated the burning of a cross on the front lawn of the house owned by an African American family. San Francisco Bay area newspapers called the cross burning the "latest in a series of hate crimes" in the Bay area. A week earlier, vandals had damaged 30 monuments and grave markers in the Jewish section of an Oakland cemetery. One week earlier, a swastika was painted on the front door of the Castro Valley, California, home of another African American family. (See also 9/19)

14 September

1921— U.S. District Court Judge CONSTANCE BAKER MOTLEY, a former Manhattan borough president and the first African American woman so appointed (by President Lyndon Johnson), was born in New Haven, Connecticut. Motley reached senior judge status in 1986.

1957— President Dwight Eisenhower withdrew Arkansas National Guard troops after then Gov. Orval Faubus used them to prevent African American students from entering Little Rock's Central High School.

1991— Virginia Gov. L. DOUGLAS WILDER, the first African American governor elected by popular vote, announced his candidacy for president of the United States and began campaigning for the Democratic nomination. Wilder later withdrew from the race.

15 September

1830— African Americans held their 1st National Convention at Mother Bethel AME Church, in Philadelphia, Pennsylvania.

1852— JAN E. MATZELIGER was born in Dutch Guiana and immigrated to the United States in 1878. He patented a shoe lasting machine in 1880. In 1883, he patented a perfected machine that became an immediate success. Shoe prices were slashed 50 percent, wages doubled and shoe exports rose from one million to 11 million pairs annually. Matzeliger died in 1889, at age 37.

1963— Four young African American girls, ADDIE MAE COLLINS, DENISE McNAIR, CAROL ROBERTSON and CYNTHIA WESLEY, each age 14, died when a bomb made of dynamite was detonated in a stairwell of the Sixteenth Street Baptist Church in Birmingham, Alabama. Two other African Americans died in rioting that followed the bombing. (See also 1990 below)

1978— MUHAMMAD ALI won a unanimous 15-round decision over World Boxing Association heavyweight champion LEON SPINKS in the New Orleans Superdome. (See also 1/17; 1/22; 4/28; 6/20; 6/28; 7/11; 8/9; 10/29; 10/30; 11/3)

1990— On a hillside in Greenwood Cemetery, a group of African Americans and Whites gathered to remember ADDIE MAE COLLINS, DENISE McNAIR, CAROL ROBERTSON and CYNTHIA WESLEY and to dedicate a state historic marker in their honor. The girls were each age 14 on this date in 1963 when a bomb made of dynamite was detonated in a stairwell of the Sixteenth Street Baptist Church in Birmingham, Alabama. All four were killed in the explosion. (See also 1963 above)

1994— Former mayor of Washington, D.C., Democrat MARION BARRY won 80 percent of votes cast in the 8th Ward's primary election (the District's poorest ward). In the November 8 balloting, Barry, as expected, did well in areas where Democrats outnumber Republicans 9 to 1. Barry then successfully campaigned against an independent African American and Republican Carol Schwartz.

16 September

1877— Levi Coffin, founder of the Underground Railroad, died.

1889— Birthday in Sanford, Florida, of CLAUDE A. BARNETT, founder of the Associated Negro Press, the first and only African American news wire service in the United States. Barnett, who died in 1967, was a 1906 graduate of Tuskegee Institute.

1925— Blues singer RIPLEY "B.B." KING was born in Itta Benna, Mississippi.

1934— Basketball great ELGIN BAYLOR was born in Washington, D.C.

17 September

1891— Cpl. WILLIAM O. WILSON, 9th U.S. Cavalry, received the Congressional Medal of Honor for bravery in action against the Sioux Indians in the Campaign of 1890.

1988— In Seoul, South Korea, for the XXIVth Summer Olympic Games, CHARLES LAKES became the first African American to compete as a gymnast in the Olympics. RON GALIMORE was a member of the 1980 Olympic team which did not compete because the United States boycotted the Moscow games. Lakes, who attended the University of Illinois, was born in 1964, in St. Louis, Missouri.

1994— A recent Gallup Poll indicates that the use of "Blacks" in exchange for "Negro" could soon become history and be replaced by "African American," a term acceptable to 18 percent of those African Americans who took part in the poll. Of the largest group, 60 percent told pollsters "it made no difference." According to the poll, those of middle age who were polled preferred "Black." In Eastern states, 35 percent of those polled said African American was preferable.

18 September

1850— In Washington, D.C., Congress passed the Fugitive Slave Act. The act imposed a $1,000 fine and six months in jail for anyone who helped an escaping or runaway fugitive slave and legalized the return of escaped slaves from free states to slave states.

19 September

1865— Atlanta University was founded by the American Missionary Society.

1943— Baseball slugger JOE LEONARD MORGAN was born in Bonham, Texas.

1990— Racist comments, slogans and swastikas written and drawn in fluorescent green, blue and orange colors screamed from the walls of buildings on the campuses of Hayward High School and Martin Luther King, Jr. Intermediate School, in Hayward, California. (See also 9/13/90)

20 September

1885— Pianist FERDINAND "Jelly Roll" MORTON, was born in New Orleans, Louisiana. Morton was a singer and composer. (See also 7/10)

1990— In New York City, the boycott of the Family Red Apple Grocery Store, a Korean-owned food market in a predominantly African American neighborhood, entered its eighth month. The boycott began January 18 after reports circulated through the neighborhood that the Koreans had beaten a Haitian woman as she allegedly tried to leave the store without paying for all of her purchases. The woman was injured slightly. After the boycott began, African Americans gathered daily outside the small store and, using bull horns, urged their neighbors to shop at other neighborhood stores. The protestors were court-ordered to stay 50 feet from the market entrance. "This is not about race, it is about respect," one neighborhood resident told the *Washington Post*. "They are taking our money out of the community and treating us like animals."

1990— Acts of vandalism, apparently the work of New York City racists, plagued small businesses selected by movie director SPIKE LEE for backdrops in the filming of the 1991 movie *Jungle Fever*. The movie is about the relationship of an African American man and an Italian woman who live in the Bensonhurst section of Brooklyn.

James Longo, owner of a flower shop where Lee filmed portions of the movie, found a smashed window on his delivery van and, a day or two later, three more broken windows in his store. According to the *Daily News*, Longo, who is not an African American, received a telephone call the day the store windows were broken. The caller told Longo: "This is what happens when you rent to niggers."

21 September

1931— Former Secretary of the Army CLIFFORD L. ALEXANDER, JR., was born in New York City.

1949— Basketball star ARTIS GILMORE was born in Chipley, Florida.

1985— MICHAEL SPINKS won a 15-round decision over Larry Holmes to win the International Boxing Federation heavyweight championship in Las Vegas, Nevada.

1989— The Senate Armed Forces Committee unanimously confirmed Army Gen. COLIN LUTHER POWELL, President George Bush's choice, as chairman of the Joint Chiefs of Staff, the nation's highest military post. As a lieutenant general, Powell succeeded Frank Carlucci as national security advisor to Ronald Reagan. After leaving the Reagan administration, Powell was promoted to full general and placed in command of all armed forces in the continental United States. (See also 4/5; 10/1; 11/4)

1989— A subcommittee of the House Government Operations panel elected to subpoena SAMUEL R. PIERCE, JR., former Housing and Urban Development Secretary during the Reagan administration. Committee members wanted to ask Pierce about mismanagement, influence peddling and favoritism for cronies of Reaganites involving government contracts and subsidized housing projects for low income and elderly persons. A number of substantial contracts were approved, netting millions for contractors and consultants but nothing for those for whom the projects were intended to benefit. Pierce honored the subpoena but refused to answer questions. (See also 9/8)

1994— In Sacramento, California, five men were arrested and charged with beating an African American man in a convenience store parking lot, according to Sacramento District Attorney Steve White.

However, federal charges were dismissed August 31 by U.S. District Judge William B. Shubb. Shubb ruled that neighborhood convenience stores are not protected under federal civil rights laws. The District Attorney's office is appealing the ruling.

Meanwhile, prosecutors say the five men — Jeremy R. Baird, 21; Gary J. Jordan, 24; Aaron J. Phillips, 22, and two others — stopped an African American male outside at a Citrus Heights 7-Eleven convenience store on May 14, 1993. According to reports, the five began shouting racial slurs and began beating the man with their feet, fists, clubs and pool cues. A Latino who attempted to help the victim also was beaten, according to prosecutors.

22 September

1862— President Abraham Lincoln read the Emancipation Proclamation to his cabinet. Public announcement was withheld for 100 days, pending a major Union victory over the Confederacy in the Civil War.

1906— Anti–African American riots in Atlanta, Georgia, left ten African Americans and two Whites dead and 70 wounded. The rioting spread two days later to Brownsville, an African American middle class suburb where police and armed Whites looted and destroyed property belonging to innocent African Americans.

1954— Actress SHARI BELAFONTE HARPER, daughter of singer Harry Belafonte, was born in New York City.

1994— The Clinton administration awarded $13.4 million to 28 historic African American colleges to help revitalize the communities around the campuses.

23 September

1896— MARY CHURCH TERRELL was born to wealth in Memphis, Tennessee. Terrell organized the National Association of Colored Women in Washington, D.C., and later helped organize Delta Sigma Theta sorority. She also addressed the International Council of Women in Berlin in English, French and German. She devoted much of her life to the end of discrimination and segregation in and around Washington, D.C., where she lived. Terrell died in Annapolis, Maryland, in 1954, just a few months after the U.S. Supreme Court declared segregation unconstitutional.

1930— Blind composer, singer and musician RAY CHARLES ROBINSON, better known as "Ray Charles," was born in Albany, Georgia.

24 September

1931— Birthday of Rep. CARDISS COLLINS, D-Illinois, in St. Louis, Missouri. Collins, a former U.S. Labor Department employee was first elected in 1973 to the seat once held by her husband, who was killed in an aircraft crash.

1957— U.S. Army paratroopers were sent to ensure nine African American students were admitted to previously all–White Central High School, in Little Rock, Arkansas.

1986— Japanese Prime Minister Yasuhiro Nakasone said United States "intelligence levels are lower than those in Japan because of African Americans, Hispanics and Puerto Ricans." Nakasone later apologized, saying his remarks were misinterpreted.

1988— The Rev. BARBARA C. HARRIS was elected suffragan for the Eastern Massachusetts diocese of the Anglican Church, the largest in the Episcopal Church in the United States. The Bishop of London, Rt. Rev. Graham Leonard, refused to recognize Harris because she is a woman. A few weeks later, the governing body within the Anglican Church of America refused to ratify Harris' election.

25 September

1951— Basketball star BOB McADOO was born in Greensboro, North Carolina.

1962— In Chicago, heavyweight boxing champion FLOYD PATTERSON was defeated by challenger SONNY LISTON, who scored a first round knock-out. (See also 5/8)

26 September

1899— WILLIAM LEVI DAWSON, composer and arranger of music, was born in Anniston, Alabama. A 1921 graduate of Tuskegee Institute, Dawson also attended Washburn College; the Kansas City, Missouri, Institute of Fine Arts; and Chicago Musical College. Among his songs: "I Couldn't Hear Nobody Pray," "Talk About a Child That Do Love Jesus" and "My Lord What a Morning."

1918— Members of the all–African American, 369th Infantry Division were cited for bravery during the battle for Argonne Forest in World War I. The battle lasted until the Armistice was signed on November 11, 1918.

1937— Singer BESSIE SMITH died in Clarksdale, Mississippi.

1990— Black leaders decide those of African decendency should be called African Americans.

1994— The U.S. Supreme Court temporarily approved a November election in a specially drawn African American majority congressional district to proceed by staying a lower court ruling against the voting plan. The district covers an estimated 250 miles across central Georgia. Its extensions nip into the suburbs of Atlanta, Savannah and Augusta, so as to include African American voters. The high court was not expected to hear the case until later.

27 September

1827— Birth date of HIRAM RHODES REVELS, who was born of free parents, in Fayetteville, North Carolina. (See also 2/25)

1912— Composer WILLIAM CHRISTOPHER HANDY, author of the famous "St. Louis Blues," and known as the "Father of the Blues," was born in Florence, Alabama. The son of a minister, Handy died in 1958.

28 September

1829— DAVID WALKER, a free African American published an anti-slavery essay, "Walker's Appeal," which called for slaves to rebel against their masters.

1962— Naval Petty Officer NELSON C. DRUMMOND became the first African American and the first of the nation's minorities to be arrested, charged and convicted of spying for the Soviet Union.

1967— WALTER WASHINGTON was sworn in as United States Commissioner of the District of Columbia. The act made Washington the first African American to become the top official in a major U.S. city.

1986— A survey of Armed Forces showed 6.4 percent of all officers were African American; 3.7 percent Hispanic.

1991— Former District of Columbia Mayor MARION BARRY was sentenced to six months in prison after his earlier misdemeanor conviction for possession of crack cocaine. The cocaine Barry used while FBI agents filmed him was provided by Rahsheeda Moore. Moore agreed to set up Barry in exchange for leniency and a reduced sentence in a West Coast drug case.

1991— Jazz trumpeter, MILES DAVIS, died at Santa Monica, California. He was 65.

29 September

1784— The FIRST AFRICAN LODGE, #459, was established with Prince Hall as its Worshipful Master. However, there was one problem: Chartering papers were missent and did not reach the lodge until 1787.

1942—The Liberty Ship *Booker T. Washington*, the first named for an African American citizen, was commissioned by Navy Capt. Hugh Muizac.

30 September

1935—Singer JOHNNY MATHIS, who was born in San Francisco, California, became known as a velvet voiced crooner. Mathis easily handled ballads including his own "Chances Are."

1943—Singer, actress and television hostess, MARILYN McCOO, was born in Jersey City, New Jersey.

1984—African Americans comprised 6.2 percent of all active duty officers in the Armed Forces. This percentage increased by .4 percent between Oct. 1, 1984, and Dec. 31, 1987.

1986—EDWARD PERKINS, a career Foreign Service officer, was appointed U.S. ambassador to South Africa by then President Ronald Reagan.

1990—A federal jury, made up of four African Americans and eight Whites, found Alabama State Rep. THOMAS REED guilty of extortion. The 60-year-old Reed was cleared of three other charges, including his acceptance of restaurant equipment, valued at $5000, as a bribe. Reed, who was also president of the Alabama National Association for the Advancement of Colored People, could be sentenced to prison for up to 25 years and fines totaling $500,000 for the conviction on the single charge. In February, Reed led a charge to the roof of the state capitol building in Montgomery, where he and several supporters tried to strike a Confederate flag hoisted earlier by diehard segregationist Southerners. Reed said his prosecution was triggered by his efforts to remove the Confederate flag. Reed was found not guilty and continued to serve as the Alabama state representative from Tuskegee.

October

What happens to a dream deferred? Does it dry up like a raisin in the sun?— Langston Hughes

This month:
1990— a Contra Costa County, California, deputy district attorney advised the author that murder charges filed against Marine Corps Pfc. Alexander Osinski were dropped. According to the attorney, Osinski used a semi-automatic weapon to pump seven shots into the body of CURTIS TERRELL. The shooting was in self defense.

1 October

1796— The African Methodist Episcopal (later Zion) Church began in a house on Cross Street, between Orange and Mulberry streets, on the east side of New York City.

1945— Minnesota Twins slugger RODNEY CLINE "Rod" CAREW was born in Gatun, Panama.

1962— Military veteran JAMES MEREDITH, by federal court order, became the first African American admitted to the University of Mississippi. (See also 6/4; 9/89)

1989— Army Gen. COLIN LUTHER POWELL assumed duties as chairman of the Joint Chiefs of Staff. In so doing, he became the first African American to serve in the nation's highest military post.

1990— The United States Supreme Court rejected appeals from three White men convicted of the death, in Howard Beach, a Brooklyn borough neighborhood, of African American MICHAEL GRIFFITH. While attempting to escape from an unexpected assault by a group of Whites, Griffith ran onto a freeway and was struck by a car. He later died of his injuries. (See also 1/7; 1/23; 12/21)

2 October

1800— Birthday of slave NAT TURNER, who was born somewhere in Virginia. Turner was executed by hanging in the fall of 1831 after his failed revolt — the first in American history — in Southampton County, Virginia.

1932— Brooklyn Dodgers baseball star MAURY WILLS, formerly one of the new African American managers in baseball and a renowned base thief, was born in Washington, D.C. (See also 9/10)

1935— Birthday of Maj. ROBERT H. LAWRENCE, USAF. Lawrence, the first African American astronaut, was killed in 1967 when his F-104 Starfighter jet crashed following a training flight while landing at Edwards Air Force Base, California. (See also 6/30; 12/9)

1967— THURGOOD MARSHALL was sworn in as the first African American justice of the U.S. Supreme Court. (See also 6/13; 7/2)

1991— Alameda County Superior Court Judge Alfred Delucchi put the life of TY-RONE ROBINSON, reputed drug dealer and prison gang member, in the hands of the jury who had listened since August 26 to evidence presented by defense and prosecution attorneys. Defense attorney Alfons Wagner told the court in closing arguments that the 27-year-old Robinson shot Huey Newton in self defense after the former Black Panther leader shot at his client. Prosecutor Kenneth Burr said Newton's body "tells you clearly" this [the shooting] was not self defense. Newton, 47, was shot three times in the head. After hearing testimony of witnesses who saw Robinson shoot Newton, the jury found Robinson guilty of murder.

3 October

1897— Birthday of JOSEPHINE RILEY MATTHEWS in Aiken County, South Carolina. Matthews was a midwife for nearly five decades. She was 17 years old when she graduated from high school and was South Carolina Woman of the Year and the state's Outstanding Older American in 1976.

1904— MARY McLEOD BETHUNE opened Sumter Girls School, in Sumter County, South Carolina. (See also 7/10)

1941— Rock and Roll singer CHUBBY CHECKER, whose stage name was a diminutive of "Fats Domino" was born ERNEST EVANS in Philadelphia, Pennsylvania. Checker was known for "The Twist," a song and a style of dance.

1951— Former major league outfielder DAVID "Dave" WINFIELD was born in St. Paul, Minnesota. Winfield played for the San Diego Padres before joining the New York Yankees, the Minnesota Twins, the California Angels and the Cleveland Indians. He retired in 1995.

1989— Former Los Angeles Raiders head coach ART SHELL, a National Football League Hall of Fame lineman, became the second African American named to lead a NFL team. The first African American NFL coach was FREDERICK "Fritz" POLLARD who, in 1923, took the helm of the Hammond (Indiana) Pros. With the hiring of Pollard, the fledgling football league became the first professional U.S. athletic organization to hire an African American coach.

1990— A computer database of indexed labor contracts that "one-time" Mississippi slaves signed in 1865-66 as free people was begun by the Mississippi Department of Archives and History. The contracts include the names of former slaves, for whom and where they worked, and the terms of their pay. In 1860, Mississippi's population was estimated at 791,305, and included 463,631 (58.6 percent) slaves, according to the Mississippi Statistical Summary of Population for 1860.

4 October

1945— Birthday of actor CLIFTON DAVIS, who was born in Chicago.

1990— CHARLES FREEMAN, owner of E. C. Records, a Fort Lauderdale, Florida, record store, was convicted on a misdemeanor obscenity charge for selling rap music albums, *As Nasty as They Wanna Be* by the group 2 Live Crew, to undercover police officers. The albums were earlier considered obscene by Federal Judge Joe Gonzales, who banned their sale. Freeman was never brought to trial, and the charge was dropped. (See also 6/8; 12/12)

5 October

1929— AUTHERINE LUCY, the first African American to attend the University of Alabama, was born in Shiloh, Alabama. Lucy graduated from Miles College and unsuccessfully attempted to enroll in the University of Alabama for post graduate work. University officials rejected Lucy's application and the issue was presented to the courts for resolution. The courts ruled in Lucy's favor but she was expelled after attending classes for a few days in February 1956. University officials rescinded the expulsion order in 1988 and invited Lucy to apply for admission.

1932 — YVONNE WATSON BRAITH-WAITE BURKE was born in Los Angeles, California. A lawyer with degrees from the University of California, Los Angeles and the University of Southern California, Burke was elected to the state assembly in 1966, served until 1972, and was twice elected to the House of Representatives from two Los Angeles districts.

1989 — Former Charlotte, North Carolina, Mayor HARVEY B. GANTT announced that he was getting into the state's Democratic primary election for the right to challenge Republican Sen. Jesse Helms. On the issue of race Gant said: "I'm audacious enough to believe North Carolinians would rise above the racial issue." Gantt won his party's primary election but lost to Helms in the general election. In 1996, Gantt unsuccessfully challenged Helms again for the state senate seat.

6 October

1871 — The FISK JUBILEE SINGERS of Fisk University, Nashville, Tennessee, began the first of many concert tours which won the University and the singers international fame.

1990 — In Naples, Florida, according to United Press International, White police officers put on blackface and posed as crack dealers. The idea was to entrap Whites looking for drugs in the predominantly African American community of River Park. Officials said they were only trying to meet the expectations of potential drug buyers. Authorities acknowledged that the Jolsonesque approach was not a good idea.

1991 — ANITA HILL, a law professor at the University of Oklahoma and a former aide to Appellate Court Judge and nominee to the U.S. Supreme Court, CLARENCE THOMAS, accused Thomas of sexual harassment. Thomas, nominated to replace retired Justice THURGOOD MARSHALL, denied the allegations and

was later confirmed and appointed as the sixteenth justice of the U.S. Supreme Court.

7 October

1857 — The birthday in Mount Pleasant, Ohio, of MOSES FLEETWOOD WALKER, believed to be the first African American to play professional baseball in the major leagues. Walker played for the Toledo Mudhens, a team still active in the American Association, which signed him in 1884 after he left Oberlin College. Walker played 41 games with the Mudhens and had a .251 batting average. His career was cut short after then Chicago White Sox manager Adrian "Cap" Anson complained and pushed enforcement of the rule that prohibited integrated baseball teams. Also affected by the ban was Walker's brother WELDAY WALKER, with whom he played six games for the Mudhens in 1884.

1934 — Playwright IMAMU AMIRI BARAKA was born Everett LeRoi Jones, in Newark, New Jersey. He attended Rutgers, Howard and Columbia universities.

1969 — The University of Wyoming football team dropped 14 African American players who defied the coach's ban on African American armbands in support of the African American Student's Alliance. The student organization called for the University to cut its ties to Brigham Young University, a school administered by the Church of Jesus Christ of Latter-day Saints (Mormons), which barred African Americans.

1988 — U.S. Army officials agreed to review records of African American World War I and II heroes. The agreement was triggered by Defense Secretary Frank Carlucci's acknowledgment that racism "could well have extended to individual decisions leading to the awarding of medals." Rep. Joseph DioGuardi, R–New York, and Rep. Mickey Leland, D-Texas, were trying to convince military officials to make posthumous awards of Medals of Honor to Army

Sgt. HENRY JOHNSON, a World War I veteran, and Navy Seaman DORIE MILLER, who died in World War II. Other World War II veterans nominated for the Medal of Honor in 1996 include 1st Lt. VERNON J. BAKER, late Staff Sgt. EDWARD A. CARTER, JR., late 1st Lt. JOHN R. FOX, late Pfc. WILLY F. JAMES, Jr., Staff Sgt. RUBEN RIVERS, late 1st Lt. CHARLES L. THOMAS and late Pvt. GEORGE WATSON. No African American soldier received the Medal of Honor, America's highest award for valor, during World War II.

1988— Jazz and ballad singer BILLY DANIELS died in Los Angeles.

8 October

1806— Inventor NORBERT RILLIEUX died in Paris.

1941— Birthday of JESSE LOUIS JACKSON, civil rights leader, former aid to the Rev. Martin Luther King, Jr., and Democratic presidential candidate in 1984 and 1988, in Greenville, South Carolina.

1990— Segregation advocate David Duke, a member of the Louisiana House of Representatives, acknowledged defeat at the hands of incumbent U.S. Sen. J. Bennett Johnston, D-Louisiana. Running as a Republican, Duke garnered just over 605,000 votes, compared with the nearly 750,000 cast for Johnston. A major plank in Duke's campaign platform was his opposition to affirmative action, proposed welfare reform and a fixed federal income tax rate. State Sen. Ben Bagert, the original Republican candidate, dropped out of the race to avoid splitting the vote three ways, thus giving Duke a chance to gain a majority.

1990— In Portland, Oregon, White supremacist Tom Metzger was held to answer a $10 million wrongful death civil suit filed by the Southern Poverty Law Center and the Anti-Defamation League. The suit alleged a connection between the beating death of JOHN SERAW, a 22-year-old Ethiopian immigrant, and Metzger, leader of the White Ayran Resistance and former grand dragon of the California Ku Klux Klan. According to the suit, Metzger's influence over a youth group known as "skinheads" was sufficient to motivate the attack on Seraw. White Ayran Resistance literature and videotapes were found by police at the residences of the three skinheads charged with the attack on Seraw. The three skinheads, members of the East Side White Pride, were convicted and sentenced to prison for the attack on Seraw.

1991— A colonial era burial site for African Americans was discovered by construction workers hired to build a new federal building in New York's Lower Manhattan. City officials said it was the only known Revolutionary era cemetery for African Americans. An estimated one dozen skeletons have been uncovered and more are expected as archeologists dig deeper than the current 15–20 feet. City records identify the site, at Broadway and Reade Street, as the northern sector of an 18th century potter's field. Once known as the "Negro Burial Ground" the site was closed in 1790.

9 October

1806— Surveyor BENJAMIN BANNEKER, planner for Washington, D.C., died in Baltimore County, Maryland. (See also 11/9)

1929— The birthday of Mayor ERNEST "Dutch" MORIAL, whose drive and penchant for public service led to a number of significant firsts, in New Orleans, Louisiana. Morial was the first African American to graduate from Louisiana State University Law School. Other firsts followed beginning in 1965, when Morial became Louisiana's first African American U.S. attorney and was elected to the state house of representatives; in 1967 he became the first African American state legislator since Reconstruction, was appointed a judge of the juvenile court in 1970, was elected to the Louisiana Court of Appeal in 1973, and was elected mayor of New Orleans in 1978, becoming the first African American to hold that office.

1991 — A jury of seven women and five men convicted TYRONE ROBINSON of the murder of Huey Newton, Black Panther leader, after four and a half days of deliberation. The panel also found Robinson guilty of being a felon in possession of a handgun. Robinson faced a maximum sentence of 32 years to life in prison.

1991 — Soon Ja Du, a Los Angeles convenience store owner shot and killed LATASHA HARLINS, an African American teenager whom Du accused of stealing a $1.79 bottle of orange juice. After a brief scuffle, the teenager put a bottle of juice on the counter, turned and began walking from the store. At that point Du picked up a handgun and shot Harlins in the back of the head. On this day Du was convicted of voluntary manslaughter and could have been sentenced to 11 years in a state prison. If convicted of second degree murder, Du could have spent the rest of her life in prison. However, Los Angeles County Judge Joyce Carlins, who heard the case, sentenced Du to 10 years probation and community service.

10 October

1788 — African Free School opened in New York City.

1897 — Birthday in Sandersville, Georgia, of ELIJAH POOLE who, in 1934, became ELIJAH MUHAMMAD and leader of the Nation of Islam.

1927 — Army Brig. Gen. HAZEL JOHNSON-BROWN was born in Westchester, Pennsylvania. Johnson-Brown was the first African American woman military officer to achieve flag rank with her 1979 promotion. She served as the chief of the Army Nurse Corps after working in a segregated unit for African American nurses which was integrated into the regular nursing corps in 1948. The general graduated from the Harlem Hospital School of Nursing and studied for advanced degrees at Villanova and Catholic universities.

1935 — *Porgy and Bess*, essentially an African American operetta with an African American cast, opened in New York City.

1946 — Actor and dancer BEN VEREEN was born in Miami, Florida. Vereen starred in the television adaptation of Alex Haley's novel *Roots*.

11 October

1922 — Retired Air Force Maj. Gen. LUCIUS THEUS was born in Bells, Tennessee.

1928 — Army Gen. ROSCOE ROBINSON, JR., was born in St. Louis, Missouri. Gen. Robinson was the Army's first African American four-star general and the second African American to reach the fourth level of flag and general officer rank.

1991 — Comedian JOHN ELROY SANFORD, better known as Redd Foxx, star of "Sanford and Son," died this day, at age 68, after suffering a heart attack on the set of "The Royal Family," a new CBS situation comedy.

12 October

1932 — Comedian DICK GREGORY was born in St. Louis, Missouri. Gregory, a civil rights activist, became a nutritionist. (See also 11/22)

13 October

1902 — In Alexandria, Louisiana, writer ARNA WENDELL BONTEMPS was born. Bontemps earned a bachelor's degree from Pacific Union College in 1923, a master's degree from the University of Chicago in 1943, and won a Guggenheim Fellowship for creative writing in 1949. Among his many novels were *God Sends Sunday*, *Popo and Fifina: Children of Haiti*, and *Black Thunder*.

1924 — Nightclub comedian and actor NIPSEY RUSSELL was born in Buffalo, New York. Russell was a frequent headliner at Small's Paradise Club in New York City, and often appeared on "Hollywood Squares," a television game show.

1942 — 301st, 302nd and 332nd Fighter groups were activated at Tuskegee Institute.

1989— Critics assailed the Rev. RALPH DAVID ABERNATHY and demanded he recant portions of his autobiography, *And the Walls Came Tumbling Down*, in which Abernathy disclosed sexual liaisons between the Rev. Martin Luther King, Jr., and three women the evening before King was assassinated. The critics, mostly former King aides or associates, included the Rev. Jesse Jackson, Andrew Young, Benjamin Hooks, and Joseph Lowery. Abernathy did not yield to the pressure before his death. (See also 1/10; 1/20)

1989— In Atlanta, Georgia, a U.S. District Court ruling, based on DeKalb County's explanation that it had "done everything possible" to desegregate the state's largest school district, was overturned by the U.S. Court of Appeals. The court further ordered the DeKalb County School District, the largest in the state, to consider "drastic gerrymandering" and forced busing to achieve integration.

14 October

1964— The Rev. MARTIN LUTHER KING, JR., was awarded the Nobel Peace Prize for his leadership in a nonviolent civil rights struggle. (See also 1/10; 1/13; 1/15; 3/11; 4/4; 4/27; 8/28; 8/29; 10/8; 12/1)

15 October

1988— Phi Beta Sigma, an all–African American fraternity, was the first minority organization to settle into a house on Fraternity Row at the University of Mississippi. The on-campus move was delayed by an arson fire that had gutted the proposed fraternity house two months earlier.

16 October

1859— John Brown and his 21-man party—16 Whites, five African Americans—raided Harpers Ferry, Virginia. (See also 12/2)

1940— In Washington, D.C., Army Col. BENJAMIN O. DAVIS, SR., was promoted to brigadier general and became the first African American officer of flag rank in the U.S. armed forces. (See also 6/1; 7/13; 12/18)

1951— Rep. ALAN WHEAT, D-Missouri, was born in San Antonio, Texas. Wheat was a member of the Missouri House of Representatives before his 1982 election to Congress.

1990— Jazz drummer ART BLAKEY, founder of the Jazz Messengers, died of lung cancer at 71 in New York. His career began at age 15 playing piano in a Pittsburgh nightclub. As Blakey tells it, his career as a pianist ended one night when a 14-year-old named Earl Garner showed up. Blakey was moved from the piano to the drums. Blakey began the Messengers in 1954, after working with the Fletcher Henderson and Billy Eckstine big bands. The original Messengers were Horace Silver, Kenny Dorham and Hank Mobley who, respectively, played piano, trumpet and saxophone. The careers of more than a dozen of today's best jazz musicians began with Blakey. Among them were Wynton and Branford Marsalis, Clifford Brown, Chuck Mangione, Freddie Hubbard, Jackie McLean, Johnny Griffin, Wayne Shorter, Keith Jarrett, Walter Davis, Lee Morgan, Donald Byrd, Cedar Walton, Woody Shaw and Billy Harper. A self taught musician, Blakey denied being a teacher for the young talent he nurtured. Blakey was born in Pittsburgh, Pennsylvania, in 1919.

17 October

1720— Birthday of JUPITER HAMMON, a writer and self-educated Calvinist. Hammon is believed to be the first African American poet to be published in the United States. He was born a slave in Queen's Village, Long Island, New York, where he spent his entire life. Hammon's first poem, "An Evening Thought: Salvation by Christ, with Penitential Cries," was printed in 1760.

1956— The birthday in Decatur, Alabama, of NASA astronaut MAE C. JEMISON, M.D., who gives Chicago as her hometown. Jemison is a graduate of Stanford and Cornell universities from which she respectively earned a bachelor of science degree in chemical engineering and a bachelor of arts in African/Afro-American studies and a doctorate in medicine. Jemison completed astronaut training in 1988, one year after being accepted as an astronaut candidate. Jemison is a mission specialist and was assigned to STS-47, Spacelab-J, a joint mission involving the Japanese that included experiments in life sciences and materials processing. The STS-47 was launched in August 1992.

18 October

1926— Rock and roll guitarist CHARLES "Chuck" EDWARD BERRY was born in San Jose, California, and later taken to St. Louis, Missouri, where he grew up. Berry, who still "duck walks" while playing the guitar, is responsible for the hits "Mabelline," "Johnny B. Good" and "Roll Over Beethoven."

1945— Singer PAUL ROBESON won the Springarn Medal for outstanding achievement in theater and on the concert stage. (See also 1/23; 4/9; 12/17)

1988— In Palo Alto, California, racism raged on the Stanford University campuses and in Washington, D.C., economic discrimination continued. Latest in the series of racist acts directed at African Americans by White Stanford university students were under investigation by university administrators. The acts included racist remarks, demonstrations and practical jokes by White students.

1988— The Associated Press reported a lawsuit filed in the District of Columbia by a dozen African American Burger King franchise owners alleging Burger King Corp. directed them to unprofitable locations, charged African American operators up to twice as much as Whites for franchises, leases and equipment, and blocked efforts of African American franchises to obtain loans for expansion.

1990— The state of Kansas honored the memory of EDWARD P. McCABE, the first African American to succeed in a statewide election. On the 140th anniversary of McCabe's birth, Kansas officials hung a portrait of McCabe in the capitol last week. A Republican, McCabe was elected state auditor in 1883 and won reelection in 1884. He was born in Troy, New York, and moved to Kansas in 1878. McCabe died in Chicago in 1920.

1991— One week after University of Oklahoma law professor ANITA HILL detailed incidents of sexual harassment for the Senate Judiciary Committee, Appellate Court Judge CLARENCE THOMAS, President George Bush's choice to replace retired Justice THURGOOD MARSHALL, was sworn in as the 106th U.S. Supreme Court Justice in a private ceremony on the south lawn of the White House. A Supreme Court spokeswoman, who later announced the swearing in, said Thomas had requested the "affair be unheralded." In attendance were Justice Thomas' wife, Virginia, Sen. John Danforth and Robb Jones, an aide to Chief Justice William Rehnquist.

19 October

1810— Birthday of Kentucky abolitionist, Cassius Marcellus Clay, somewhere in Kentucky.

1923— GEORGIA MONTGOMERY DAVIS POWERS was born in Springfield, Kentucky. In 1967, Powers was the first African American woman elected to the Kentucky State Senate. She completed a fifth four-year term in 1989.

1936— Birthday of JOHNETTA BETSCH COLE the first African American woman appointed president of Spelman College, a school for women.

1983— Grenada's U.S. educated Prime Minister MAURICE BISHOP was killed in a military coup.

1990— In Washington, D.C.'s Union Station, labor and union leaders gathered to unveil a statue of ASIA PHILIP RANDOLPH who, more than six decades ago, organized the Sleeping Car Porters Union. Randolph died in 1979. (See also 4/15)

20 October

1967— In Meridian, Mississippi, seven men, among them a Ku Klux Klan official and a deputy sheriff, were convicted of violating the civil rights of slain civil rights workers, JAMES E. CHANEY, ANDREW GOODMAN and MICHAEL H. SCHWERNER.

1986— A U.S. Department of Agriculture Soil Conservation Service employee documented a pattern of racism and discrimination against African American farmers. He was fired from his job and his Forest City, Arkansas, home was destroyed by an arsonist after a suit against the Department of Agriculture was settled.

1989— U.S. District Judge ALCEE HASTINGS was impeached by a U.S. Senate vote of 69–26 on charges of conspiracy. The charges involved an alleged payment of $150,000 to Hastings in exchange for reduced sentences of two defendants in a drug case heard in Hastings' Florida courtroom. Hastings was acquitted of the same charges in an earlier court trial. (See also 8/8; 10/23)

1990— In Florida, the rap music group 2 Live Crew was acquitted of obscenity charges relating to the sexually explicit lyrics on their 1989 album. *As Nasty as They Wanna Be*; some critics claim the lyrics also demean women. Group leader LUTHER CAMPBELL and members MARK "Brother Marquis" ROSS and CHRIS "Fresh Kid Ice" WONGWON, were each looking at a year in the Broward County Jail and fines of $1,000. After a two-week trial, the jury deliberated just over two hours before finding the group innocent of all charges. The charges were brought after the group completed an adults-only concert on June 10 in Hollywood, Florida. Campbell and other members of the group were arrested after the concert.

21 October

1917— Birth date of trumpeter JOHN BIRKS "Dizzy" GILLESPIE, father of bebop, who was born in Cheraw, South Carolina.

1950— In Lake City, South Carolina, the birthday of NASA astronaut RONALD E. McNAIR, Ph.D. McNair, a mission specialist, earned a bachelor of science degree in physics from North Carolina A & T University and a doctorate in physics from Massachusetts Institute of Technology. McNair's first space mission was in the shuttle *Challenger* on February 3, 1984, when two communications satellites were placed in orbit. (See also 1/28)

1986— Responding to a $10 million suit brought by Democrats, Republicans agreed to halt the party's so-called "Voter Integrity" program, which Democrats said was designed to intimidate African Americans and Hispanic voters nationwide. (See also 11/9)

1989— Businessman PETER C.B. BYNOE acquired the Denver Nuggets National Basketball Association franchise for $54 million. Bynoe, the first African American to own a major share of a professional athletic team was joined in the deal by Robert J. Wussler, president of Comsat Video Enterprises, Inc.

1990— Japan's justice minister, Seiroku Kajiyama, who defamed African Americans with a racial slur uttered in September of this year, was asked by Tsuruo Yamaguchi, general secretary of the Japan Socialist Party, to resign before the scheduled visit — six days later — of South Africa's NELSON MANDELA. Kajiyama had been justice minister for four days when he compared Tokyo prostitutes with African Americans during a press conference. When either group moves into a neighborhood, Kajiyama said, it deteriorates.

22 October

1936— Birthday of BOBBY SEALE, in Dallas, Texas, co-organizer and former chairman of the Black Panther Party.

1990—In Portland, Oregon, jurors in the trial of Tom Metzger heard the White supremacist caution them against finding him guilty. Such a verdict, Metzger said, could imperil their constitutional right to free speech. Metzger, a former Grand Dragon of the California Ku Klux Klan, and his son John were accused of inciting the killing of MULUGETA SERAW, an Ethiopian immigrant who was beaten to death by three so-called skinheads in November 1988. Prosecutors in the case accused the Metzgers of sending an agent to Portland to organize skinheads. The jurors, ignoring Metzger's warning, decided that he, his son and their organization, WAR (White Aryan Resistance), helped create a climate of violence and hate among Portland's skinheads that resulted in the beating death of Seraw. The panel proceeded to order damages paid to Seraw's family. (See also 10/28)

23 October

1945—First baseman JACKIE ROBINSON, the fifth African American to play major league baseball, began his career with the Brooklyn Dodgers' Montreal farm team. (See also 10/7)

1989—Former U.S. District Judge ALCEE HASTINGS filed formal papers declaring his candidacy in the 1990 race for governor of Florida. Hastings' action came three days after a U.S. Senate voted 69–26 for his impeachment. Hastings ran unsuccessfully for the U.S. Senate in 1970 and the state Public Service Commission in 1974. (See also 8/8; 10/20)

1989—In Miami, the trial of William Lozano, a Colombian-born police officer began. Lozano was charged with manslaughter in the shooting death of CLEMENT LLOYD, an African American, and the death of ALLAN BLANCHARD, also an African American. Lozano had said Lloyd, who was operating a motorcycle on which Blanchard was a passenger, tried to run him (Lozano) down with the two-wheeled machine. Lozano claims to have shot Lloyd in self-defense. Blanchard died

of injuries received when the motorcycle crashed after Lloyd was shot.

1990—In Washington, D.C., President George Bush vetoed the Civil Rights Act of 1990, a bill with which Congress intended to restore civil rights laws overturned by U.S. Supreme Court rulings in the past year. The president said the veto was necessary because, in its present form, the new civil rights act would require businesses to use quotas in hiring new employees. The president offered a bill of his own upon which Congress did not act.

1991—*San Francisco Chronicle* sports writer Ira Miller told San Francisco 49er fans that wide receiver JERRY RICE was assured a spot in football history and "if Rice doesn't catch another pass" he'll still earn induction to the NFL Hall of Fame. Miller listed Rice's statistics after something less than seven years with the 49ers: catches: 480 in 99 games; yardage: 8,484 (second only to Hall of Famer Lance Alworth); touchdown catches: 87 (fourth on a list behind Steve Largent, Don Hutson and Don Maynard). After the 1995 season, Rice was the NFL's all-time leader in all three categories.

24 October

1948—Birthday of Rep. KWEISI MFUME, D-Maryland, who was born Frizzell Gray in Baltimore, Maryland. Mfume was elected to the seat once held by Rep. PARREN MITCHELL, who retired in 1986. Mfume, a former Baltimore city council member, won Mitchell's seat by winning 87 percent of the vote in the 1986 general election. In 1996 Mfume became president of the NAACP.

1972—Baseball player JACKIE ROBINSON died in Stamford, Connecticut. (See also 1/31)

1988—Boxing champion HENRY ARMSTRONG died at age 75 of heart failure in Los Angeles. Considered by some to be the best in boxing history, Armstrong became the only boxer to concurrently hold championships in the featherweight, lightweight and welterweight classes.

25 October

1917— Heart surgeon WALTER CARL GORDON, JR., was born, in Albany, Georgia. Gordon attended Hampton Institute, Tuskegee Institute and McHarry Medical College and is a former director of Florida A & M University. (See also 4/18)

1990— The Senate, despite a Democratic majority, failed to override a presidential veto of the Civil Rights Act of 1990. A key vote in the proceeding was that of Sen. Pete Wilson, later elected governor of California, who voted to sustain the veto. Had Wilson voted to override, the act would have become law.

1991— Former District of Columbia Mayor MARION BARRY began serving a six-month prison sentence for possession of crack cocaine. Barry was sent to a minimum federal facility at Petersburg, Virginia.

1994— BENJAMIN CHAVIS, dismissed two months before from his job as the NAACP CEO by the National Association for the Advancement of Colored People, was fired because he took NAACP funds — without board approval — to settle a lawsuit filed against him by former aide Mary Stansel. Stansel accepted the cash, saying Chavis had promised to find her a job in the "$80,000 range, but failed to do so." Board members were unaware that Chavis had given Stansel $332,400. In a press interview earlier this month, Chavis said the NAACP Board members were "mean-spirited" in their decision to fire him. Taking into consideration that Chavis' wife is expecting twins, the board agreed to cover two mortgage payments on Chavis' $478,000 residence in Ellicott City, Maryland. Chavis earned $200,000 a year as CEO of the NAACP.

26 October

1749— British Parliament legalized slavery in the colony known now as the state of Georgia.

1919— Birth date in Washington, D.C., of former U.S. Senator EDWARD WIL-LIAM BROOKE, a Republican whose 1966 election to the 90th session of Congress made him the first African American senator from Massachusetts. The third African American to win a senate seat since Reconstruction, Brooke served as Massachusetts Attorney General from 1962 to 1966 and was editor of the Boston University Law Review from 1946 to 1948.

1990— District of Columbia Mayor MARION BARRY, found guilty of drug possession after a 10-week trial, was sentenced to six months in prison and a $5,000 fine. The conviction on only one count stemmed from an FBI sting in which Bureau agents brought Hazel Rasheeda Moore, a former close friend of Barry, to the District to lure him to her hotel room and offer him crack cocaine while federal agents captured the event on videotape from their hidden vantage point in an adjoining room. (See also 1/18; 1/20; 3/6; 7/7; 7/27; 8/14)

27 October

1923— Birth date of actress RUBY DEE, who was born in Cleveland, Ohio.

28 October

1789— Birth date of Levi Coffin, in New Gardin, North Carolina. Coffin was the founder and head conductor of the Underground Railroad. (See also 9/16)

1990— After finding Southern California White supremacist Tom Metzger and his son John guilty of causing the death of Ethiopian immigrant MULUGETA SERAW, a Portland, Oregon, jury further awarded a $12.5 million civil judgment to be paid to Seraw's family by the Metzgers and WAR (White Aryan Resistance). Attorneys representing Seraw's family planned to seize the Metzger home, in Fallbrook, California, and any bank accounts and cash sent to WAR, which Metzger founded. (See also 10/22)

29 October

1945— Birth date of actress MELBA

MOORE. Moore was born in New York City.

1990— Of the 408 African Americans recently questioned by a *New York Times*/CBS News telephone survey:

29 percent believe the AIDS epidemic stems from a government plot against African Americans.

60 percent believe the federal government ensures the availability of drugs in African American neighborhoods.

77 percent believe government agencies are involved in investigating African American politicians as a means of discrediting them.

30 October

1912— In Fort Scott, Kansas, on this day, photographer and filmmaker GORDON PARKS was born. Parks' early work was almost exclusively for *Time* and *Life* magazines. In 1966, Parks became the first African American film director with *The Learning Tree.*

1925— Rep. GUS SAVAGE, D-Illinois, was born in Detroit, Michigan. A lawyer, Savage also worked as a journalist, and as editor and publisher of the Citizen Community Newspapers from 1975 until a year before his election to the House of Representatives in 1980. As 1989 came to an end House members showed no interest in investigating charges of sexual harassment lodged against Savage by a Peace Corps volunteer Savage had met in March during a tour of Zaire. (See also 2/1)

1933— WALLACE MUHAMMAD was born in Hamtramack, Michigan. Muhammad attended Muhammad's University of Islam, where he received vocational training as a welder.

1974— MUHAMMAD ALI regained his heavyweight championship title by knocking out George Foreman in the eighth round of a title fight in Kinshasa, Zaire.

31 October

1864— The Lincoln administration succeeded in getting Nevada admitted as the 36th state in the Union. Lincoln needed Nevada's vote to ratify his proposed Constitutional amendment banning slavery.

1900— ETHEL WATERS, singer and actor, was born in Chester, Pennsylvania. Waters spent years singing in dives and smokey nightclubs until she substituted for Florence Mills at New York's Plantation Club in 1923. Waters' presentations of "Dinah," "I'm Coming, Virginia" and other hits of the era endeared her to audiences and her career was launched. At age 12, Waters earned $4.75 a week as a maid and laundress in a Philadelphia hotel. At age 37, she commanded $2,000 per week.

November

The right of citizens of the United States to vote ... shall not be denied or abridged by the United States or any State by reason of failure to pay any poll tax or other tax. — Article XXIV of the United States Constitution

This month:

1945 — Publisher JOHN H. JOHNSON distributed the first issue of *Ebony* magazine. Johnson and *Ebony* celebrated their 50th anniversary in 1995.

1951 — Educator and writer W.E.B. DU BOIS was tried for failing to register as a subversive. He was acquitted. (See also 2/23; 5/31)

1 November

1964 — The Cleveland Browns' JIM BROWN became the first football player to rush for more than 10,000 yards, ending the '64 season with 10,135 yards rushing in his career. In 1965, his last year in football, Brown had rushed for a then record 12,312 yards.

1990 — The National Center of Institutions and Alternatives released a report indicating 33 percent of African American men in California, from ages 20 to 29, were in jails, prisons or under the supervision of the courts while on parole or probation.

1991 — The California Supreme Court overturned a death sentence given to JOSE LEON FUENTES, a Cuban immigrant charged with the murder of an armored car guard during a 1980 robbery attempt.

Fuentes' attorney appealed the sentence, telling the court that the prosecution "improperly" excluded African American jurors under a 1975 state supreme court ruling that barred the exclusion of jurors because of their race. Of the 13 prospective jurors, 10 were African American. However, all 13 were successfully challenged. Fuentes lost his appeal and remains a prisoner of the California prison system.

2 November

1983 — Legislation designating January 15 a national holiday in celebration of the birthday of the Rev. MARTIN LUTHER KING, JR., was signed in the White House Rose Garden by President Ronald Reagan. (See also 1/14)

1990 — The election of Louisiana trial judges in ten districts were put on hold when the U.S. Supreme Court temporarily agreed with a group of African Americans who said the scheduled elections violated the Federal Voting Rights Act of 1965. In their emergency request to the court, the plaintiffs argued that the districts and the scheduled election date were invalid because Louisiana had not sought and received Justice Department approval as required by the Voting Rights Act.

1991—While reviewing 72 hours of radio transmissions made in 1990, Alameda, California, police officials discovered transmissions in which four White officers used racial slurs and comments in a series of radio exchanges about African American residents of this mostly military city across the Bay from San Francisco. The officers apparently were unconcerned about jokingly discussing killing a "nigger" or dressing up in Ku Klux Klan regalia. The following are transmissions made late afternoon on Oct. 27, 1990, as reported by the San Francisco *Chronicle*:

5:12 P.M. "Nigger night."

5:13 P.M. "Don't do this to me."

8:18 P.M. "I hear those drums a poundin', they're poundin' round the bend, I ain't been to (Name deleted) since I don't know when, stuck in Alameda going to kill me a nigger."

8:41 P.M. "Was that Johnny Cash or Credence Clearwater Revival? Either way I like it. Makes me proud to be an American. Ain't it great to be a honky?" (Although some officers were either suspended or fired, the transmissions angered NAACP officials and set the stage for a lengthy debate among Alameda residents, conservatives, liberals and minorities.)

3 November

1933—Birth date of Health and Human Services Department Secretary LOUIS SULLIVAN in Atlanta, Georgia.

1949—Boxer LARRY HOLMES was born in Cuthbert, Georgia. After dropping out of school at age 13, Holmes became an amateur boxer and began working for the heavyweight title, which he won in 1970. He won the World Boxing Council Championship after a bout with KEN NORTON, and later became International Boxing Federation Champion. Holmes beat Norton in a 1978 re-match, Muhammad Ali in October 1980, and won decisions over Trevor Berbick and LEON SPINKS. MICHAEL SPINKS ended Holmes' championship reign in September 1985 with a unanimous 15-round decision.

Holmes defended his title 21 times and came out of retirement numerous times in an attempt to regain his title.

4 November

1987—Army Lt. Gen. COLIN LUTHER POWELL was chosen national security advisor to President Ronald Reagan. The former commander of the 5th Army Corps in West Germany, Powell succeeded Frank Carlucci, who became secretary of defense with the resignation of Caspar Weinberger. (See also 4/5; 9/21; 10/1)

5 November

1931—In Clarksdale, Mississippi, the birthday of singer and musician IKE TURNER. He was Ike in the "Ike & Tina Turner Review" and was once married to Tina Turner. (See also 11/26)

1968—SHIRLEY CHISHOLM of New York City became the first African American woman elected to the House of Representatives and the first African American to run for president of the United States. (See also 11/30)

6 November

1746—ABSALOM JONES, founder of St. Thomas Episcopal Church of Philadelphia, was born in Sussex, Delaware. Jones learned to read with the help of a clerk in a store where he once worked. He later married a slave woman and, working together, the Joneses purchased the wife's freedom first because the status of the child was determined by the mother. By 1784 both were free and the Joneses acquired their own home and built two others. Jones became well known in St. George's Methodist Episcopal Church. However, after White trustees at St. George's hauled the Jones and (Richard) Allen families from their knees during worship, Jones and Allen founded Mother Bethel AME Church which opened in 1794. St. Thomas was opened by Jones the same year. Jones was instrumental in forming an African American infantry unit for the War of 1812 and was the first African American Grand Master of Masonry in the United States. (See also 9/1)

1946— Jazz pianist ART TATUM died in Los Angeles. He was 46.

1973— CLARENCE LIGHTNER of Raleigh, North Carolina, and COLEMAN YOUNG of Detroit, Michigan, were elected mayors of their respective cities. His election marked the fifth term for Young.

1990— The Arizona electorate rejected a ballot initiative that would have recognized MARTIN LUTHER KING, JR's birthday as a state holiday. (See also 11/20)

7 November

1775— Lord John Murray Dunmore, the last royal governor of Virginia, offered freedom to those male slaves who joined the British armed forces in the Revolutionary War. There are no records to show how many slaves accepted Dunmore's offer.

1950— Birthday, in Lansing, Michigan, of ALEXA CANADY, the first African American woman to become a neurosurgeon. Canady studied medicine at the University of Michigan.

1967— CARL B. STOKES was elected mayor of Cleveland, Ohio. In winning the election, Stokes became the first African American elected mayor of a major U.S. city. Cleveland, at the time of Stokes' election, was the seventh largest American city in the nation.

1975— ANGELA DAVIS returned to teaching for the first time since her 1969 ouster from the University of California at Los Angeles faculty. Davis began a series of lectures on Black Women for the Black Studies Center at the privately owned Claremont colleges in Southern California. (See also 1/26)

1989— Off-year election summary:
* Virginia Lt. Gov. LAWRENCE DOUGLAS WILDER became the nation's first popularly elected African American governor after defeating a Republican challenger. Wilder, Virginia's first African American state senator, defeated J. Marshall Coleman by an estimated 8,000 votes. State election officials honored Coleman's demand for a recount. There are no significant changes in the election results. (See also 1/14; 1/17; 1/26; 11/27)
* Manhattan borough president DAVID DINKINS handily beat back a challenge by former U.S. Attorney Rudolph Giuliani to become New York City's first African American mayor.
* Detroit Mayor COLEMAN YOUNG defeated Tom Barrow for a fifth term. It was Barrow's second attempt to unseat Young.
* Ohio State Senator MICHAEL WHITE was elected mayor of Cleveland, Ohio.
* Five-term State Senator JOHN DANIELS became the first African American mayor of New Haven, Connecticut.
* Seattle, Washington, residents chose Councilman NORMAN RICE as their mayor. Rice will be the first African American elected to head this Pacific Northwest city.
* In Houston, Texas, city council candidate BEVERLY CLARK unseated longtime Councilman James Westmoreland. During a pre-election council meeting to discuss renaming the Houston Airport for the late Rep. Mickey Leland, Westmoreland cracked to reporters that the airport should be named "Nigger International" if it was renamed for Leland. Westmoreland denied being a racist and apologized for his remark. Apparently, his actions were too little too late.

1990— The National Association of Black Journalists' hierarchy reversed an earlier decision to provide, at the request of the New York *Daily News*, names of association members whom *News* officials intended to hire as replacements for striking employees. Association officials decided earlier to provide the *News* with a list, but decided against that action after being criticized. One day later the National Association of Hispanic Journalists and the Asian-American Journalists Association declined to be drawn into the bitter and violent dispute between the *News* and its striking employees.

1990—A massive boycott of Dade County, Florida, public schools was staged by African American students, teachers, and bus drivers as a protest against the appointment of a Cuban-American as school superintendent. African Americans supported one of their own, TEE S. GREER, who was interim superintendent during the selection process. The boycotters pointed out that Greer is more experienced and has a doctorate in education, both attributes lacking in the appointee, Octavio Visierdo.

1991—Baltimore Mayor KURT SCHMOKE handily defeated Republican attorney Samuel Culotta by winning 72 percent of the votes cast.

1991—Rock legend JIMI HENDRIX was inducted into the Rock and Roll Hall of Fame. Hendrix died a drug-related death on September 18, 1970.

8 November

1933—Actress ESTER ROLLE was born in Pompano Beach, Florida.

1988—On Election Day, Democrats in Orange County, California, accused Republicans of voter intimidation by hiring uniformed security guards to ask minority voters what "qualifications" did they have that entitled them to vote. The guards, posted in minority-dominant precincts, also carried signs announcing: "Non-citizens Can't Vote." The Orange County district attorney, the California attorney general and the Federal Bureau of Investigation are investigating. The Associated Press reports "at least 12 Hispanics said they were intimidated by the guards and did not vote." Hispanic voters filed a lawsuit claiming that they and other ethnic minorities were threatened by the guards. A $480,000 settlement was reached. The county registrar of voters settled for $20,000, the security agency $60,000, and the Orange County Republican Party settled for $400,000. In addition, workers at

the polling sites were given extra training about illegal activity in or around a polling place. California State laws were also amended to prevent reoccurrence of this type of political action. (See also 10/21)

1990—FBI agents arrested and jailed Walter Leroy Moody, Jr., on a 70-count indictment, including making the two mail bombs that killed ROBERT ROBINSON, a Savannah, Georgia, alderman, lawyer and NAACP activist, and Federal Judge Robert S. Vance, who sat on the Atlanta District U.S. Court of Appeals. Moody also is charged with mailing bombs to the NAACP's Jacksonville, Florida, office.

1991—In Inglewood, Los Angeles Lakers basketball star EARVIN "Magic" JOHNSON announced that he had tested positive for the AIDS virus and that he planned to retire from professional basketball. Johnson played again in the '92 Olympics Games and came out of retirement to coach the Lakers in 1994 and play again in 1996. Johnson announced his second "retirement" at the end of the 1996 season to focus on his business ventures.

1991—Sacramento Superior Court Presiding Judge James Ford turned aside the attempt by Placer County prosecutor Roland Iverson to challenge Judge James Long, who was assigned the retrial of KENNETH WILLIAMS, a man charged with the rape and murder of a 22-year-old Roseville, California, woman a dozen years earlier. Williams is an African American and his alleged victim was White. Judge Ford's action was in response to a petition by the state attorney general to accept Iverson's challenge of Judge Long.

9 November

1731—BENJAMIN BANNEKER was born free in Elicott Mills, Maryland. He was a mathematician, inventor, astronomer and one of a team of surveyors headed by Pierre Charles L'Enfant, who was appointed by President George Washington to plan a permanent site for a U.S. Capitol. L'Enfant left and Banneker took charge, assuming responsibility for the project's completion. Banneker's legacy is now known as Washington, D.C. In 1761, Banneker invented a wooden clock, the first built in the United States of America. He authored six almanacs, such as *Benjamin Banneker's Pennsylvania, Delaware, Maryland, and Virginia Almanac* between 1791 and 1797. In September of 1987, archaeologists aided by volunteers were involved in a dig at Banneker's Maryland homestead at Oella, 15 miles west of Baltimore.

1935— Former St. Louis Cardinal pitcher BOB GIBSON was born in Omaha, Nebraska. Voted into the Baseball Hall of Fame in 1981, Gibson spent 17 seasons with the St. Louis Cardinals. He won 251 games and lost 174 in the 3,884 innings that he pitched. Gibson's World Series record was seven wins against two losses, between 1964 and 1968.

1990— Police in Phoenix City, Alabama, frequently checked a wooded area where, in early October, a group of African American children reported being chased by people dressed in costumes not unlike those worn by members of the Ku Klux Klan. Less than a week before that incident, an African American man with an electrical cord twisted around his neck was found hanging from a tree. In July, the body of a second African American man was found in the Chattahoochee River. Assistant Police Chief PRESTON ROBINSON said authorities believe someone chased the children, ages 7 to 9. However, the children's accounts are inconsistent and "difficult to substantiate," Robinson added.

10 November

1898— In Wilmington, North Carolina, White supremacists invaded the "Negro district," burned houses, killed and injured people and chased the remaining African Americans out of town.

1990— Standard University historian CLAYBORNE CARSON while reviewing the writings of the Rev. Martin Luther King, Jr., discovered King used material plagiarized from the writings of Jack Boozer and Paul Tillich/Henry Nelson Weiman while working on his dissertation at Boston College. King earned a doctorate in theology from Boston College in 1955. King's widow, Coretta King, was told about the discovery more than a year earlier. (See also 1/10; 1/12; 1/13; 1/14; 1/15; 1/19; 3/11; 4/4; 4/11; 4/27; 8/25; 8/28; 8/29; 10/8; 10/13; 10/14; 11/2; 11/7; 11/11; 11/20; 11/21; 12/1; 12/9)

11 November

1914— Author and newspaper publisher DAISY BATES was born in Huttig, Arkansas. A past president of the Arkansas chapter of the National Association for the Advancement of Colored People, Bates' family established the *Arkansas State Press*. Bates is the author of *The Long Shadow of Little Rock*.

1928— Birthday of jazz vocalist ERNESTINE ANDERSON, in Houston, Texas. Anderson sang and travelled with several major bands in the transitional period when swing, while remaining popular, gave way to rock and roll. For example, Anderson worked with blues artist Johnny Otis and jazz vibraphonist Lionel Hampton.

1946— Birth date of MILTON L. OLIVE in Chicago, Illinois. In 1996, he was posthumously awarded the Congressional Medal of Honor for heroism in Vietnam.

1987— U.S. Interior Secretary Donald Hodel announced plans for a national memorial to the 5,000 African American Civil War veterans in Constitution Gardens, between the Lincoln Memorial and Washington Monument. The memorial is not for African Americans, according to lawyer Maurice A. Barboza, who started the project, but rather a memorial to the struggle for freedom.

12 November

1896— First Sgt. MOSES WILLIAMS, 9th U.S. Cavalry, received the Congressional Medal of Honor for bravery under fire in action against "hostiles" in the Cucillo Negro Mountains of New Mexico Territory.

1922— Six teachers in Indianapolis, Indiana, founded Sigma Gamma Rho sorority based on a desire to raise the standards of teachers in normal and other schools, a goal proposed by MARY LOU ALLISON LITTLE. Little was joined by DOROTHY HANLEY WHITESIDE, VIVIAN WHITE MARBURY, NANNIE MAE GAHN JOHNSON, HATTIE MAE DUBLIN REDFORD, BESSIE M. DOWNEY and CUBENE McCLURE. Little, who now lives in Los Angeles, and Marbury, who still lives in Indianapolis, are the sole surviving founders. The sorority is headquartered in Chicago.

1933— California State Senator DIANA WATSON was born in Los Angeles, California.

1989— In Lafayette, Louisiana, Creole PAUL CLUSE helped found Creole, Inc., to help nearly one-half million French speaking African Americans preserve their southwestern Louisiana culture.

1990— A collection of documents relating to the history of the Black Panthers was returned to ELDRIDGE CLEAVER, a former Panther leader. Cleaver temporarily forfeited ownership of the papers pending a $500 settlement for $900 in overdue fees for storage space Cleaver rented in Berkeley. The papers were sold for $25 at an auction by owners of the rental facility. However, they were returned to Cleaver on this date. Cleaver said the collection included tapes of telephone conversations between foreign governments and Panther Party officials. He has promised to donate the material to the Bancroft Library at the University of California, Berkeley, along with other documents and tapes stored in Oakland and Paris.

13 November

1956— The U.S. Supreme Court ruled unconstitutional a Montgomery, Alabama, law calling for segregated buses in that city's transit system.

14 November

1915— BOOKER T. WASHINGTON died of a heart attack at Tuskegee Institute.

1990— New York's African American-owned Freedom National Bank was declared insolvent by the Federal Deposit Insurance Corp. The FNB had deposits of $101.9 million and 92 employees, and most of its depositors were non-profit, charitable organizations. The FDIC paid depositors 50 cents for every dollar on deposit at FNB, compared to full value for those with money in the Bank of New England, which failed a few weeks later.

15 November

Basketball great BILL RUSSELL, named coach of the Boston Celtics, became the first African American to coach a National Basketball Association team. (See also 2/12; 4/18)

16 November

1967— Birthday of actress LISA BONET. Bonet was born in San Francisco, California.

1991— The U.S. Commission on Civil Rights announced plans to investigate racial problems across the nation. The announcement came almost three decades after Bill Moore, a White ex–Marine, was shot to death in Keener, Alabama. Moore, apparently a compassionate man who believed in fairness, doggedly worked at his own anti-segregation protest. Moore's activities, a cross country walk, ended with the crack of a rifle near a walnut tree in Keener. Keenerites cut the tree down, fearing it might attract tourists. Everything else in Keener is pretty much the same as it was April 23, 1963, when Moore was shot to death. An investigator found the weapon believed used in the shooting but local law enforcement officials, reportedly have failed to press prosecutors to bring the guilty to justice. That also has not changed.

A number of civil rights–related deaths remain to be solved, according to the Southern Poverty Law Center. Herbert Lee was advised to stop helping African Americans register to vote. In September 1961, Lee was shot to death inside a cotton gin in Liberty, Mississippi. A state legislator fired the weapon, but a coroner's jury based its verdict on the later-recanted testimony of an African American witness, who testified that Lee had a tire iron.

LOUIS ALLEN, who witnessed the Lee shooting, promised to tell the truth about the shooting if given federal protection for his family. He was ambushed, in 1964, and shot to death in his driveway. No one has ever been charged with his murder. The investigation failed to solve any of these crimes.

1991— Soon Ja Du, a Korean shopkeeper, shot and fatally wounded LATASHA HAR-LINS, 15, after the two scuffled over a bottle of orange juice valued at $1.79. Harlins had turned her back on Du and was leaving the store when Du shot her in the head. Los Angeles County Superior Court Judge Joyce Karlin sentenced Du to five years' probation and 400 hours of community service. Judge Karlin's seemingly light sentence ignored a probation report that recommended a maximum sentence of 16 years.

17 November

1801— AMOS FORTUNE, a former slave and resident of Jaffrey, New Hampshire, died at age 91. Fortune left the city of Jaffrey $233 to be used for educational purchases, and another $100 for the Jaffrey Congregational Church to buy a pewter communion service. The outgrowth of that bequest was the Amos Fortune Fund, which has grown significantly. Fortune, who gained prominence as a tanner, was

born in Africa, brought to the colonies in 1725 at age 15, and sold at auction in Boston.

1901— Birthday of GLADYS MER-RITT ROSS, co-founder of Phi Delta Kappa International, the African American teachers sorority. Ross was born in Jersey City, New Jersey. (See also 5/6)

1911— The Omega Psi Phi fraternity was founded at Howard University by EDGAR A. LOVE, OSCAR J. COOPER, ERNEST E. JUST and FRANK COLE-MAN.

1916— Civil rights activist WINSON HUDSON was born in Carthage, Mississippi. (See also 7/29)

1945— Basketball standout ELVIN HAYES was born in Rayville, Louisiana.

18 November

1955— ROY WILKINS was named executive secretary of the National Association for the Advancement of Colored People.

1991— California Lt. Gov. Leo Mc-Carthy said there is evidence that the Ku Klux Klan and other White supremacist groups are recruiting members from among school-aged children attending California schools.

19 November

1921— Birth date in Homestead, Pennsylvania, of former Brooklyn Dodgers catcher ROY CAMPANELLA, who was paralyzed by an automobile accident.

20 November

1867— Howard University was founded.

1925— U.S. Attorney General Robert Kennedy was born in Brookline, Massachusetts.

1989— Air Force Col. FREDERICK C. GREGORY became the first African American astronaut to command a space shuttle mission with the launch of *Discovery* from Cape Canaveral, Florida. (See also 1/7)

1990— The celebration of Martin Luther King, Jr. Day became a reality for employees of Pima County, Arizona, while the remainder of the state debated the merits of another federal holiday. Supervisors expressed hope that their Maricopa County peers would follow their lead and spur the state legislature to action. Two proposals creating a King holiday in the state were rejected by the Arizona electorate in the general election held earlier this month. (See also 11/6/90)

1990— The U.S. Treasury Department's Bureau of Engraving and Printing officially ended what have been called "practices to keep African American workers in low-paying, low-skilled jobs." The agreement involves nearly 250 current and past Bureau employees and ends eight years of litigation during which African American employees said they were denied higher paying jobs as bookbinders, printers and press operators. The agreement, reached in U.S. District Court for the District of Columbia, suspended written tests for selected apprentices for craft jobs and reduced the apprenticeship period. It also set aside 72 bookbinder and press operator apprenticeships to be filled from within the Bureau. Previously, White workers, brought in from private industry by friends and relatives, received preferential treatment.

1990— Led by Rep. RONALD DELLUMS, D-California, 45 Democrats in the House of Representatives joined in a lawsuit seeking to prevent President Bush from declaring war against Iraq. Iraqi President Saddam Hussein ordered his armed forces to invade and occupy the tiny sheikdom of Kuwait. The lawsuit failed, but a sympathetic court commented that the suit would have had greater merit had more members of the House joined the effort. At issue was a dispute between Bush's staff and the House over the president's need for Congressional approval before declaring war on another nation.

1991— A conviction of drug dealing charges earned TOMETRIUS PAXTON a four-year sentence to quarters in a California state prison. The charges against Paxton were dismissed after an investigation disclosed that the arresting officer had made up details about Paxton's behavior to support the arrest. The 19-year-old Paxton, a passenger in a car, fled after police made a routine traffic stop. Officers who took Paxton into custody reportedly found less than two dozen rocks of crack cocaine in his pockets and a handgun believed to belong to the teenager. According to the *San Francisco Chronicle*, Sgt. Benny Pugh of the East Palo Alto Police Department said he recognized Paxton as a wanted fugitive. San Mateo County District Attorney James Fox, later determined that Pugh could not have known about any outstanding warrants. There was no legal reason for Paxton's arrest, according to Fox.

21 November

1949— Baseball great JACKIE ROBINSON was awarded the Freedom Foundation Medal by President Dwight D. Eisenhower.

1990— Bearing the sting of charges of racism, the Illinois State Police issued public apologies after finding a Missouri mother and three of her seven children in their car floating in the Cache River eight weeks after the occupants were reported missing. The family's car was only a few hundred feet from a state police substation. Relatives had reported RUBY LEE FELTUS and three of her seven children missing when they failed to return to their home in Hayti, Missouri, after attending an October 2 birthday party in Mt. Vernon, Illinois. The trip would have been a four-to-five hour drive. The relatives were unable to convince authorities to conduct a search. Law enforcement authorities took no action until the Illinois relatives contacted Johnny Scott, president of the local NAACP chapter. Police wanted to know if the family was involved with drugs and, when told no, suggested the family may have just "taken a vacation." There were no news reports on the missing mother and her children until Scott telephoned local newspapers. Strangely, a trooper spotted the partially submerged car but felt the vehicle looked older and rustier than Feltus' Camaro and ignored it. The car was spotted November 15 by a television news helicopter that radioed Missouri authorities, who passed the information to Illinois troopers at the substation near the car. Authorities claimed that the car had been investigated and that it was not the right one. A November 19 decision by Illinois police at the substation to check the car yielded the decomposed bodies of Feltus and two of her children. A search was begun for the third and was eventually found.

22 November

1930 — The African American Black Muslim movement was organized in Detroit, Michigan.

1942 — Air Force Col. GUION S. BLUFORD, JR., was born in Philadelphia, Pennsylvania. Assigned to NASA as an astronaut, Bluford, a fighter pilot, became the first African American in space as a crew member on a 1985 mission aboard the shuttle *Columbia*. Bluford is a 1964 graduate of Pennsylvania State University. He earned a master of science degree in aerospace engineering from the Air Force Institute of Technology in 1974, and a doctorate in the same field with a minor in laser physics four years later.

1943 — Navy Messman DORIE MILLER died of wounds he received while defending the USS *Arizona* during the December 1941 attack on Pearl Harbor, Hawaii. (See also 11/24)

1963 — President John F. Kennedy was assassinated in Dallas, Texas.

1990 — Businessman, peace advocate and former comedian DICK GREGORY began a fast in protest of the military buildup in Saudi Arabia. The fast began at Plymouth Rock, Massachusetts. Gregory vowed to continue the fast until all U.S. military personnel then in Saudi Arabia were back in the United States. (See also 10/12)

1990 — The U.S. Census Bureau admitted its census workers undercounted residents of Detroit, Michigan, by more than 22,000. The recount included residents serving in the military at out of city/state bases when the first count was taken, and people out of the city at winter homes. The revised count meant continued federal funds for the mostly African American populated city.

1990 — Voters in several states, including California, approved ballot initiatives that limit to two the terms of elected state and municipal government law makers. In Kansas City, Kansas, incumbent city council members CHARLES HAZLEY, an African American, and Robert Hernandez, who is Hispanic, filed suit after discovering Kansas' new law would bar their re-election. Hazley and Hernandez say the law conflicts with the Voting Rights Act of 1973 in that it restricts the choice of candidates for minority voters.

23 November

1922 — With full page advertisements in the *New York Times*, *Atlanta Constitution* and several other leading newspapers of the day, the National Association for the Advancement of Colored People began its anti-lynching campaign. Earlier the NAACP had persuaded Rep. L. C. Dyer of Missouri to sponsor a bill "to assure to persons within the jurisdiction of every state the equal protection of the laws, and to punish the crime of lynching." The measure was adopted by the House of Representatives by a 230–119 vote, but died in the Senate where Southern states blocked a vote with a well organized filibuster. (Other legislation intended to outlaw lynching was introduced in 1935 and in 1940, but each failed in the face of still Southern opposition.)

24 November

1865 — The state of Mississippi passed the so-called "Black Codes" that barred African Americans from jury service, testifying against Whites in trials, bearing arms and attending White schools.

1868 — Composer and musician SCOTT JOPLIN was born in Texarkana, Texas. Joplin was the best known of the ragtime composers. His "I'm Just Wild About Harry," became a national hit.

1870 — ROBERT SENGSTACKE ABBOTT, born this day on St. Simons Island off the Georgia coast, became a printer at the *Savannah News*. Abbott left the South, moving to Chicago where he earned a law degree from Kent College of Law and began a practice in Chicago, Illinois, and Gary, Indiana. Abandoning his law practice, Abbott — with 25 cents and a lot of help from friends — published the first edition of the *Chicago Defender* newspaper. Abbott died in 1940 and, in 1944, the U.S. Maritime Commission named a Liberty Ship — the *Robert S. Abbott* — in his honor. (See also 5/5)

1935 — Rep. RONALD V. DELLUMS was born in Oakland, California.

1938 — OSCAR ROBERTSON, star professional basketball player, was born in Charlotte, Tennessee.

1919 — Naval hero DORIE MILLER was born in Waco, Texas. Miller joined the Navy at age 19 and, as most African Americans who joined the Navy in that era, became a mess attendant aboard the USS *Arizona*. During the attack on Pearl Harbor, Miller, although untrained as a gunner, manned an anti-aircraft gun and shot down four Japanese aircraft. Miller was the first hero of World War II and, in May 1942, was awarded the Navy Cross for heroism by Admiral Chester W. Nimitz. Several efforts have been made to upgrade Miller's award to the Medal of Honor, but none have been successful. He is still one of the few sailors to be personally decorated by Admiral Nimitz.

25 November

1908 — ADAM CLAYTON POWELL, JR., civil rights activist, past minister of Abyssinian Baptist Church and U.S. Congressman, was born in New Haven, Connecticut. Powell was educated at Townsend Harris Preparatory School, which accepted only students with an "A" average, City College (New York) and Colgate University. In 1944, he was elected to a seat in the House of Representatives which he held more than six consecutive terms. Powell became chairman of the House Labor and Education Committee, a position he used to bargain for the rights of African Americans. (See 1/10; 3/1; 4/4; 4/11)

1937 — College and professional basketball standout and NBA coach LENNY WILKENS was born in the Brooklyn, New York, community of Bedford-Stuyvesant. Former coach of the Seattle Supersonics and the Cleveland Cavaliers, Wilkens then coached the Atlanta Hawks. Wilkens is the all-time NBA leader with more than 1,000 coaching victories, and he also coached the 1996 U.S. Olympic team.

1990 — A resolution setting aside a day to honor FRED HAMPTON, a leader of the Black Panther Party, triggered a pitch battle between Chicago elected city officials — those who support the measure and those who do not. Hampton and MARK CLARK, another Black Panther leader, were shot to death in bed during a 1969 Chicago police raid on their apartment. After giving unanimous approval for a Fred Hampton Day, one White alderman said their action was an error, and that the majority of the aldermen believed the day was to honor then Chicago Bears defensive tackle Dan Hampton, who is White. Sixteen aldermen changed their votes, while the remainder — 12 White, 18 African American and four Hispanics — still favored the resolution. It was hoped the measure would soothe feathers ruffled over past racial disputes and promote racial harmony, according to the *New York Times*. (See also 12/4)

1991 — Virginia Gov. L. DOUGLAS WILDER disclosed that his gubernatorial campaign received a financial boost from three African American fraternal organizations whose existence began at Howard and Virginia Union universities. The groups are the Boules (Sigma Phi Phi), Guardsmen (Omega Psi) and Ques (Phi).

26 November

1797 — SOJOURNER TRUTH (originally named Isabella Baumfree) was born a slave in Ulster County, New York. An illiterate, Truth knew the Bible by heart and was a most effective speaker for the abolition of slavery and an advocate of women's rights. Truth won her freedom under the New York Emancipation Act of 1827. When nearly 70 years of age, Truth worked in refugee camps, the Freedman's Hospital and, it is said, used her spare time to integrate Washington, D.C., streetcars. She died in Battle Creek, Michigan, in 1883.

1938 — Pop/soul singer Tina Turner was born ANNIE MAE BULLOCK in Nutbush, Tennessee. She and Ike Turner, to whom she was once married, comprised the "Ike & Tina Turner Review." Later she had a Grammy-winning career as a solo artist. (See also 11/5)

1946 — Former Oakland Raiders offensive tackle and former team coach ART SHELL, a graduate of Maryland State Eastern Shore College, was born in Charleston, South Carolina. (See also 10/2)

27 November

1894 — Sgt. JOHN DENNY, 9th U.S. Cavalry received the Congressional Medal of Honor for bravery under fire 15 years earlier at Las Animas Canyon, New Mexico.

1944 — The late Rep. MICKEY LELAND, D-Texas, was born in Lubbock, Texas. Leland was killed when the plane in which he was a passenger crashed somewhere in southwestern Ethiopia. Leland was en route to a refugee camp during a visit to Ethiopia.

1989 — The Virginia Board of Elections certified the results of the state's November 7 general election in which Lt. Gov. L. DOUGLAS WILDER, a Democrat, defeated Republican J. Marshall Coleman by less than 6,800 votes. Coleman earlier announced his intent to demand a recount if

Wilder's victory margin was less than 9,000 votes. However, unlike Republican party officials, Coleman's priority seemed to be more about becoming governor and less about the image of the party should a recount support Wilder's slim victory margin. Wilder garnered 57 percent of the vote in his successful 1985 run for lieutenant governor. (See also 1/14; 1/17; 1/26; 11/7; 11/9; 11/25)

28 November

1929 — Motown recording executive BERRY GORDY, JR., was born in Detroit, Michigan.

1949 — Dancer BILL "Bojangles" ROBINSON died in New York City.

29 November

1780 — Birthday of LEMUEL HAYNES, in Torrington, Connecticut. Haynes was the first African American Congregational minister licensed to preach in a White church.

1900 — In Jasper County, Mississippi, the birthday of the late GILBERT LINDSAY, a 27-year member of the Los Angeles city council who represented the city's Ninth District. (See also 12/28)

30 November

1924 — Birthday of former Rep. SHIRLEY CHISHOLM, a 1969 candidate for president of the United States of America. Chisholm was born in the borough of Brooklyn, New York. (See also 11/5)

1953 — Rep. MIKE ESPY, D-Mississippi, was born in Yazoo City, Mississippi. Espy was an assistant attorney general in charge of consumer protection prior to his election, in 1986, to the House of Representatives.

1986 — An African American Citadel cadet and the NAACP sued the military academy following an incident in which White students wearing sheets broke into the African American student's room, chanted obscenities, and left a burning paper cross.

December

I would never be of any service to anyone as a slave.

— Nat Turner

1 December

1955 — ROSA PARKS was arrested after refusing to give up her seat on a Montgomery, Alabama, transit bus for a White man. The Montgomery bus boycott, led by the Rev. Martin Luther King, Jr., began two days later. (See also 2/4)

1990 — U.S. Navy Rear Admiral ROBERT L. TONEY retired from active duty in Oakland, California, where he attended elementary school after his family migrated to the Bay Area from Monroe, Louisiana, where Toney was born August 30, 1934. Toney will draw on his 32 years as a naval officer in his new non-military post as president of the Oakland chamber of commerce. Toney studied two years at Youngstown University, but graduated from California State University, Chico, in 1957, and was commissioned an ensign in the fall of 1957. Toney was executive officer of two ships before a posting to his first command, the ammunition ship *Kiska*. Toney was given command of the fleet oiler *Roanoke* in 1983 and promoted to flag rank in September 1984. Toney was promoted to rear admiral in May 1988.

1991 — According to the *San Francisco Examiner*, 82 percent of California schoolteachers are White. Of their students, 54 percent are minorities, many of whom speak one or more of the 90 languages now spoken in California schools.

2 December

1859 — Abolitionist John Brown, leader of the assault on Harpers Ferry, was executed in Charles Town, West Virginia. (See also 5/9)

1898 — BLANCHE K. BRUCE, the second African American elected to the U.S. Senate, died at his District of Columbia home. (See also 3/1)

1987 — Novelist JAMES BALDWIN died in France. (See also 8/24)

1989 — Dancer and choreographer ALVIN AILEY, founder 31 years earlier of the Alvin Ailey American Dance Theater, died. Ailey's ballets have been a part of the repertoires of other companies. Among them are the American Ballet Theater, Joffrey Ballet, London Festival Ballet, Paris Opera Ballet and the Royal Danish Ballet. (See also 1/5)

1991 — West Coast newspapers recently discovered savings and loans — many are now called "savings banks" — rejected 39 percent of the African Americans and Hispanic Americans who applied for home loans in 1991. Rejection rates for African Americans and Hispanics are respectively 67 percent and 64 percent higher than those for White applicants. California legislators have held hearings on the matter and more are planned. However, the Assembly and Senate have not discussed what action should be taken.

3 December

1986 — In Gretna, Louisiana, the sheriff of Jefferson Parish announced plans to stop and question all African Americans found in the New Orleans suburb. Sheriff Henry Lee, who is Chinese, said the stops will reduce crime in the area. (See also 12/4)

1991 — Tom Metzger, the former grand dragon of the California Ku Klux Klan, was sentenced to six months in jail, three years' probation and 300 hours of community service for his part in a 1983 cross burning. Metzger, a long time White supremacist, once hired bikers to handle security for Klan functions in Southern California. Stanley Witek and Brad Kelley received the same sentences as Metzger.

4 December

1906 — Alpha Phi Alpha fraternity was founded at Cornell University. The founders were HENRY CALLIS, CHARLES CHAPMAN, EUGENE JONES, GEORGE KELLEY, NATHANIEL MURRAY, ROBERT OGLE and VERTNER TANDY.

1969 — FRED HAMPTON, Chicago leader of the Black Panther Party, was shot to death by police while in his bed. The chief of security for the Panthers was an undercover police officer assigned to the FBI whose actions were part of the Bureau's counter-intelligence program against African American Nationalist groups in the U.S. Killed in the same raid was MARK CLARK, also a Chicago Black Panther Party leader. (See also 11/25)

1986 — In Gretna, Louisiana, Sheriff Henry Lee rescinded his order to stop and question African Americans found in Gretna, an affluent suburb of New Orleans. The practice was considered questionable under provisions of the U.S. Constitution. (See also 12/3)

5 December

1784 — Poet PHILLIS WHEATLEY died at age 30. In 1776, Gen. George Washington invited Wheatley to visit his Cambridge, Massachusetts, headquarters. Washington personally expressed his appreciation for poems Wheatley had written in his honor.

1870 — Novelist and playwright ALEXANDRE DUMAS died in Dieppe, France. (See also 7/24; 7/27)

1871 — Cowboy and rodeo performer BILL PICKETT, creator of bulldogging, was born to T. J. Pickett and Mary Virginia Elizabeth Gilbert in the Jenks-Branch Community, Travis County, Texas. Pickett's exact date of birth was perhaps his most closely guarded secret. Pickett died in 1932 from injuries received when he was kicked by a horse. During his life, Pickett demonstrated his considerable riding and roping skills in hundreds of performances, including one in London in 1914, for King George V and Queen Mary of England. (See also 4/2)

1935 — RICHARD WAYNE PENNIMAN, best known as Little Richard, was born in Macon, Georgia. Penniman's hits, including "Long Tall Sally," "Good Golly Miss Molly," "Tutti Fruitti" and "Ready Teddy," resulted in Penniman's billing himself as the "Georgia Peach" of soul music.

1990 — In Georgia it became a misdemeanor crime for Ku Klux Klan members to wear hooded masks in public after the State Supreme Court upheld a 1951 ban on masks. In their ruling, the justices called the law an expression of Georgia's interest in avoiding violence and intimidation. The challenge to the 39-year-old law was brought by Klansman Shade Miller, Jr., who was charged with wearing a mask in public. Miller's attack centered on his belief that the wearing of a mask was "symbolic speech" and thus subject to First Amendment protection. Miller argued successfully in lower court; however, the high court carried the day. The ruling was explicit. The ban on masks followed an era of "harassment, intimidation and violence against racial and religious minorities" carried out by masked Klansmen and other hate groups, according to an Associated Press report. (See also 11/9)

6 December

1869—The Colored National Labor Union was formed in Washington, D.C.

1990—In Riverdale, Georgia, two police officers resigned their jobs after a phony training tape they had made, which contained racial slurs directed at African Americans, was aired by a local television station. The tape was intended to be a spoof on handling African American suspects, but viewers heard one officer say "most blacks are criminals."

1990—In Atlanta, employees of the Federal Centers for Disease Control, who seem to spend much of their time compiling statistics about African Americans, released new data about the lifespan of African American males age 15 to 24. According to a CDC study, fatal shootings in California, Florida, Michigan, Missouri, New York and the District of Columbia accounted for 51 percent of the deaths of young African American men in 1987. Of all African American males in the 15 to 24 age group, 29 percent live in those five states and the District. The CDC data also showed 2,741 young men, age 15 to 24, were slain in 1988, an increase of 67 percent over 1984.

7 December

1874—A race riot in Vicksburg, Mississippi, left 75 African Americans dead.

1990—YOLANDA KING and ATALLAH SHABAZZ, respectively the daughters of the Rev. Martin Luther King, Jr., and Malcolm X, opted to meet an earlier commitment to perform in a play at the University of Arizona in Phoenix, despite November 6 voter rejection of a ballot initiative that would have established King's birthday as a state holiday. Shortly after the election, National Football League Commissioner Paul Tagliabue recommended the 1993 Super Bowl, scheduled to be held in Phoenix, be moved to another state, and this did ocur. (See also 12/9)

1990—Democratic members of the North Carolina legislature elected the first African American speaker of its House of Representatives since Reconstruction. The honor went to DANIEL BLUE, a lawyer. Blue said he plans to put together winning majorities in the 120 member House.

8 December

1925—Singer, dancer and actor SAMMY DAVIS, JR., was born in New York City. (See also 5/16; 5/18)

1989—In Capps, Florida, five of Ted Turner's neighbors were without electricity because Turner ignored their requests to allow power lines to cross a portion of his 8,100 acre estate. The estate manager said Turner was "complying with a former owner's restrictions."

1989—In Miami, Florida, a jury convicted Colombian born police officer William Lozano of manslaughter in the deaths of motorcyclist CLEMENT LLOYD and his passenger, ALLAN BLANCHARD. Lloyd was shot to death by Lozano, and Blanchard died of injuries he received when the motorcycle struck a car after Lloyd was shot. Lozano said he shot in self-defense because Lloyd was trying to run him down. When Lozano was acquitted in court, riots broke out in the streets. The acquittal still stood.

9 December

1922—In St. Louis, Missouri, comedian, actor and television star Redd Foxx was born JOHN ELROY SANFORD.

1938—Football great DAVID "Deacon" JONES was born in Eatonville, Florida.

1966—In Opelika, Alabama, a jury of 12 White men needed only 70 minutes of deliberation to find Marvin L. Segrest, 67, innocent of the fatal shooting of SAMUEL YOUNGE, JR., a 21-year-old Tuskegee Institute student. (See also 1/3)

1967 — At Edwards Air Force Base, California, Air Force Maj. ROBERT H. LAWRENCE, the first African American military pilot to complete astronaut training, was killed when his F-104 Starfighter jet crashed upon landing after a training flight. Lawrence was to have taken part in the Air Force's Manned Orbiting Laboratory program. (See also 6/30)

1990 — Actress YOLANDA KING, daughter of the Rev. MARTIN LUTHER KING, JR., who was assassinated in 1968 by James Earl Ray, opted not to honor a commitment to perform in Tucson, Arizona. King was to have appeared in the play *Stepping into Tomorrow* but changed her mind. King said it became apparent that her presence in Arizona "could and would be misconstrued" to be in conflict with the goals of a national King holiday proponents. (See also 1/13; 1/14; 5/15; 11/20; 11/21; 12/6)

10 December

1948 — The United Nations declared this date Human Rights Day in celebration of universal human rights.

1989 — Composer, arranger, musician, producer QUINCY JONES released his first new music in eight years with the album *Back on the Block*. Jones was backed up by the late Ella Fitzgerald, Dizzy Gillespie and rappers Ice-T and Kool Moe Dee. Others taking part included the late Sarah Vaughn, George Benson, Al Jarreau, James Moody, Barry White, Take 6, Herbie Hancock and the late Miles Davis. (See also 3/14)

11 December

1816 — The state of Indiana was admitted to the Union. Slavery was outlawed but African American residents were denied the right to vote and to serve in the state militia.

1929 — Army Maj. Gen. JOHN MITCHELL BROWN was born in Vicksburg, Mississippi.

1954 — Singer JERMAINE JACKSON, a member of the original Jackson Five, was born in Gary, Indiana.

1991 — Houston City Councilwoman BEVERLY CLARK cited racism as the culprit after she lost a runoff election to lawyer Gracie Saenz. Clark said she received an estimated 30 telephone calls from Houston voters who said they were "glad" that an African American was removed from public office.

12 December

1870 — JOSEPH H. RAINEY became the first African American seated in the U.S. House of Representatives.

1961 — Montgomery, Alabama, police arrested 737 of those who took part in a march protesting the trial of 11 Freedom Riders. As a result, African Americans organized a boycott of White Montgomery merchants.

1990 — In Fort Lauderdale, Florida, record store owner CHARLES FREEMAN was fined $1,000 plus court costs for selling the 2 Live Crew record album *As Nasty as They Wanna Be*, after a federal judge ruled it obscene. Freeman, owner of E. C. Records, could also have been sentenced to one year in federal prison. Elsewhere, three members of the rap group were acquitted of having performed the songs illegally at an adult only concert in October. And, in Texas, charges similar to those against Freeman, but lodged against a Texas record store owner, were dropped two days before fines were levied against Freeman. The earlier conviction of an Alabama record shop owner was overturned in February after review by an appellate court. (See also 6/8; 6/12; 10/4; 10/20)

1991 — Jazz trumpeter BUCK CLAYTON was born WILBUR DORSEY CLAYTON at Parsons, Kentucky, in 1911. He died December 8, 1991, in New York City. Clayton was once a leading soloist with Count Basie's band and accompanied singer Billie Holiday. In the '50s he formed the Buck Clayton Sextet, and he often worked with pianist Joe Buskin and musicians Tony Parenti and Jimmy Rushing. He appeared in the movies *The Benny Goodman Story* and *Jazz on a Summer's Day.*

13 December

1916— Light heavyweight boxing champion Archie Moore was born ARCHIBALD LEE WRIGHT in Benoit, Mississippi. Moore was secretive about his age, so the year of his birth is based on estimates by sports authorities and historians. He moved to San Diego in 1938 and enjoyed a successful, active boxing career for more than 25 years. Moore won the light heavyweight championship from Joey Maxim December 17, 1952, in St. Louis, Missouri. He was light heavyweight champion of the world from 1952 to 1961. He also made two unsuccessful challenges for the World Heavyweight Championship. Moore had 220 fights as a professional and won 136 of them by knockouts. Moore lived in San Diego, where he worked with troubled and disadvantaged youth, some of whom he had taken into his home. In his spare time, Moore worked to improve his near flawless Ping Pong play.

1921— Retired Army Maj. Gen. JAMES FRANK HAMLET, was born in Alliance, Ohio.

1944— A Presidential Order admitted African American women to the Navy WAVES (Women Accepted for Volunteer Emergency Service).

1986— The U.S. Air Force announced an additional 1600 jobs available to women. Included were crew positions on reconnaissance and electronic warfare planes.

1991— KEOVAN THOMPSON, a guest in the Los Angeles home of two White women, attacked his hosts after learning "Nigger" was the name of their pet black cat. According to police, one of the women told Thompson the cat's name, adding that she hoped he would not be offended. Thompson tried to strangle one woman and charged the other with a knife. Thompson was arrested and pleaded no contest to battery and was sentenced to two years' probation.

1991— Attorneys for ELMER GERONIMO PRATT, a former Black Panther Party leader and member, continued to work to free their client, who had been imprisoned 21 years. His attorneys said they had evidence that Pratt was at a Black Panther Party meeting the night of the robbery and murder for which he was convicted. The new information came from a wire tap log maintained by an FBI surveillance team. Pratt's case was transferred to Los Angeles, where his appeal failed.

14 December

1829— JOHN MERCER LANGSTON, the first African American elected to public office in the United States, was born on a plantation in Virginia. Langston was elected to the House of Representatives from Virginia in 1889, and served one term. En route to Congress, Langston gained experience as a member of the Brownhelm, Ohio, City Council; Oberlin, Ohio, Board of Education; school inspector general of the Freedmen's Bureau, dean of the Howard University Law School; minister-resident to Haiti; and president of Virginia Normal and Collegiate Institute.

1902— Businessman and politician BARNEY L. FORD died at Denver's St. Joseph's Hospital. He was 80. (See also 1/22)

1929— Baseball standout ELSTON GENE HOWARD died in New York City. Howard worked behind the plate, played first base and tracked down towering hits in the outfield during the 13 years he played America's favorite sport. (See also 2/23)

1963— Jazz and blues singer DINAH WASHINGTON, born RUTH JONES, died from an overdose of sleeping pills. (See also 8/29)

1990— Attorney MICHAEL L. WILLIAMS, assistant education secretary for civil rights, was unknown to most Americans outside Washington, D.C., until he called a December 12 press conference to comment on federal scholarship programs for minority students attending colleges and universities. Williams caught a lot of people off guard, including President Bush, when he told the media "race-exclusive scholarships," and those based on "ethnic origin" were illegal because they would be discriminatory. Colleges and universities awarding such scholarships could lose federal subsidies. Williams immediately gained Bush's attention and that of affected students and university administrators. Williams' interpretation of federal law — Title VI of the Civil Rights Act of 1964 — prohibits discrimination based on race, color or national origin in any program or activity receiving federal dollars. The president's call for a review of Williams' announcement put on hold any implementation of a new policy in this area.

15 December

1791— The first 10 amendments to the U.S. Constitution, known as the "Bill of Rights," were ratified. They are celebrated on this date, which is Bill of Rights Day.

1870— The Christian and or Colored Methodist Episcopal Church was formed in Tennessee and Georgia by disgruntled former members of the African Methodist Episcopal Zion Church, who were unhappy with church leadership.

1944—American troops in Belgium were almost surrounded by German infantry and armored divisions before the battle in the Ardennes Forest, known as the Battle of the Bulge, began. The American forces were victorious largely because of land and air support provided by African American infantry and Air Corps units, notably the 99th Pursuit — later Fighter — Squadron.

1988— Singer JAMES BROWN, the "Godfather of Soul," was sentenced to six years in a South Carolina state prison after an Aiken, South Carolina, jury debated for three hours before convicting Brown, 55, of aggravated assault and failure to stop for police during a vehicle chase in September. What began as a simple traffic stop led to a chase that started in Georgia and ended in South Carolina. Brown was found not guilty of a charge of assault with intent to kill. Brown worked in the kitchen of the State Park Correctional Center, a minimum security prison near Columbia, South Carolina. Prison officials turned down requests from hundreds of the singer's fans wanting to visit him. (See also 4/19; 6/17; 12/24)

16 December

1976— President Jimmy Carter appointed ANDREW YOUNG United States ambassador to the United Nations. Young served Carter well, but was forced to resign in 1979 after it was disclosed that he had had an unauthorized meeting with PLO chairman Yassar Arafat at a New York City hotel. (See also 2/4; 3/12; 7/27; 10/13)

17 December

1951— PAUL ROBESON and WILLIAM L. PATTERSON presented a petition to the United Nations charging the United States with a policy of genocide against African American citizens.

1990— Self-styled bigot and racist Byron de La Beckwith was arrested in Signal Mountain, Tennessee, and, for the second time, charged with murder in the 1963 assassination of MEDGAR EVERS, a Mississippi civil rights activist. Evers was shot in the back as he left his car outside his Jackson, Mississippi home.

Chronology of Events
June 12, 1963 — Medgar Evers assassinated.

June 21, 1963 — FBI agents arrested Beckwith on a civil rights charge after finding his fingerprint on the telescopic sight of a weapon found near Evers' home after the shooting. Beckwith told authorities the rifle had been stolen earlier from his home.

Jan. 27, 1964 — Beckwith's trial began before an all–White jury.

Feb. 7, 1964 — The trial ended in a hung jury.

April 6, 1964 — Beckwith's second trial began, also with an all–White jury.

April 17, 1964 — Jurors advised the court they were deadlocked.

1969 — Murder charges against Beckwith were dismissed.

Fall 1989 — The prior existence of the Mississippi Sovereignty Commission, a segregationist watchdog agency, was disclosed. The Commission screened potential jurors for Beckwith's second trial. Prosecutors announced they found no evidence of jury tampering. The commission had been dissolved in 1973.

Oct. 3, 1989 — MYRLIE EVERS, widow of Medgar Evers, asked that the case be reopened.

March 11, 1990 — District Attorney Ed Peters announced that there were new leads in the case.

Dec. 17, 1990 — Beckwith was arrested in Tennessee on a fugitive warrant issued by Mississippi.

Feb. 22, 1991 — Beckwith appeared in a Chattanooga, Tennessee, court for a hearing on the charges. He was later found guilty and remanded to the Tennessee state prison system.

1990 — Evidence presented in a Los Angeles County courtroom indicated continued discrimination in housing despite the adoption of federal and state laws banning such acts. NATHAN BEAMS, a title insurance executive, received part of the $317,000 settlement in a lawsuit brought on Beams' behalf by the Fair Housing Congress of Southern California. After moving to Southern California, Beams made an appointment to look at an Encino apartment near his office. Beams' action was based on a newspaper advertisement listing several vacant units. When Beams showed up for his appointment, the complex manager, an employee of Beaumont Property Management Co., Inc., told him there were no vacancies. The Fair Housing Congress later sent African American and White test applicants to the complex to establish that African Americans were treated differently from Whites and were often told there were no vacancies, despite advertising to the contrary.

18 December

1865 — The 13th Amendment to the U.S. Constitution, which banned slavery, was declared ratified by a proclamation from the U.S. secretary of state. (See also 2/1)

1912 — Air Force Lt. Gen. BENJAMIN O. DAVIS, JR., was born in Washington, D.C. The son of Army Brig. Gen. BENJAMIN O. DAVIS, SR., the younger Davis was a graduate of West Point. He was the first African American military officer to reach three-star military rank and the first African American Air Force flag/general officer. Lt. Gen. Davis retired in 1970. (See also 5/22; 6/1; 7/13; 10/16)

1917 — Actor OSSIE DAVIS was born in Cogdell, Georgia. Davis attended Howard University. His first movie, *No Way Out*, was released in 1950. Davis built a reputation on his performance in the Broadway production of *No Time for Sergeants*.

1961 — African Americans and Montgomery, Alabama, officials negotiated an agreement that included the desegregation of public facilities and reduced charges against the so-called Freedom Riders in exchange for an end to the boycott and protest marches.

19 December

1875 — CARTER GOODWIN WOODSON was born in New Canton, Buckingham County, Virginia. A graduate of Douglass High School in Huntington, Virginia, and Berea College in Berea, Kentucky, Woodson taught in Fayette County, Virginia, after becoming a teacher in 1898. Woodson's abilities greatly impressed other educators. As a result, they later selected him to be principal of Douglass High School. Woodson also taught in the Republic of the Philippines while taking classes during the summer at the University of Chicago. After three years in the Philippines, Woodson traveled and studied in Asia and Europe, and did graduate work at the Sorbonne. He earned a doctorate in history from Harvard University in 1912. Woodson, founder of African American History Week, retired from teaching in 1922 and devoted his time to cataloguing the history of Africans and African Americans in the United States. He became an expert on the subject in the process. The first issue of Woodson's *Journal of Negro History*, a quarterly publication of the Association for the Study of Negro Life and History, was circulated January 1, 1916. Woodson died in 1950.

1930— Air Force Lt. Gen. WINSTON D. POWERS was born in New York City.

1933— Birthday of Emmy Award–winning actress CICELY TYSON in New York City. Tyson was once married to the late jazz trumpeter Miles Davis.

1991— Tensions mounted at California's Berkeley High School as students struggled to cope with the appearance of racist Ku Klux Klan leaflets on the school campus. Two White students, ages 17 and 16, were beaten and kicked by a group of African American students who accused them of distributing Klan literature similar to that passed out at a Hayward, California, BART (Bay Area Rapid Transit) station . An African American youth reported that a White woman gave him and several other African American students copies of a racist leaflet that referred to the Klan and congratulated African Americans for killing each other.

20 December

1893— The state of Georgia passed an anti-lynch law. History indicates that enforcement of the law was hardly enthusiastic.

1988— In Oakland, California, MAR-

CUS FELDER held a press conference to announce the filing of a civil lawsuit on his behalf alleging discrimination by Cherry Hill Photos. Felder accused the photo studio of refusing to hire him to work as a Santa Claus because of his race. Felder produced photographs of himself dressed in Santa's regalia, and said he "plays a decent Santa." Court records indicate that the suit was never filed; however, the Cherry Hill Photo Studio has since gone out of business in Oakland.

1988— The "ABC Evening News" anchor MAX ROBINSON died of AIDS at Howard University Hospital. Robinson was 49.

21 December

1986— The Associated Press reported that African American residents in a Selma, Alabama, community called "Slave City," lacked running water. Selma city officials said they would extend the water and sewer system to Slave City "as quick as we can." (A trip to Selma in June 1989 disclosed that residents of Slave City still lacked running water and indoor plumbing.)

1986— MICHAEL GRIFFITH, one of three African Americans fleeing a gang of white teenagers armed with tree limbs and baseball bats, was hit and killed by a car after he was chased onto a freeway in the Howard Beach community in the borough of Queens, New York City. The trio was chased from a pizza parlor where they had stopped to use a telephone after their car broke down in the predominantly White community. (See also 1/7; 1/8; 1/23; 3/29; 10/1)

22 December

1988— RONALD BROWN, a former member of Jesse Jackson's 1988 presidential campaign, made public plans to replace Paul Kirk as national chairman of the Democratic Party. Brown was successful as party chairman and was appointed secretary of commerce by President Bill Clinton in 1994. Brown was killed in a plane crash on April 9, 1996, while promoting U.S. trade in Croatia.

23 December

1815— Birthday of HENRY HIGH-LAND GARNET, minister and reformer, in Delaware. Ordained a Presbyterian minister in 1842, Garnet was active in post–Civil War politics and in 1881 was appointed minister to Liberia. While serving in this capacity, he died in Monrovia, the Liberian capitol.

1867— MADAM C. J. (SARA BREED-LOVE) WALKER, who made her money from the manufacture of cosmetic products for African Americans, became the nation's first African American woman millionaire.

1985— RANDY MILES JEFFRIES, employed as a messenger for a copying service, became the fourth African American charged with espionage. Miles attempted to sell copies of documents from Congressional hearings to undercover FBI agents whom he believed to be Russian KGB agents.

1990— Soundly criticized after an editorial implied a connection between birth control and poverty as the two issues relate to African Americans, the *Philadelphia Inquirer* issued a public apology. Critics of the newspaper said the editorial was racist because it suggested birth control (specifically the new Norplant contraceptive) was the solution to poverty among African Americans. "We left the impression that our cure for poverty was to reduce the number of [African American] people," the newspaper offered as an apology.

24 December

1865— "Kyklos," Greek for "circle," and "Klan" are the roots of the name "Ku Klux Klan," a new White supremacist organization that appeared for the first time in Giles County, Tennessee. The first grand wizard: Gen. Nathan Forrest. (See also 4/12)

1845— Wealthy San Franciscan businessman WILLIAM LEIDESDORFF first introduced San Francisco to steamships by bringing the SS *Sitka* into San Francisco Bay.

1954— Rhythm and Blues singer JOHNNY ACE died of a gunshot wound while playing Russian roulette backstage at the Houston City Auditorium. (See also 6/9)

1989— Former New Orleans, Louisiana, Mayor ERNEST "Dutch" MORIAL died of a heart attack. (See also 10/9)

1990— On this Christmas Eve, JAMES BROWN, the Godfather of Soul, entertained an estimated 10,000 soldiers at Ft. Jackson, South Carolina. Christmas leaves were cancelled for the soldiers because of the Persian Gulf crisis. It was the first public appearance/performance for Brown since his imprisonment two years earlier. He was released from custody Sunday to begin a four-day Christmas furlough. (See also 4/19; 6/17; 12/15)

25 December

1907— Band leader and musician CAB CALLOWAY, the Heidi Ho King of early soul swing, was born in Rochester, New York. Calloway, the last of the big swing band leaders, often performed at Harlem's Cotton Club.

26 December

1908— Boxer JACK JOHNSON of Galveston, Texas, defeated Canadian Tommy Burns after a 12-round fight for the heavyweight boxing championship of the world. (See also 3/31)

27 December

1939— Actor JOHN AMOS was born in Newark, New Jersey.

28 December

1816— Free African Americans in Northern states, with help from liberal White abolitionists, formed the American Colonization Society. The society's goal was to relocate free African Americans in Liberia.

1990— GILBERT W. LINDSAY, the first African American elected to the Los Angeles City Council 27 years before, died at age 90 of a heart attack. Lindsay's death was attributed to a massive September 2 stroke that left him speechless and almost immobile.

29 December

1893— JOHN JAMISON MOORE, an African Methodist Episcopal Zion minister and educator, died. Born a slave in 1804, Moore left his native Virginia for California in 1852. He remained in the Golden State for 14 years and established the first school for African American children in San Francisco.

1917— Four-term Los Angeles Mayor THOMAS BRADLEY was born in Calvert, Texas. Bradley worked 20 years as a Los Angeles, California, police officer. He was elected to three terms as a city council member beginning in 1961, and was first elected mayor in 1973.

1990— Phoenix, Arizona, took another financial hit, this time from the Episcopalian Church. Church leaders had scheduled a triennial convention in Phoenix but decided a second look was necessary. The Episcopalians began having second thoughts when Arizona voters spurned a ballot initiative that would have put the Rev. MARTIN LUTHER KING, JR.'s birthday on the books as a recognized federal holiday. There were no estimates as to how many of the 2.5 million church members planned to attend the convention.

30 December

1928— Composer and musician BO DIDLEY was born in McCombs, Mississippi. He is known for his classic blues arrangements.

1970— Former heavyweight boxing champion CHARLES "Sonny" LISTON, died in Las Vegas, Nevada. (See also 5/8)

31 December

1930— ODETTA HOMES FELIOUS GORDON, better known simply as ODETTA, the well-known singer, was born in Birmingham, Alabama.

Appendix: Inventors and Their Patents

If you have no confidence in self you are twice defeated in the race of life, with confidence you have won even before you have started. —Marcus Garvey

ALBERT, Albert P., of New Orleans, Louisiana — Designed a cotton picking machine that used air to separate cotton from the bolls in which it grew. Patented July 9, 1912.

ATHERTON, Fisher C., of Buffalo, New York — Improved the clip used to attach brake levers to velocipede handlebars. Patented May 29, 1894.

BAILEY, Leonard C., of Washington, D.C. — Designed improvements in folding beds. Patented July 18, 1899.

BEARD, Andrew J., of Eastlake, Alabama — Designed the automatic car-coupling for railroad cars. Patented May 28, 1901.
*Invented improvements to rotary engines. Patented July 5, 1892.

BERKELEY, Arnold D., and **BOLD,** Eugene W., both of Potomac; **JEFFERSON,** Donald E., and **ZELLER,** Gerard A., of Silver Spring and Ellicott City, Maryland, respectively. Jointly developed a data processing system for computers. Patented October 31, 1972, and assigned to Computer Retrieval Systems, Inc., of Bethesda, Maryland.

BLAIR, Henry — Invented the corn husker. Patented in 1834.

BOYKIN, Otis F., of Chicago, Illinois — Invented a precision wire wound resistor that is adaptable to a variety of space and electrical circuit configuration requirements. "The Boykin resistor was designed to meet stringent induction (electrical current) requirements without the need for reverse windings in bobbin-type resistors, and can be made cheaply and quickly," Boykin wrote in the patent application. Patented February 21, 1961, and assigned to CTS Corporation, Elkhart, Indiana.
*Constructed an electrical capacitor designed to provide high capacity, small volume, high dielectric breakdown (at or near zero electrical non-conductivity) and low dissipation. Boykin used a mixture of lead titanate lead tantalate, tantalum and titanium oxides (ceramic materials) resistant to, rather than acting as a conductor of, electric current but capable of holding electrical charges (the primary task of capacitors) or discharging current at specific intervals, according to the design of the circuit of which the capacitor is a part. Patented June 22, 1965, and assigned to CTS Corporation, Elkhart, Indiana.

153

*Invented an electrical resistance element and a means of manufacturing it. Patented September 6, 1966, and assigned to CTS Corporation, Elkhart, Indiana.

BROOKS, Charles B., of Newark, New Jersey — Invented improvements to street sweepers. Patented March 17, 1896.

BURR, John Albert, of Agawam, Massachusetts — Improved operation of "common types" (manually operated) of lawn mowers by designing a casing to house the "operating gearing" to prevent the "gearing" from clogging or damage by obstructions. Patented May 9, 1899.

BURRIDGE, Lee S., and **MARSHMAN,** Newman R., of New York, New York — Invented the type-writing machine. The intent of the inventors was to design an "inexpensive yet complete machine of very few parts" that was not "liable to get out of order." Patented April 7, 1885.

BUTLER, Francis E., of Washington, D.C., and **WOLF,** Sylvan, of College Park, Maryland — Invented the watertight electrical connector for drill mines submerged in up to 400 feet of water. Patented July 4, 1961, and assigned to the United States government represented by the Secretary of the Navy.

CHERRY, Matthew A., of Washington, D.C. — Invented a velocipede to accommodate three people, only one of whom need pedal. Patented May 8, 1888.

CLAY, Percy, and **WASHINGTON,** G., both of New Orleans, Louisiana — Designed what they described as "new and useful improvements in Signal-Lanterns." Clay and Washington's improvements included a redesign of the "normally hidden" colored signal-lantern globes that enabled lantern users to reposition the globes so the lantern's flame would be seen as a "colored" light instead of a clear one. The redesigned lanterns were patented August 13, 1912.

CROSTHWAIT, David N., Jr., of Marshalltown, Iowa — Invented improvements

in refrigeration and the required apparatus. Patented August 30, 1932. Patent later assigned to the C.A. Dunham Company, Marshalltown, Iowa.

DAVIDSON, Shelby — Invented rewind devices for tabulating and adding machines; received patent in 1910.

DAVIS, William D., of Fort Assinniboine, Montana — Invented a military "Spring Seat" riding saddle with "Spring Stirrups," for use by troops assigned to light cavalry or artillery units. Patented October 6, 1896.

DICKINSON, Samuel L., of Cranford, New Jersey — Created an attachment for pianos that mechanically recorded notes by using the force of impact of each key struck when a selection was played on the keyboard. The notes were translated into perforations on a special cylinder with a wax coating. The device was patented February 2, 1915.

Invented improvements in the construction and operation of player pianos to make certain that "proper regulation of pneumatic playing mechanisms may be secured." The piano, with Dickinson's improvements, was patented April 15, 1913.

DORTICUS, Clatonia Joaquin, of Newton, New Jersey — Designed a photographic print or negative "washer or bath, in which photographic bromide and platinotype or gelatin negatives can be successfully washed," to remove sodium hyposulfite and other chemicals from photo prints or negatives "in a short time." Patented April 23, 1895.

EVANS, John H., of Cleveland, Ohio — Invented a convertible settee and bed that, perhaps, was the first of what are now two-tiered bunk beds with centered supports for the upper bunk. Patented October 5, 1897.

FLEMING, Robert F., Jr., of Melrose, Massachusetts — Designed a guitar with wooden sides but "instead of wooden heads, parchment or vellum heads are stretched over the sides." The location of the heads also was slightly different from conventional guitar construction. The patent was issued March 30, 1886.

GRANT, William S., of Cleveland, Ohio — Invented improvements in the design of curtain rod supports "especially adapted to the class of supports" designed for use with curtains. Patented August 4, 1896.

GREGG, Clarence, of Pitt Bridge, Texas — Designed changes in the construction of machine guns, including one that resulted in the simultaneous discharge of a "plurality of cartridges therein and the projection of the bullets therefrom, in a manner such as will sweep the path of travel thereof." Patented August 27, 1918.

GUNN, Selim W., of Agawam, Massachusetts — Invented improvements to the shoe that included a two-part sole "slidably connected at the heel [and] combined with the upper and inserted pieces at the sides, which are adapted to be let out and taken up according to the length of the shoe." Patented January 16, 1900.

HALL, Lloyd A., of Chicago, Illinois — Invented the process of sterilizing hospital and physicians' supplies to eliminate bacteria, molds and yeasts and the spores thereof. "It is applicable to a wide variety of hemostatic dusting powder, cotton rolls and balls, rolled gauzes, gauze bandages, catgut (animal source), sutures ... and other hospital products, many of which are variously medicated," Hall wrote in his patent application. "These are comprehended by the term hospital and physicians' supplies of animal and vegetable origin." Patented May 31, 1960, and assigned to the Griffith Laboratories, Inc., Chicago, Illinois.

HARNEY, Michael C., of St. Louis, Missouri — Designed improvements to the lantern or lamp. Improvement included a "wick-raising" device. Patented August 19, 1884.

HAWKINS, Joseph F., of West Windsor, New Jersey — Invented the then-called "Gridiron for Broiling" meats and other solid foods. Patented March 26, 1845.

HEARNS, Robert, of St. Paul, Minnesota — Designed detachable car fender for use with "rapid-transit street cars and other vehicles" in order to prevent individuals or objects "from being run over by the wheels of the vehicle(s)." Patented July 4, 1899.

HINES, Samuel J., of Plaqukemine, Louisiana — Invented a life-preserver in the form of a waterproof garment. The preserver was fitted with a belt, to which four inflatable balls were secured, that circled the waist and kept the wearer dry as well as afloat and above water. The preserver was patented May 4, 1915.

HOWARD, Elijah D., of Lynn, Massachusetts — Improvements were made to the arrangement of cutters for sole channeling machines. Patented February 27, 1872.

JACKSON, Benjamin F., of Cambridge, Massachusetts — Designed improvements for the "water-tube" steam boiler. The most significant changes in Jackson's boiler included structural alterations for enhancing strength while improving the process of superheating steam and vaporizing liquid fuel. Patented January 7, 1902.

*Invented improvements in automobiles, including an interchangeable motor and generator that could be removed from one vehicle and used in another vehicle. Patented April 30, 1901.

*Invented improvements to the hydrocarbon gas furnace. Using Jackson's plans, the furnace burner was reconstructed so that the burning of gases occurred near the "convex bottom of the utensil sustained above the burner," and so that a "large supply of air [is] delivered to the products of combustion to be consumed therewith," Jackson's attorneys wrote in the patent application. Jackson was awarded a patent December 4, 1906.

JEFFERSON, Donald E., of Silver Spring, Maryland, and **VERMILLION, Ronald G.,** of Rockville, Maryland — Invented a digital data storage system. Patented July 18, 1972, and assigned to the United States represented by the Secretary of the Navy.

JENNINGS, Thomas L.— The first African American to patent an invention (in 1821), designed a dry-cleaning process.

JOHNSON, Willis, of Cincinnati, Ohio — "The object of my invention is to provide a machine wherewith eggs, batter, and other similar ingredients used by bakers, confectioners, can be beaten or mixed in the most intimate and expeditious manner." Johnson's egg beater was patented February 5, 1845.

JONES, Albert A., and Long, Amos E., of Philadelphia, Pennsylvania — Developed a cap that "relates to the closure of vessels [intended] to be used but once and is adapted to indicate, by its condition, whether the vessel upon which it is secured has been opened or not." Patented September 13, 1898.

*Invented the two-cycle gasoline engine which has the piston rods and crankshaft extending into a common crankshaft chamber and provides double pistons and double cylinders, one part of each piston and cylinder operating as a charging chamber. Patented May 29, 1945, and assigned to U.S. Thermo Control Co., of Minneapolis, Minnesota.

*Designed other modifications for the two-cycle gasoline engine to "provide a multi-cylinder, two-cycle, gas engine which is valveless and wherein all gas and exhaust control passages, as well as the inlet and gas control passages, are in effect unitary gas chambers which serve both cylinders and are operative alternately for controlling inlet and exhaust to and from one or the other of the cylinders." Patented March 11, 1947, and assigned to U.S. Thermo Control Company, of Minneapolis, Minnesota.

*Invented improvements in the two-cycle internal combustion engine. Jones' modifications resulted in an engine that used one cylinder for combustion and the other to "pre-compress a fluid charge which may be air or a hydrocarbon mixed with air, with a simplified form of passage for transmitting the pre-compressed charge to the combustion cylinder." Patented No-

vember 28, 1950, and assigned to U.S. Thermo Control Co., of Minneapolis, Minnesota.

JONES, Harry L., of Geneva, Illinois — Invented improvements and modifications to that class of corn harvester "wherein the cutting, carrying and binding mechanism are mounted on suitable carriage or truck wheels and drawn by horses, the same consisting of ... novel features in the combination, arrangement, and operation of the several parts." Patented June 3, 1890.

JULIAN, Percy L., of Maywood, Illinois, and two others — Invented improvements to margarine. Patented November 22, 1955, and assigned to the Glidden Company, Cleveland, Ohio. Associates on the patent are Herbert T. Iveson, of Berwyn, Illinois, and Marian L. McClelland, of Harvard, Illinois.

KELLEY, George W., of Norfolk, Virginia — In his application for patent, Kelley explained that his invention involved improvements to existing steam-tables "for keeping viands warm in hotels, restaurants, dining rooms, and the like; and the object is to provide a simple, convenient and effective device for this purpose." Kelley's steam-table, the prototype for today's modern versions, was patented October 26, 1897.

LEWIS, Anthony L., of Evanston, Illinois — Designed a flexible, squeegee-type window cleaner with a reservoir "to carry a supply of water sufficient for washing a number of windows and a scraper of customary construction so arranged that by going over the window with the working side of the reservoir, it will be thoroughly wet and, by again going over it with the scraper, the water will be removed," Lewis explained in the patent application. The cleaner was patented September 27, 1892.

LEWIS, James E., of Washington, D.C.— Created an antenna feed for coordinate tracking radar(s). Patented June 11, 1968, and assigned to the United States, represented by the Secretary of the Navy.

LOVE, John Lee, of Fall River, Massachusetts — Invented a pencil-sharpener that doubled as a paper-weight or other ornamental desktop object. The sharpener was patented November 23, 1897.

LUTTGENS, H. A., of New York, New York — Designed a device that was connected to the governors of steam engines and controlled engine speed by the cut-off. The regulator was patented October 21, 1851.

McCOY, Elijah, a mechanical engineer born in Colchester, Ontario, Canada — Designed the first automatic lubricator. The lubricator was patented July 2, 1872.

MILES, Alexander, of Duluth, Minnesota — Created a mechanism for automatically closing off openings to passenger and freight elevator shafts. Patented October 11, 1887.

MORGAN, Garrett A., of Cleveland, Ohio — Designed a hood-like headcovering fitted with a floor-length breathing tube that allowed firefighters to breath uncontaminated air from the floor. Morgan's device was patented March 24, 1914.
*Invented additional improvements to the breathing device that were patented October 13, 1914.

NUMERO, Joseph A. and **JONES,** Frederick M., of Minneapolis, Minnesota — Invented air conditioning for vehicles, including railroad cars, trucks and other carriers of perishable goods. Patented December 1, 1942, and assigned to U.S. Thermal Control Company and an association that included Numero and one M. Green.

PARKER, Alice H., of Morristown, New Jersey — The gas-fueled heating-furnace, for which Parker developed improvements, was intended for use in heating residences and commercial buildings. Parker's furnace ensured that "the economy of labor and fuel cost is effected" while maintaining increased flexibility during operation. The furnace was patented December 23, 1919.

PENNINGTON, Harold C., of East Orange, New Jersey — Invented the electric steam radiator. Patented July 5, 1932, and assigned to Joseph B. Grison, of New York,

New York, and Charles B. Morton, of Summit, New Jersey.

PICKERING, John F., of Gonaives, Republic of Haiti — Invented an air ship or air launch with a gas-filled dome to provide bouyancy. The patent information does not indicate whether helium was the gas used to keep his craft airborne. The airship was patented February 20, 1900.

PURVIS, William B., of Philadelphia, Pennsylvania — The objective of improvements to the fountain pen Purvis designed was to "provide a fountain pen of simple, durable and inexpensive construction for general use." In Purvis' words, "through the mediation of the ink-feeding devices, ordinary writing causes the ink to flow into the pen from the reservoir in volume commensurate with the duty required of the pen." Patented January 7, 1890.
*Electric Railway. This device, designed by Purvis, automatically lifted portions of an electric conductor until it came in contact with sections of conduit that held the conductor in place. Through contact, the conduit transferred current to a motor for a car or other vehicle that used electric power for propulsion. Patented May 1, 1894.

RHODES, Jerome Bonaparete, of Shreveport, Louisiana — Invented an attachment for the commode, then known as a water closet. The attachment, which Rhodes called a "spray tube," was strategically placed so the user was able to "spray and wash the rectum, which is sometimes very important when that part of the human body is diseased." Mounted on the left side of the water closet was a lever used to operate Rhodes' spray tube. His device was patented December 19, 1899.

RICHARDSON, Albert C., of South Frankfort, Michigan — Designed a device for lowering caskets into graves. The device was invented to provide a "simple, durable device" that fit inside the grave, accepted a casket and held loose soil at the edge of the grave. The device also prevented caskets from tipping and falling into graves, then a frequent occurrence. The device was patented November 13, 1894.

RICKMAN, Albert Longo, of Scio, Ohio — Redesigned the overshoe to offer a "light and elastic overshoe sole that attached easily to shoes." Patented February 8, 1898.

SAMMONS, Walter H., of Philadelphia, Pennsylvania — Invented the (hot) comb (curling iron). Sammons' device appears to have been the forerunner of the manually operated curling iron heated by an open fire or stove burner. Patented December 21, 1920.

SAMMS, Adolphus, of Yuma Test Station, Arizona — Designed the multiple stage rocket. Patented August 10, 1965, and assigned to the United States of America.

SAMPSON, George T., of Dayton, Ohio — Invented the clothes-drier, which he also called a drying frame. Patented June 7, 1892.

SCHALLER, Michael D., of Durhamville, New York — Designed roofing tongs, which enabled one man, "without the use of other tools," to do the work of two. Patented August 24, 1915.

SCOTT, Robert P., of Cadiz, Ohio — Invented a corn-silker that automatically removed the "silky fiber" from green corn after the fiber was cut from the ear. The machine was patented August 7, 1894.

SCUDDER, John, of New York, New York — Designed apparatus and system for preserving blood, which was known to deteriorate if not transfused almost immediately into the body of another. Patented November 10, 1942, and assigned to Dr. Charles R. Drew, of Washington, D.C.

SMITH, Elijah S., of Good Hope, Illinois — Designed improvements in windmills, including the creation of such machines with folding wheels. Patented September 17, 1878.

SMITH, James, of Oakland, California — Improved steering and propelling devices in aeroplanes and a "novel type" of airframe. Patented December 17, 1912.

SMITH, Joseph H., of Washington, D.C. — Created the lawn sprinkler, which looks startlingly similar to sprinkler heads in use today. Patented May 4, 1897.

SMITH, Peter D., of Springfield, Ohio — Invented improvements to the potato-digger. The machine was designed to "harvest potatoes safely, quickly and profitably." Patented January 27, 1891.

SPIKES, Richard B., of San Francisco, California — Invented improvements to the automatic gear shift system for motor-driven vehicles. Patented December 6, 1932.

STANARD, John, of Newark, New Jersey — Invented improvements to the refrigerator, including an air duct to enhance circulation of cold air from the ice chamber. Patented July 14, 1891.
*Invented the oil stove with redesigned attachments that allowed concurrent cooking of a variety of meats, vegetables and other foods. Patented October 29, 1889.

STEWART, Marvin C., of Hempstead, New York — Designed the arithmetic unit for digital computers. Patented July 30, 1968, and assigned to Sperry Rand Corporation of Delaware.

SWEETING, James A., of New York — Invented the cigarette rolling machine. Patented November 30, 1897.

TURNER, Madeline M., of Oakland, California — Designed improvements for the fruit press. Turner's invention permitted extraction of juices from citrus fruits. Patented April 25, 1916.

WASHINGTON, Wade, of Huntington, West Virginia — Invented improvements to the corn-husking machine. Patented August 14, 1893.

WHITE, Charles F., of Philadelphia, Pennsylvania — Designed the timing device for use in racing events. Patented February 27, 1912.

WHITE, John T., of New York — Invented the lemon squeezer. Patented December 8, 1896.

WOODS, Granville, of Cincinnati, Ohio — Designed an apparatus for transmitting messages by electricity over the same line without changes in transmitting instruments. Patented April 7, 1885. Assigned to the American Bell Telephone Co. of Boston, Massachusetts.

*Designed improvements to the steam boiler furnace. Patented June 3, 1884.

*Woods, Granville & Lyates, of New York, New York— Invented the railway brake apparatus that enabled the automatic stoppage of rail cars in the event of an emergency or the disabled status of a railroad motorman. Patented July 18, 1905.

*Developed the telephone system and related apparatus that allowed the transmission of speech over electrical wires. Patented Oct. 11, 1887. It later was assigned to the Woods Electric Company.

Bibliography

Adams, Russell L. *Great Negroes, Past and Present.* 3rd ed. Afro-Publishing Co., 1981.

The Alabama Journal. Editions of Oct. 25 and Nov. 10, 1966.

Allen, Robert L. *The Port Chicago Mutiny.* New York: Warner Books, 1989.

Amer, Mildred L., analyst. *Black Members of the United States Congress, 1789–1987.* Report No. 87–253. Washington, DC: Congressional Research Service 1987.

Barone, Michael, and Grant Ujifusa. *The Almanac of American Politics.* Washington, DC: Barone & Company, 1981.

_____, and _____. *The Almanac of American Politics.* Washington, DC: National Journal, 1990.

Bean, Walton. *California: An Interpretive History.* New York: McGraw Hill, 1968.

Beasley, Delilah L. *The Negro Trail Blazers of California.* New York: Negro Universities Press, 1919. (Reprinted: New York: Greenwood, 1969.)

Bennett, Lerone, Jr. *Before the Mayflower: A History of the Negro in America, 1619–1964.* Penguin Books, 1962.

_____. *Wade in the Water.* Chicago: Johnson, 1979.

Blair, Clay. *The Forgotten War: Americans in Korea.* New York: Doubleday, 1987.

Bonner, T.D. *The Life and Adventures of James P. Beckworth.* New York: Harper & Brothers, 1856.

Bontemps, Arna. *Great Slave Narratives.* Boston: Beacon Press, 1969.

California State Department of Education. *Afro-American Contributors to American Life.* Sacramento: California State Series, 1972.

Carroll, John M., ed. *The Black Military Experience in the American West.* Liveright, 1971.

Carruth, Gorton. *What Happened When: A Chronology of Life in America.* New York: Harper & Row, 1989.

_____, and Eugene Ehrlich. *Facts & Dates of American Sports from Colonial Days to the Present.* New York: Harper & Row, 1988.

Centralia, Citizens of. *Centralia's First Century: 1845–1955.* Tumwater, WA: Quality Printing, 1977.

Chase, William, and Helene Chase. *Chase's Annual Events.* New York: Contemporary Book, 1987.

Clifford, Mike, consultant. *The Illustrated Encyclopedia of Black Music.* New York: Harmony Books, 1982.

Cook, David C. *Black America Yesterday and Today.* David C. Cook, 1969.

Councill, W. H., president. *Lamp of Wisdom, or Race History Illuminated.* Normal, AL: A & M College for Negroes, 1898.

Dannett, Sylvia G. L. *Negro Heritage Library. Profiles in Negro Womanhood,* vol. 1, 1619–1900. Yonkers, NY: Educational Heritage, Inc., 1964.

Davis, John P,. ed. "The American Negro Reference Book" in *Negro Heritage Library.* Englewood Cliffs, NJ: Prentice-Hall, 1966.

De Coy, Robert H. *The Blue Book Manual of Nigritian History: American Descendents of African Origen.* Los Angeles, CA: Nigritian, Inc. 1969.

Dennis, R. Ethel. *The Black People of America.* New Haven, CT: Readers Press, 1970.

Durham, Philip, and Everett L. Jones. *The Negro Cowboys.* New York: Dodd, Mead, 1965.

Eppse, Merl R. *The Negro Too: In American History.* Chicago, Nashville, New York: National Education, 1938.

Facts on File, vol. XXV, no. 1274. March 25–31, 1965.

Facts on File, vol. XXVI, no. 1315. January 1–12, 1966.

Facts on File, vol. XXX, no. 1830. December 6, 1975.

Famous Black Americans. Indianapolis: The Saturday Evening Post, 1976.

Faw, Bob, and Nancy Skelton. *Thunder in America: The Improbable Presidential Campaign of Jesse Jackson.* Austin: Texas Monthly Press, 1986.

Flemming, James and Christian E. Burckel, eds. *Who's Who in Colored America.* Yonkers, NY: Christian Burckel & Associates, 1950.

Foner, Eric. *Reconstruction: America's Unfinished Revolution, 1863–1877.* New York: Harper & Row, 1989.

Foner, Philip S. *The Voice of Black America: Major Speeches by Blacks in the United States 1797–1973.* Capricorn Books, 1975.

Franklin, John Hope. *From Slavery to Freedom: A History of Negro Americans,* 4th ed. New York: Alfred A. Knopf, 1974.

_____. *Henry Ossawa Tanner: American Artist.* Chicago: University of Chicago Press, 1969.

Gibbs, Miflin Wistar. *Shadow & Light: An Autobiography* (1902). Introduction by Booker T. Washington. Reprinted, New York: Arno Press/The New York Times, 1968.

Guide to Congress, 3rd ed. Washington, DC: U.S. Government Printing Office, 1982.

Halway, John. *Voices from the Great Black Baseball Leagues.* New York: Dodd Mead, 1975.

Hanes, Colonel Bailey C. *Bill Picket, Bulldogger.* Norman: University of Oklahoma Press, 1977.

Harris, Middleton, ed., with Morris Levitt, Robert Furman and Ernest Smith. *The Black Book.* New York: Random House, 1974.

Hart, James David. *A Companion to California,* 2nd ed. Berkeley: University of California Press, 1987.

Higgins, Chester, Jr., and Orde Combs. *Some Time Ago.* Garden City, NY: Anchor Press/Doubleday, 1980.

Hughes, Langston, and Milton Meltzer. *Black Magic.* New York: Bonanza Books, 1967.

_____, _____, and C. Eric Lincoln. *A Pictorial History of Black Americans,* 5th ed. New York: Crown Publishers, 1983.

Indianapolis News. Indianapolis: Star News, June 22, 1989.

International Library of Negro Life and History: Medicine. New York, Washington and London: Publishers Co.; The Association for the Study of Negro Life and History, 1976.

Jackson, George F. *Black Women: Makers of History a Portrait.* Sacramento: Fong & Fong, 1977.

Jet Magazine, vol 74, nos. 15, 23 and vol. 76, no. 11.

Katz, Loren. *Black People Who Made the Old West.* New York: Thomas Y. Crowell, 1977.

_____. *The Black West,* 3rd ed. Seattle: Open Hand, 1987.

Lanker, Brian. *I Dream a World: Portraits of Black Women Who Changed America.* New York: Stewart, Tabori & Chang, 1989.

Lapp, Rudolph M. *Afro-Americans in California.* Boyd and Fraser, 1979.

_____. *Blacks in Gold Rush California.* New Haven, CT: Yale University Press, 1977.

Litwack, Leon, and August Meier. *Black Leaders of the Twentieth Century.* Champaign: University of Illinois Press.

Lowe, W. A., and Virgil A. Clift. *Encyclopedia of Black Americans.* New York: McGraw-Hill, 1981.

Magarshack, David. *Pushkin: A Biography.* New York: Grove Press, 1967.

The Montgomery Advertiser. Editions of Jan. 5, Jan. 6, Jan. 12, Mar. 14, Dec. 8 and Dec. 9, 1966.

The National Encyclopedia of the Colored Race, vol. 1. Montgomery, AL: National Publishing, 1919.

The New York Times. Editions of June 10 and 13, 1989.

Panger, Daniel. *Black Ulysses.* Athens: Ohio University Press, 1982.

Parker, Marjorie H. *Alpha Kappa Alpha: In the Eyes of the Beholder.* Washington, DC: Alpha Kappa Alpha Sorority, 1979.

Parkhill, Forbes. *Mister Barney Ford: A Portrait in Bistre.* Denver: Sage Books, 1963.

Pico, Pio. *Dn. Pio Pico's Historical Narrative.* Translated by Arthur P. Boteko, edited by Martin Cole and Henry Welcome. Glendale, CA: The Arthur H. Clark Co., 1973.

Ploski, Harry A., and James Williams, eds. *The Negro Almanac: A Reference Work on the Afro-American,* 4th ed. New York: John Wiley & Sons, 1983.

_____, and Warren Mar II. *The Negro Almanac: A Reference on the Afro-American,* 3rd ed. New York: John Wiley & Sons, 1976.

Prewar Days at Tuskegee: A Historical Essay on Tuskegee Institute. Roman Publications, 1971.

Quarles, Benjamin. *The Negro in the Civil War.* New York: Da Capo Press, 1989.

Rand McNally Contemporary World Atlas. New York, Chicago, San Francisco: Rand McNally, 1986.

The Ring Record Book and Boxing Encyclopedia. New York: Ring Publishing, 1988.

Robinson, Wilhelminia S. *International Library of Negro Life and History: Historical.* New York, Washington & London: Publishers Co.; The Association for the Study of Negro Life and History, 1969.

Ross, L. Thomas. "William Leidesdorff" in *The Far Westerner.* Stockton, CA: Stockton Corral of Westerners, April 1987.

_____. "A Man to Match the Mountains" in *Old West.* Stillwater, OK: Western Publications, Fall 1987.

Savage, Sherman. *Blacks in the West.* Westport, CT, and London: Greenwood, 1976.

Sterling, Dorothy B. *Black Foremothers: Three Lives.* Old Westbury, NY: The Feminist Press, 1979.

Talmadge, Marian, and Iris Gilmore. *Barney Ford, Black Baron.* New York: Dodd, Mead, 1973.

Tinkham, George H. *California: Men and Events, Time 1769–1890,* 2nd ed. Stockton, CA: Record Publishing Company, 1915.

Toll, Robert C. *On with the Show.* New York: Oxford University Press, 1976.

Toppin, Edgar, and David McKay. *Biographical History of Blacks in America Since 1528.* New York: David McKay, 1969.

U.S. Coast Guard. *Commandant's Bulletin: A U.S. Coast Guard Magazine.* Washington, DC: Department of Transportation, 1989.

U.S. Department of Defense. *Black Americans in Defense of Our Nation.* 1985.

U.S. Department of Transportation. *The History of Blacks in the Coast Guard from 1790.* Washington, DC: Department of Transportation.

Wallace, Irving & David Wallechinsky. *The People's Almanac.* Garden City, NY: Doubleday, 1975.

_____, and _____. *The People's Almanac, #2.* New York: William Morrow, 1978.

_____, and _____. *The People's Almanac, #3.* New York: William Morrow, 1981.

Walls, William Jacob. *The African Methodist Episcopal Zion Church: Reality in the Black Church.* Charlotte, NC: AME Zion Publishing House, 1974.

Warner, Lucille Shulberg. *From Slave to Abolitionist: The Life of William Wells Brown*. New York: The Dial Press, 1976.

Weisbrot, Robert. *Father Devine*. Boston: Beacon Press, 1983. Reprint from *Blacks in the New World*. "Father Devine and the Struggle for Racial Equality." Normal: University of Illinois Press.

Wesley, Charles H., and Patricia W. Romero. *Negro Americans in the Civil War from Slavery to Citizenship*. New York, Washington & London: Publishers Co.; The Association for the Study of Negro Life and History, 1968.

Who's Who, 1986–1988 editions.

Who's Who Among Black Americans. Northbrook, IL: Who's Who, 1980, 1981.

Who's Who in the West, 1986–1987.

Wilson, Elinor. *Jim Beckworth*. Norman: University of Oklahoma Press, 1972.

Woodson, Carter G. *Important Events and Dates in Negro History*. Washington, DC: The Association for the Study of Negro Life and History, 1936.

The World Almanac and Book of Facts. New York: Newspaper Enterprise Association, 1979 to 1996.

World Book Encyclopedia. *Negro: The Story of Black Americans Yesterday and Today*. A World Book Encyclopedia reprint.

Index